Pre-Press: 71 FILM Ltd., Bangkok, Thailand
Pre-Press & Printing: EASTERN PRINTING Co., Ltd., Bangkok,
Thailand
PRINTED IN THAILAND

THE HOLY LAND SATELLITE ATLAS

STUDENT MAP MANUAL
ILLUSTRATED SUPPLEMENT
VOLUME 1

PHOTOGRAPHY AND SATELLITE CARTOGRAPHY

RICHARD CLEAVE

ROHR PRODUCTIONS

Contents

SATELLITE IMAGERY: Future Developments

All the satellite imagery in this atlas was recorded during a single pass of NASA's "Landsat 5" satellite at 9.30 am on Sunday January 18th., 1987. That was a cold, exceptionally clear and almost cloudless morning: the very best of all possible mornings for a single contemporary image of the whole area.

This period is a magical time in the Holy Land. Parts of the country have not yet fully emerged from winter, whereas others are in the greenest flush of spring or are already turning yellow in the strengthening sun. Look at the maps at the front and back of the book: trace the gradual transition from the green sources of the Jordan around Dan, in the North, to the withered yellow fields around Beer Sheba, in the South; follow the same from the Golan to Moab and Edom. This is the mid-point when spring is turning into summer and here in this atlas the satellite has preserved it all, for us to study, region by region, at our leisure.

The Landsat 5 satellite looks down vertically as it scans the Earth below, generating "vertical" or two-dimensional (2D) imagery. All the satellite imagery in this atlas is of this "vertical" type, which is ideal for mapping the area in photo-realistic detail and for defining the geographical limits of the various Biblical regions into which the Holy Land is traditionally divided.

However, it is possible to get much more out of the satellite data than this. If the height of the terrain is also known, it is possible, with computers, to "calculate" three-dimensional (3D) or perspective views and then to "animate" sequences of such 3D views to generate simulated flights, which provide optimal visualization.

Such oblique views are much more realistic than the vertical ones.

Rohr Productions is now preparing a 2 1/2 hour videotape of 3D satellite animation, specifically designed for use with this atlas. This will have a 20 minute Introduction and 13 Regional Segments, each of approximately 10 minutes duration.

Each Regional Segment will start with the 2D satellite map, to help place the selected Region in its general geographical context. Then, as the "flight" zooms closer, the view will become "oblique", giving a 3D side-look at the terrain. Then follow three specific circuits: the first, at relatively high altitude, to show the major geographical features and then two more, at much lower altitude, to show specific sites: first from the Old Testament and then the New. The spoken commentary in the video will be descriptive, designed to reinforce the regional commentary printed in the book.

Relevant low-level aerial photographs (selected from the book) will be inserted into the "flight path", providing familiar details of the major Biblical/historical sites and geographical features, each presented in its appropriate regional context.

Therefore all three of the most important elements in the atlas will be fully represented in the videotape: viz. the regional commentary, satellite imagery and low-level aerial photography. The videotape will provide optimal visualization and the book optimal documentation. To be fully effective, both systems are necessary.

Also planned for use with this videotape is another book, a companion volume to the present atlas, in which all the satellite imagery is of the 3D "oblique" type, consisting of selected frames from the videotape. These views will be generated from satellite data of much higher resolution, with enlargement up to 1: 25,000 (compared to 1: 150,000 in the present volume). The main emphasis in the oblique views will be historical, rather than geographical: designed to illustrate specific Biblical events, especially those already cross-referenced in this atlas to the Student Map Manual.

These oblique views will also be made available as sets of standard 35mm color slides and overhead projection transparencies, for classroom use. Rohr Productions is publishing a completely new package of teaching aids, based on this satellite resource, with materials designed specifically for both teachers and students.

THE HOLY LAND ON CD-ROM

In the case of the above videotape of simulated flights over the Holy Land, the actual flight paths have been pre-determined for use in conjunction with the regional satellite maps in the atlas. Thus the viewer cannot alter these animation sequences in any way. Such personal intervention or "interactivity" is only possible if the 3D satellite data is supplied in digital format (on **CD-ROMS**), for use on the computer. Such use is already possible, of course, but only on the more powerful graphic work stations. We must still wait for comparable processing power and storage capacity in the **PC** world to provide this interactive option to a much wider group of Bible students, **but it cannot be more than a few years away !**

****

SAMPLE VIDEOTAPE OF 3D SATELLITE ANIMATION

A sample videotape of "Simulated Flight" over the Holy Land is now available; also a brochure with much more detailed information. Anyone interested should write or fax directly:

TO: ROHR PRODUCTIONS Ltd.
P.O. Box 3312, Nicosia, Cyprus
Telefax: + 357 2 477350

Introduction

This book is a visual and narrative introduction to the Holy Land, Sinai and Egypt. It contains 196 aerial and panoramic views of Palestine, Trans-Jordan, Sinai, and Egypt (Goshen). The photographs chosen for their quality and content are arranged by region to present a systematic view of the Holy Land. With so many photographs, it is possible to memorize the land of the Bible much as you would memorize the words of a text. Then, as you read the Bible, you will visualize "the whole region of Galilee" (Mark 1:28), "the whole region of the Jordan" (Matt. 3:5), and "throughout Judea and Samaria" (Acts 8:1). In addition, you will better appreciate biblical passages that use the land to convey important thoughts or ideas. Consider, for example, this verse from the Psalms:

As the mountains surround Jerusalem, so the Lord surrounds his people both now and forevermore (Ps.125:2).

Some of the effect of this verse is lost if you have not been to the Holy Land or if you cannot picture the mountains rising above and around Jerusalem. The ability to visualize simple expressions like, "so Joseph also *went up* from the town of Nazareth in Galilee to Judea" (Luke 2:4; italics added), or "A man *was going down* from Jerusalem to Jericho" (Luke 10:30; italics added), will help fix biblical events in your mind. The imagery of many other expressions, such as, "make straight in the wilderness" (Isa. 40:3), or "the grass withers and the flowers fall, because the breath of the Lord blows on them" (Isa. 40:7), become clear when you can picture the Judean Wilderness and know that the grass withers and dies almost in a day when the warm east winds of summer begin to blow. Those who go to the Holy Land will not remember everything they see. Indeed, a short time after most people return, they find it difficult to remember the location and setting of many different sites and regions. This volume enables you to visit the Holy Land again and again, until you know it well.

Historical Geography

People who study the historical geography of Palestine use information derived from the Bible, inscriptions and other ancient texts, topography, geology, and archaeology. Even a limited knowledge of these subjects can illuminate biblical events and lead to a better understanding of the Bible itself. Two of the most useful books on the historical geography of Palestine are *The Historical Geography of the Holy Land* by George Adam Smith and *The Land of the Bible* by Yohanan Aharoni. The first edition of Smith's book appeared in 1894. In the introduction to the 1931 25th edition, H. H. Rowley summarizes the contribution of Smith's book:

George Adam Smith's *Historical Geography of the Holy Land* is a classic which has fascinated and instructed generations of students and which has passed through a remarkable number of editions. I remember the impression it made on me when I first read it in my youth. It illuminated for me many Biblical passages and helped me to realise, as I had not realised before, the close interrelation between geography and history, and to understand the history better.

Geography is a descriptive science that deals with the earth's surface features (topography). It also deals with plants, animals, natural resources, soils, climate, and people. Smith was one of the

first to discuss geography as an important element in the history of the Holy Land. His descriptions of the land's surface features are wonderfully detailed. Still, the image he creates of the Holy Land will be different for people with different backgrounds. A good example comes from Smith's description of the descent from the region of Lower Galilee to the Sea of Galilee: "You feel you are passing from the climate and scenery of Southern Europe to those of the barer tropics. The sea-winds which freshen all Galilee and high Hauran beyond, blow over this basin, and the sun beats into it with unmitigated ardour" (Smith, 285). Some people will understand sea winds, and almost everyone will understand the heat of the sun, but one would have to be familiar with Southern Europe to picture the scenery.

In another example, Smith describes the western shore of the Sea of Galilee: "In contrast to the *green open slopes* of the north, these dark, *imprisoning cliffs*, with their black <u>debris</u>, impose upon this part of the coast a sombre, sinister aspect" (Smith, 287; italics added). Green open slopes and imprisoning cliffs will mean one thing to one person and another thing to someone else. For those who have not been to the Holy Land, forming a correct picture of the land will depend on one's experience with the words used to describe it. Now, read again the above description while looking at photograph **B1-2** (see below, p. 32). The effect is much different; the words have more impact when viewed with the photograph. Even without Smith's description, the photograph has an impact of its own that will contribute to understanding the land of the Bible.

Like Smith, Yohanan Aharoni combined history and geography to help us better understand biblical events in their ancient Near East setting. The Bible deals with the religious history of God's people and was not meant to be a textbook on geography or the secular history of Israel. The people who wrote the Bible understood the historical background of their times and took for granted their special knowledge of the land and current events. Most people today are detached from the biblical world by both distance and culture. Yet most will agree that knowing something about the land of the Bible is important for understanding the history of the Bible. Aharoni wrote:

It is not too much to say that the geographical position of this little land has always dominated its history.

Thus, in the land of the Bible, geography and history are so deeply interwoven that neither can be really understood without the help of the other (Aharoni, ix).

This volume does not purport to be a true historical geography of the Holy Land and cannot replace the two books just mentioned. It uses brief historical and geographical sketches to describe the relationship between the land and the history of ancient Israel. This book adds a new dimension to Bible study by showing with photographs what others have tried to describe with words. The text of this book explains how 28 independent regions influenced the history of the Holy Land. The captions to the photographs correlate much of the history and geography for sites within each region. While detailed studies about the people, their history, the geography of the Holy Land, and archaeology can be found in books about each of those particular subjects, this book will teach Bible students what the land looks like and introduce new meaning to many biblical passages.

A good example of how this happens comes from the story of David and Goliath. The Philistines had camped in the lowlands west of the Judean Hill Country (see **Unit J1**). This region, called the Shephelah (see **Unit J2**), was crossed by several strategic valleys. If the Philistines could control the valley where the scene of David's slaying of Goliath is set, there would be nothing to stop them from attacking the cities of Judah via Bethlehem (northern Judah) and Hebron (southern Judah). Controlling the Shephelah, then, was one of the first steps to conquering all of Judah. David's valiant act came at a critical moment in the history of Israel. Knowing where the battle took place and what the Philistines were trying to accomplish adds much to an already dramatic story. Seeing the actual valley and the nearness of the Judean Hill Country that the Israelites were meant to defend (see **J2-1**) gives the story a new sense of reality (see 1 Sam. 17). For such reasons, this new and comprehensive set of photographs on the Holy Land was produced.

Palestine in the 19th Century

Many of ancient Palestine's geographical features were still evident in the 1800s. Extensive swamps and forests, as well as many kinds of animals, were described by early travelers to Palestine. These included men like J. L. Burckhardt (1812), Charles Irby and James Mangles (1818), Edward Robinson (1838), William Thomson (1857), James MacGregor (1869), and George Adam Smith (1897). Some of the best descriptions were given by Robinson, Thomson, and Smith. Another man, Carl Ritter, never visited the Holy Land, but he examined the different geographies and compiled a valuable summary of what was known in 1866. Much of what these explorers described disappeared in the first half of the 20th century. The greatest changes took place in the Plain of Sharon (see **Unit E1**) and the Upper Jordan Valley (see **Unit A2**), where swamps were drained and turned into farm land. [The 19th century descriptions quoted in this book are followed by an author's name and a page number. The full reference is given in the bibliography under the name of the author.]

A concern of the men and women who wrote about Palestine in the 19th century was to provide their readers with "clear visions" of the Holy Land. Thomson, for example, wrote:

In many departments of Biblical literature the student in Europe or America, surrounded by ample libraries, is in a better situation to carry on profitable inquiry than the pilgrim in the Holy Land, however long his loiterings or extended his rambles. *But it is otherwise in respect to the scenes and the scenery of the Bible*, and to the living manners and customs of the East which illustrate that blessed book. Here the actual observer is needed, not the distant and secluded student.

A new generation of readers and students of the Sacred Scriptures has arisen, and the interest in Biblical studies has been greatly increased and extended. Any work designed to meet the wants of those who now daily search the Scriptures *should abound in illustrations, both textual and pictorial*, which are accurate and reliable in detail (Thomson 1: iv–v; italics added).

To achieve accuracy, the pictorial illustrations in Thomson's book were prepared "from photographs taken by the author, and from the best existing materials, and they [were] drawn and engraved ... by artists in London, Paris, and New York" (Thomson 1:v). Another writer, Edward Robinson, regarded his own work "as a beginning, a first attempt to lay open the treasures of Biblical Geography and History." He wished that he could do it again, "furnished too with suitable instruments" that would allow him to "lay before the Christian world results far more important and satisfactory" (Robinson 1: xii–xiii). Both Thomson and Robinson knew it was important to use the best technology available in their day to help their readers see and understand important details about the land of the Bible.

John Fulton, who traveled to Palestine in the 19th century, told the experience of a minister who wanted to know more than the events of the Bible; he wanted "to appreciate the Gospel story in its *sublime reality of place and circumstance*" (Fulton, vii; italics added). Fulton's friend read many books on the subject of the Holy Land, including the books by several authors listed in the bibliography (see below, p. 253). While this approach taught Fulton's friend much about the land, he still had to go to Palestine to learn what the land looked like.

George Adam Smith explained, from his point of view, how to obtain a vision of the land:

> **There are many ways of writing a geography of Palestine, and of illustrating the History by the Land, but some are wearisome and some vain. They do not give a vision of the Land as a whole, nor help you to hear through it the sound of running history. What is needed by the reader or teacher of the Bible is some idea of the outlines of Palestine—its shape and disposition; its plains, passes and mountains; its rains, winds and temperatures; its colours, lights and shades. Students of the Bible desire to see a background and to feel an atmosphere; to discover from "the lie of the land" why the history took certain lines and the prophecy and gospel were expressed in certain styles; to learn what geography has to contribute to questions of Biblical criticism; above all, to discern between what physical nature contributed to the religious development of Israel, and what was the product of moral and spiritual forces. On this last point the geography of the Holy Land reaches its highest interest** (Smith, 17).

Of all the early writers, Smith probably came the closest to giving his readers a vision of the land and a feeling for its "shape and disposition." As is true today, the majority of the people who wanted to go to the Holy Land in the 19th century could not; they had to experience the land through the writings of those who did go. The value derived from reading the descriptions of these early travelers to the Holy Land is the same today as it was in the 19th century. Their writings are an important source for learning about the land of the Bible. Their books, however, lacked photographs and could show the land only through sketches and drawings.

The need for seeing the land is illustrated by the fact that many readers of the Bible do not realize that Palestine has a wide variety of landscapes. In Galilee, for example, there are trees and green grass, hills and valleys, and small streams (see Deut. 11:11; **Units B1, B2**, and **C1**). In the south are desert lands, dry and foreboding (see **Unit L**). Aerial photography and panoramic photographs enable anyone today to have a better understanding of the land of the Bible.

The Near East Setting

The Mediterranean Sea is enclosed by the southern coast of Europe, and by Asia Minor, the Levant, and North Africa. From early history, the Mediterranean has been the basis for commercial and cultural exchange among the countries of the ancient Near East. The coast of Palestine lacks the good harbors such as Tyre and Sidon, but there were ports at Dor, Jaffa and Acco (see **Unit C2**). The Israelites were not the seafarers like their Phoenician neighbors to the north. For most of biblical history, the coastal plain was under the control of Tyre in the north and the Philistines in the south.

Palestine's role in the history of the Near East was largely determined by its position between two continents. Aharoni stresses the influence of geography on the history of Palestine:

> **The history of any land and people is influenced to a considerable degree by their geographical environment. This includes not only the natural features such as climate, soil, topography, etc., but also the geopolitical relationships with neighbouring areas. This is especially true for Palestine, a small and relatively poor country, which derives its main importance from its unique centralized location at the juncture of continents and a crossroads for the nations.**

Palestine was a land bridge between the continents of Asia and Africa. It was frequently invaded and became subject to foreign rulers who wanted to control, more than anything else, the lines of communication and transportation. As George Adam Smith explained in 1894:

> **Syria's** [the Holy Land] **position between two of the oldest homes of the human race made her a passage for the earliest intercourse and exchanges of civilisation. There is probably no older road in all the world than that which can still be used by caravans from the Euphrates to the Nile, through Damascus, Galilee, Esdraelon** [Jezreel]**, the Maritime Plain, and Gaza"** (Smith, 32)**.**

The Fertile Crescent

Palestine was a part of the western leg of what James Henry Breasted called the "Fertile Crescent." From Egypt the Fertile Crescent curved northward through Palestine to the Euphrates then southward through Mesopotamia to the Persian Gulf, forming a rough semicircle, with the sea on the west, mountains on the west, north, and east, and the Syrian and Arabian deserts in the center and on the south (see Near East map, pp. 10–11). Breasted described this area and the struggle to control it:

> **This great semicircle, the Fertile Crescent, may also be likened to the shores of a desert bay, upon which the mountains behind look down—a bay not of water but of sandy waste, some five hundred miles across, forming a northern extension of the Arabian Desert. This desert bay, a part of the Southern Flatlands, is a limestone plateau of some height—too high, indeed, to be watered by the Tigris and Euphrates, which have cut canyons obliquely across it. Nevertheless, after the meager winter rains, wide tracts of the northern desert bay are clothed with scanty grass, and spring thus turns the region for a short time into grasslands. The history of Western Asia may be described as an age-long struggle between the mountain peoples of the north and the desert wanderers of these grasslands—a struggle which is still going on—for the possession of the Fertile Crescent, the shores of the desert bay** (Breasted, 135).

The following brief descriptions are of key lands and names associated with the Fertile Crescent and the history of Israel.

Mesopotamia

The Greek word Mesopotamia means "the land between the rivers." It was the region bounded on the east by the Tigris River and on the west by the Euphrates River. Both rivers originate in the highlands of Turkey near Lake Van before descending to the Persian Gulf. The northern part of Mesopotamia was settled by Aramean tribes who called their land *Aram-naharaim*, "Aram of the two rivers" or "Aram of the great river bend." The Hebrew patriarch Abraham was from this region (Gen. 12:5).

Assyria

The Assyrian Empire was the major political force of northern Mesopotamia that reached its zenith in the 9th through the 7th centuries B.C. It dominated all the countries of the Fertile Crescent, including Israel and Judah. The Assyrian empire brought about the fall of Israel during the reign of King Hoshea (722–21 B.C.; 2 Kgs. 17). The capitals of Assyria included Ashur (from which the name Assyria is derived), Calah, and Nineveh. In the Bible, the prophet Jonah was sent to call the people of Nineveh to repentance. The book of Nahum, on the other hand, celebrates Nineveh's fall.

Babylonia

The Babylonian Empire was the major political force of southern Mesopotamia—the floodplain region of the Tigris and Euphrates Rivers, also known as "Shinar" (Gen. 10:10). Babylonia dominated virtually all the lands of the Fertile Crescent on two occasions: 1792—1750 B.C. during the reign of Hammurabi, and during the 7th and 6th centuries B.C. The second Babylonian Empire conquered the kingdom of Judah and caused the exile of Jews to Babylon (ca. 597–586 B.C.; 2 Kgs. 24–25).

Aram/Syria

The boundaries of Aram are indefinite but generally comprised the region of the upper Euphrates River extending southward to Damascus and west to the Mediterranean. The Semitic name Aram was rendered "Syria" by the Greeks and Romans, and is translated as Syria in the older English translations of the Bible. Aram was a powerful confederation of city-states that clashed with Israel for control of the desert trade routes. The Aramean kingdoms were brought to an end in 732 B.C. by Tiglath-pileser III of Assyria, just before Assyria conquered Israel (ca. 722–721 B.C.).

Hatti/Anatolia

Hatti was the land of the Hittites in central Anatolia (the central portion of Turkey today). They were an Indo-European people who established a strong kingdom rivaling that of the Egyptians, Assyrians, and Babylonians from the 17th through the 13th centuries B.C. After the breakup of the Hittite Empire ca. 1200 B.C., smaller Hittite kingdoms covered parts of Anatolia and Syria. These smaller kingdoms never achieved the greatness of the Hittite Empire that had competed on equal terms with Egypt and Assyria. (For mention of Hittites in the Bible, see Gen. 23:10; 26:34; 1 Sam. 26:6; 2 Sam. 11:3.)

Mitanni

Mitanni was an important empire in northern Mesopotamia (ca. 1600–1330 B.C.), apparently responsible for the introduction of chariot warfare in the Near East. Mitanni was Egypt's chief rival for 100 years (ca. 1520–

1420 B.C.) before peace finally came in 1420 B.C. Mitanni was defeated by the Hittites in the 14th century B.C. A century later, the Assyrians destroyed what was left of this once mighty empire. The site of Haran, which figured prominently in the Abraham narrative (Gen. 11:29–32), was situated in the land of Mitanni.

Persia

At the height of its expansion, the Persian Empire extended from Greece and Cush in the west to India in the east. It began when Cyrus the Great conquered the Medes (ca. 550 B.C.) and continued until it was brought down by Alexander the Great (ca. 330 B.C.). After Cyrus conquered the Babylonians (ca. 538 B.C.), he allowed the Jews to return to Judah and rebuild the temple in Jerusalem (see 2 Chron. 36:22–23; Ezra 1; 3:7; Isa. 44:28; 45:1).

Hellas / Greece

The Greek peoples occupied the western seacoast of Asia Minor, the Greek peninsula and the islands of the Aegean. They established colonies from the Black Sea in the east to Spain in the west.. They confronted the East in the Persian Wars of the Fifth Century B.C.. The conquests of Alexander the Great led to the Hellenization of Asia Minor, the Eastern Mediterranean regions (including Palestine), and Egypt. Greek influence affected politics, religion and culture from 300 B.C. to A.D. 640. The Ptolemies (Egyptian Greeks) controlled Palestine until 198 B.C.; control passed to the Seleucids (Syrian Greeks) under Antiochus III, who defeated Ptolemy V at the Battle of Panias. Events centering around the legitimacy of the high priest led to the proscription of Jewish religion by Antiochus IV; the Maccabean Revolt was the Jewish response. An independent Jewish state was finally achieved by 142 B.C.; this lasted until the intervention of the Romans under Pompey in 63 B.C.

Rome

Pompey, invited to settle the dispute between Hyrcanus II and Aristobulus, decided in favor of Rome. Rome eventually put down two revolts (A.D. 70 and 135) and destroyed the temple and Jerusalem in the process.

Egypt

Egypt's cultural traditions were very different from those of the Fertile Crescent, and the two areas remained culturally distinct throughout their history. The Sinai peninsula was historically part of Egypt and a land bridge to the countries of Asia. The turquoise mines of Sinai were an important source of income, as were the trade routes through Sinai that brought merchant caravans from beyond the Red Sea. Sinai was most important, however, as a buffer zone that helped give further protection to an already isolated and naturally-protected Egypt. The ancient road between the Nile Delta and Gaza (southern coast of Palestine) was the road through the Philistine country. The Israelites took instead the desert road toward the Red Sea, a route through the heart of Sinai (Ex. 13:17–18). They probably did this to avoid the Egyptian military bases that controlled the strategic route across northern Sinai (see **Unit P3**).

Egypt played a role in God's dealings with Abraham and his descendants (Gen. 12:10; 46:3–4). Jacob went to Egypt, where he lived with his sons and their families, including Joseph, who had risen to a high and influential position in the Egyptian government (see Gen. 37–45). Some time later, Moses was called to deliver the descendants of Abraham from Egyptian bondage (see Ex. 2–14), fulfilling God's promise to Jacob: "Do not be afraid to go down to Egypt, for I will make you into a great nation there. I will go down to Egypt with you, and I will surely bring you back again" (Gen. 46:3–4). Egypt, in an attempt to control Palestine, came into conflict with the Hittites, Assyrians, Babylonians and Persians before being incorporated into the Greek Empire under the Ptolemies. Egypt was an imperial Roman province during New Testament times, when Joseph and Mary fled to Egypt to escape King Herod (see Matt. 2). Egypt enjoys a special status in the history of the Holy Land, partly because of its role as an international power, but mostly because it was the birthplace of Israel as a nation. In Rev. 11:8 Egypt is the symbol for evil oppression.

Transjordan

In addition to the empires and kingdoms described above, there were smaller kingdoms closer to home that faced Israel from the east. These smaller kingdoms also wanted to control the desert trade routes, and, as a result, engaged in intermittent warfare with Israel. A major trade route, known as "The Kings Highway," stretched from Damascus to Eilat, and other routes fed off this to Egypt, Palestine and Phoenicia. The main kingdoms of Transjordan are briefly discussed below.

Ammon

The Ammonites were descendants of Abraham's nephew, Lot (Gen. 19:30–38). They settled the region east of Mt. Gilead and south of the Jabbok River. The rise of the Ammonite kingdom coincides with that of the kingdoms of Moab, Edom, and Israel during the Late Bronze and early Iron Age (1500–1000 B.C.). The capital of Ammon was Rabbah (modern Amman), near the sources of the Jabbok River and at the junction of the King's Highway and the desert road (see **Unit N**; Judg. 11; 1 Sam. 11; 2 Sam. 10; 11:1; 12:9, 26, 31; Amos 1:13ff.; Zeph. 2:8; 2 Kgs. 24:2; Ezek. 25:2ff.; Neh. 4; 1 Macc. 5).

Moab

The Moabites are reckoned as the descendants of Lot's eldest daughter (Gen. 19:37), and occupied the lands east of the Dead Sea. Their territory was divided into two parts by the Arnon River (Wadi Mujib). The flatland north of the Arnon River is called the "Mishor" or tableland (Deut. 3:10; Josh. 13:9), and was part of the territory allotted to the tribes of Reuben and Gad (Judg. 5:16; 1 Sam. 13). As a result, there was constant warfare between Israel and Moab for control of the Mishor (see **Unit O**; Num. 22–25; Judg. 3:12–30; 11:17; 2 Sam. 8:2; 2 Kgs. 3:6–27; 13:20; 24:2; 1 Chron. 18:2; 2 Chron. 20:1–25).

Edom

The Edomites are reckoned as the descendants of Esau, the brother of Jacob. They occupied the high plateau south of Moab called Mt. Seir (Gen. 32:3; 36:9; Deut. 2:5, 12, 22). The border between Edom and Moab was the Zered River. Edom's chief source of wealth came from controlling the trade routes to Arabia. This led to constant conflicts with Israel who wanted to control these same trade routes (see **Unit O**; Num. 20:14 ff.; 21:4; Judg. 11:17; 1 Sam. 14:47; 2 Sam. 8:13–14; Jer. 27:3; 49:7–22; Ezek. 35:3–15).

The Decapolis

In 62 B.C., a league of ten cities was established by Rome in the northeastern part of Palestine. Pliny named the original members as Scythopolis (Beth Shean, the only city west of the Jordan River), Damascus, Hippus, Gerasa, Gadara, Dion, Raphana, Kanatha, Pella, and Philadelphia. Ptolemy included other towns in a list of 18 cities in the 2nd century A.D. These were important centers of Hellenistic culture and religion. Gadara was the birthplace of Philodemus, an Epicurean philosopher of the 1st century B.C., and the home of Menippus, a Greek cynic and satirist of the 3rd century B.C. Jesus traveled to the Decapolis according to Mark 5:1–20; 7:31. The Jewish church moved to Pella before the war of A.D. 70.

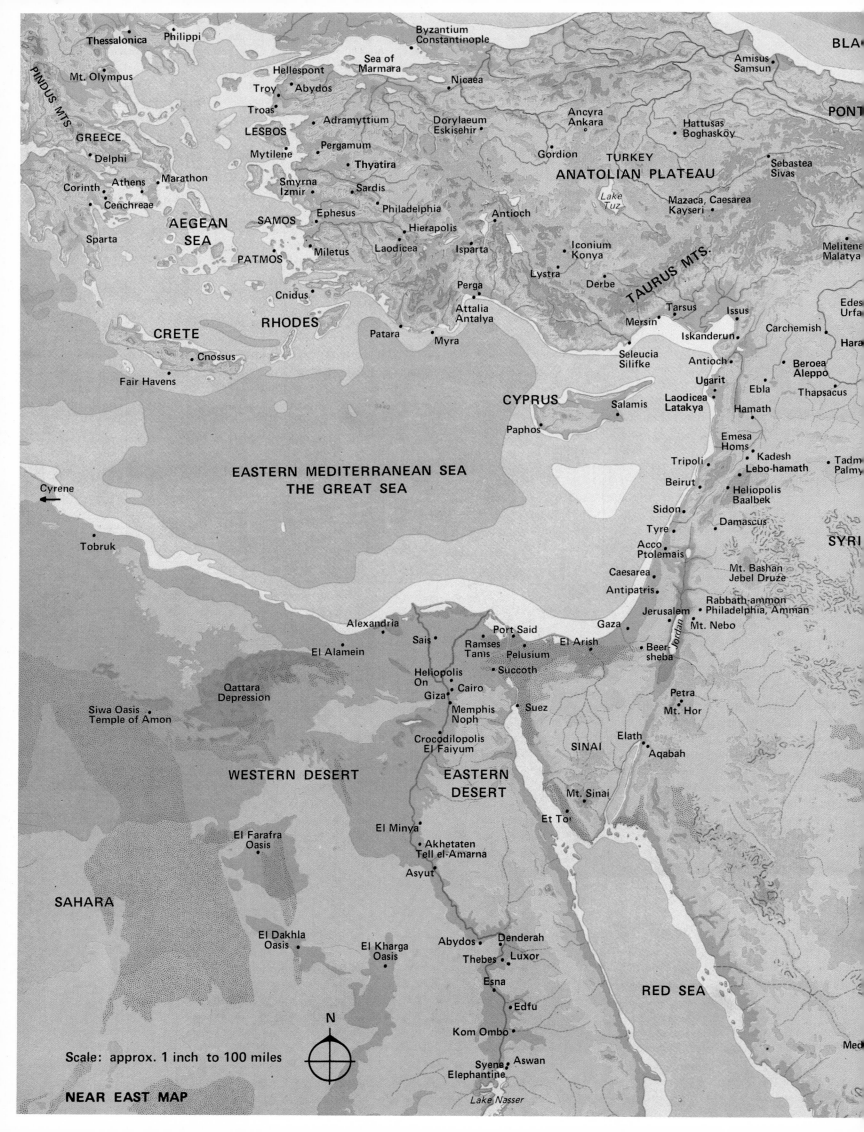

In the introduction to his book, *The Land and the Book*, William Thomson wrote that Palestine "has had an all-pervading influence upon the costume and character of the Bible." Thus he traveled through the land with the following objective in mind:

> **Let us, therefore, deal reverently with it, walk softly over those acres once trodden by the feet of patriarchs, prophets, and sacred poets, and most of all by the Son of God himself ... There is design in this grouping of mountains and plains, hills and valleys, lakes and rivers, the desert and the sea, with all their vegetable and animal products, and in the marvelous and miraculous incidents and phenomena in the sacred record. These things were not the result of blind chance, were not merely natural, but beyond and above that, for we see in them the supernatural and the divine** (Thomson 1: 3).

Thomson also described the diverse scenes one can expect to see while traveling through Palestine:

> **There are within the borders of the Holy Land lofty mountains covered with snow; hills and valleys and wide plains carpeted with gay flowers; lakes, rivers, and streams baptized with beauty; and sacred sites and scenes innumerable, and of the very deepest interest** (Thomson 1: 6).

Before the Israelites

Our focus here is on biblical times, but one does well to remember that Palestine was home to human occupation for vast stretches of time before we have any historical record. Stone Age human families occupied caves and open sites on Mt. Carmel, at a number of sites in the Galilee and the Upper Jordan Valley, and in the wadis of the Central Hill Country. Jericho the oldest "city" in the world, represents the more recent end of this long stretch of time.

A Land of "Milk and Honey"

As God was preparing to bring the children of Israel out of Egypt, he said to Moses: "So I have come down to rescue them [Israel] from the land of the Egyptians and to bring them up out of that land into a good and spacious land, a land flowing with milk and honey" (Ex. 3:8). "Flowing with milk and honey" was a proverbial expression meaning that Canaan was fruitful and productive in husbandry and agriculture. It was "a land with wheat and barley, vines and fig trees, pomegranates, olive oil and honey; a land where bread will not be scarce and you will lack nothing; a land where rocks are iron and you can dig copper out of the hills" (Deut. 8:8–9). These promises of fruitfulness and prosperity are conditional, depending on Israel's continuing devotion to God (Deut. 7:11–14). The same land, with its uncertain rainfall and changeable patterns of temperature, can become a curse in the face of disloyalty.

The "Rain of Heaven"

Canaan was not like Egypt, with its flat lands watered by the Nile River. Canaan was a "land of mountains and valleys that drinks rain from heaven." The children of Israel were told that if they would faithfully obey the commands of God—"to love the Lord … and to serve him" with all their heart and soul—then God would give to Israel "rain on your land in its season, both autumn and spring rains, so that you may gather in your grain, new wine and oil." But if Israel served other gods, then the heavens would be "shut ... so that it will not rain and the ground will yield no produce" (Deut. 11:9–17). Rain fell primarily on the west of the central hills; the east slopes are in a rain shadow.

The rains of autumn marked the beginning of the agricultural season, putting moisture back into the ground left dry by the hot summer months. After these rains, lightweight plows could break up the hard surface of sun-baked fields. The spring rains helped the crops to ripen and ensured a good harvest. If the agricultural season was wet in the beginning but dry at the end, it was possible to have an agricultural drought, even though the annual rainfall reached its average. The importance of this complete cycle is reflected in numerous passages from the Bible:

> **When a king's face brightens, it means life; his favor is like a rain cloud in spring** (Prov. 16:15).

> **"Let us fear the Lord our God, who gives fall and spring rains in season, who assures us of the regular weeks of harvest"** (Jer. 5:24).

> **I also withheld rain from you, when the harvest was still three months away, ...** (Amos 4:7). [Barley was ready to be harvested in May, and wheat about four weeks later. The harvest of grapes and olives took place in late summer and into the fall.]

> **Be patient, then, brothers, until the Lord's coming. See how the farmer waits for the land to yield its precious crop and how patient he is for the fall and spring rains** (James 5:7).

A Land Divided

Two factors challenged Israel's ability to prosper in the land. First, Canaan was a land occupied by another people: seven nations larger and stronger than Israel. The people might ask, "How can we drive them out?" God answered, "Do not be afraid of them; remember well what the Lord your God did to Pharaoh and to all Egypt" (Deut. 7:1,17–18). The fact that so many nations could exist side by side in Canaan suggests a second problem: the natural features of the land worked against unification. The mountains and valleys tended to separate Canaan into independent districts, each with its own ruler. A strong, well-organized government was required to unify a land with so diverse a topography.

During the Amarna Age (the reigns of Amenhotep III and IV when the capital of Egypt was moved to Amarna, ca. 1400 to 1350 B.C.), Canaan was ruled by numerous kings, each controlling different regions of the country. In the central hill country, the two main centers were Shechem and Jebus (Jerusalem). The main centers in the Jezreel Valley were Taanach and Megiddo. The king of Megiddo complained to Pharaoh:

> **Labayu [king of Shechem] has carried on hostilities against me, and we are not able to pluck the wool, and we are not able to go outside the gate in the presence of Labayu, since he learned that thou hast not given archers [i.e., Pharaoh had removed military support from his vassal kings]; and now his face is set to take Megiddo, but let the king protect his city, lest Labayu seize it** (*ANET*, 263).

The division evident in the Amarna Age also existed at the time of the Israelite conquest. After the report of the conquest of Jericho and Ai, Joshua faced five kings of the Amorites who tried to stop him at Gibeon (see Unit F2). The Bible also speaks of other groups of people living in Canaan: Kenites, Kenizzites, Kadmonites, Hittites, Perizzites, Rephaites, Amorites, Canaanites, Girgashites and Jebusites (Gen. 15:18–21). This division of the land and its inhabitants was the main challenge Israel faced before the land was finally unified under King David.

Roads and Highways

Important political and commercial centers grew up along the international highway, earlier called the Via Maris, which ran from Mesopotamia through Palestine to Egypt, including Gaza, Dor, Megiddo, Hazor, and Damascus in the Old Testament era, Caesarea and Capernaum in the New Testament era. Merchant caravans like the one that carried Joseph into Egypt traveled this route, carrying their products and other items for sale or trade in the cities of Egypt and Mesopotamia (see Gen. 37). Providing for the needs of these caravans and protecting them from bandits was an important source of income for whatever nation controlled the route. It was in use in all historical periods and was the prime objective of Egypt when it sought to conquer Palestine. We will refer to this main highway as the Coastal Route.

When Moses sent messengers from Kadesh, in Sinai, to the king of Edom, requesting permission to pass peacefully through his land, he promised the king that Israel would not pass through their fields or drink water from their wells; instead, Israel would "travel along the king's highway" (Num. 20:17). The King's Highway ran the length of Transjordan near the desert and served at times as an alternative to the Coastal Route. Important branch routes from the King's Highway led to Egypt across the Negev (see **Unit L**) and Sinai (see **Unit P1**), or to Arabia across the desert and along the shores of the Red Sea. The King's Highway facilitated the export of many goods from southern Arabia, including precious perfumes. The Queen of Sheba, for example, presented the following items to King Solomon:

120 talents of gold, large quantities of spices, and precious stones. Never again were so many spices brought in as those the queen of Sheba gave to King Solomon (1 Kgs. 10:10).

After the Queen of Sheba left Jerusalem, Solomon benefited from trade with the "merchants and traders and from all the Arabian kings and the governors of the land" (1 Kgs. 10:15). At Ezion-geber, the northern port of the Red Sea where Solomon had his fleet of ships (see **P1-6**), the King's Highway branched either to Damascus through Edom, Moab, and Gilead (see **Unit N** and **Unit O**) or northwest through the Negev (see **Unit L**) to Jerusalem and the coast of Palestine.

These international highways, as well as other routes, served both the soldier and the merchant. Egypt's kings embarked on numerous military campaigns that resulted in disaster for both the Canaanites and Israelites. Two campaigns in particular were those of Thutmose III (ca. 1468 B.C.) and Shishak (ca. 924 B.C.). Thutmose defeated a Canaanite coalition in the Jezreel Valley near Megiddo, and Shishak devastated both the northern kingdom of Israel and the southern kingdom of Judah in an attempt to weaken Israel's hold on the routes through the Jezreel Valley and Negev (see **Unit D1** and **Unit L**). In view of Palestine's unique geographical position among nations, God's promise to Moses on Mount Sinai seems almost incredible:

And I will grant peace in the land, and you will lie down, and no one will make you afraid ... *and the sword will not pass through your country* (Lev. 26:6; italics added).

Flora and Fauna

The basis of Palestine's economy has always been the cultivation of the land and the breeding of livestock. The most important crops were wheat, barley, vines, fig trees, pomegranates, olive oil, and honey (Deut. 8:8). Consider, also, this passage from Psalm 104:13-15:

He waters the mountains from his upper chambers;...bringing forth food from the earth: wine that gladdens the heart of man, oil to make his face shine, and bread that sustains his heart).

These products became a symbol of prosperity and peace when the enemies of Israel would have no power to conquer or control the land. The prophet Joel referred to such a time:

The Lord will reply to them: "I am sending you grain, new wine and oil, enough to satisfy you fully; never again will I make you an object of scorn to the nations.

Be glad, O people of Zion, rejoice in the Lord your God, for he has given you a teacher for righteousness. He sends you abundant showers, both autumn and spring rains, as before. The threshing floors will be filled with grain; the vats will overflow with new wine and oil" (Joel 2:19, 23–24).

An account by an Egyptian official named Sinuhe (ca. 1950 B.C.) confirms the description of the land found in the Bible:

It was a good land, named Yaa. Figs were in it, and grapes. It had more wine than water. Plentiful was its honey, abundant its olives. Every kind of fruit was on its trees. Barley was there, and emmer (Pritchard 1: 7).

Other plants were available for eating: almonds (Gen. 28:19), pistachio nuts (Gen. 43:11), and figs (1 Kings 10:27) The palm produced dates, which grew well in the Jericho area (Deut. 34:3, *War* 4.8.3) Several woods were used for lumber: cedar, oak and pine. Flax was used for the manufacture of linen.

Palestine was also a land of sheep and goats, both of which were used for their meat (Deut. 14:4). From the goat came milk for food (Prov. 27:27), skins for making containers (Gen. 21:14; Josh. 9:4), and hair for making tents. The roof of the tabernacle, for example, was made of goat hair (Ex. 26:7; 36:14–15). Goats were hardy animals, able to survive on the scanty vegetation of the desert, and thus use land that was not suitable for agriculture.

Sheep, which are mentioned more than 500 times in the Bible, required grazing ground and thrived on the stubble left after the harvests of wheat and barley. The shepherd was in constant search of greener pastures (see 1 Chr. 4:39–40). Joseph, for example, went looking for his brothers in the fields around Shechem. When he asked a man where his brothers were feeding their flocks, he was told they had moved on to Dothan, a broad plain leading into the Jezreel Valley (Gen. 37:15–17). Sheep provided milk, meat, hides, and wool. Their horns were used both as containers for oil and as musical instruments (Deut. 32:14; 1 Sam. 14:32; Heb. 11:37; Job 31:20; 1 Sam. 16:1; Josh. 6:4; et al.). The wool of sheep was an important item of trade. The annual tribute of the king of Moab to Israel was 100,000 lambs and 100,000 rams, "with the wool" (2 Kgs. 3:4). In both the Old (see Psalm 23, Ezekiel 34) and New Testaments, sheep are symbolic of people. Jesus compared Israel to sheep lost and without a shepherd, announcing that he was the shepherd who was willing to give his life for the sheep (John 10:7–9; see Matt. 9:36; 10:6; 12:11; 18:12; 25:33; Isa. 53:6; Ezek. 37:24).

In addition to domesticated animals (oxen, sheep and goats), many wild animals found in Palestine were used for food: deer, gazelle, roe deer, wild goat, ibex antelope, and mountain sheep (Deut. 14:5). Some birds, especially the dove and pigeon, were eaten. Fish provided another source of food (Neh. 13:16; Matt. 13:47). Josephus mentions several kinds of fish found in the Sea of Galilee that were "different both to the taste and the sight from those elsewhere" (*War* 3.10.7).

The ass or donkey was used as a beast of burden and outnumbered all other animals for this purpose (Ezra 2:66–67). The dog was considered a scavenger and ran wild in packs (Ps. 22:16–20). The fox and jackal were much alike and often confused. The fox is a solitary animal; the jackal is gregarious. Since the jackals stay together in packs, the "three hundred" animals that Samson caught (Judges 15:4) were probably jackals. The bear and lion are mentioned as two of the largest and strongest beasts of prey. They symbolized strength and terror (Amos 5:19).

A1-1 Mt. Hermon (foothills) & Nimrud castle

View: SW

A1-2 Gamala

View: W

A1-3 Mt. Hermon: sunrise　　　　　　　　　　　　　　　　　　　　　**View: NW**

Mt. HERMON & GOLAN　　　　　　　　　　**Unit A1**

Mt. Hermon is the southern peak of the Anti-Lebanon mountain range. It was called Sirion by the Phoenicians and Shenir by the Amorites (Deut. 3:9), although these names may have designated the entire Anti-Lebanon range and not just Mt. Hermon (Song 4:8). The tribes of Israel took from the Amorites the territory east of the Jordan, from the Arnon Gorge as far as Mount Hermon (Deut. 3:8). The territory between Arnon and the River Jabbok ("half mount Gilead") was given to the tribe of Reuben (see **Unit N**). The remaining territory north of the Jabbok to Mt. Hermon, including all of Bashan, was given to the half tribe of Manasseh (Deut. 3:12–13).

South of Mt. Hermon is the region of Old Testament Bashan, well-known for its rich pasture lands that supported the fattened animals from Bashan (Ezek. 39:18). Golan was a district in the western part of Bashan that overlooked the Upper Jordan Valley and Sea of Galilee (see **A1-4** and **A1-6**). Golan was important because of the highways that crossed it, connecting Damascus with Hazor (see **Unit A2**) and the Sea of Galilee, as well as Damascus with Beth-shan and the Jezreel Valley (see **Unit D1** and **Unit G1**). Solomon's wealth, for example, was based in part on his controlling the important trade routes through Canaan (see 1 Kgs. 4:21–34; 9:15–19). These routes included the one from Damascus to Beth-shan, which was used by an Egyptian scribe from the time of Ramses II (13th century B.C.). The scribe, whose name was Hori, told about his travels from Kadesh in the valley of Lebanon to Damascus, and from Damascus via the Golan region to Beth-shan (*ANET*, 477). This route was an extension of the Coastal Route, which merged with the King's Highway in Bashan.

PHOTO CAPTIONS

A1-1 The castle-fortress of Nimrud (center) is one of the best preserved Crusader sites in the Holy Land. A former stronghold of the Assassins (an Islamic sect founded at the end of the 11th century by the Persian Hasan as-Sabah, and which used assassination as its chief political weapon), it was conquered first by the Crusaders and then by the Mamelukes. It was strategically located on a mountain spur that overlooks the entire Upper Jordan Valley (see **Unit A2**). The castle is 1 mile east of Banias (Caesarea Philippi). The valleys and ridges in the foreground of this photograph are part of Mt. Hermon. The view is to the southwest. The Golan region is to the southeast (in the upper left-hand corner of the photograph).

A1-2 The site of Gamala (Gamla) is about 6 miles east of the Sea of Galilee on a hill (center) that "falls away sharply on both sides and in front in impassable ravines" (*War* 4.1.1). Sometimes referred to as the "Masada of the north" (see **H1-5**), Gamala was one of the last cities in northern Palestine to fall before the Roman general Vespasian in the First Jewish Revolt against Rome (68 B.C.). Jewish resistance inside the walls of the city was so intense that the Romans were forced to retreat with heavy losses. After this first defeat, it required the skill of Vespasian to restore the morale of his men and resume the fight. In the end 5,000 Jewish men, women, and children met their deaths by throwing themselves "into the artificial ravine that had been excavated to a vast depth well below the citadel" (*War* 4.1.10).

A1-3 The highest peak of Mt. Hermon is some 9,230 feet above sea level. It looks down on Bashan to the south, the Upper Jordan Valley to the southwest, and the Valley of Lebanon (Josh. 11:17; the Beq'a of modern Lebanon) to the west. Every year Mt. Hermon receives about 70 inches of precipitation in the form of dew, rain, and snow. Much of this water is absorbed into the porous rocks and feeds the springs at the base of the mountain that form the headwaters of the Jordan River. The dew of Hermon was a sign of blessing in antiquity, "even life forevermore" (Ps. 133:3). Its majestic peak, snow-capped for several months of the year, could be seen from many parts of Canaan and was considered a sacred place by the original inhabitants of Canaan (cf. "Baal Hermon" in Judg. 3:3). According to one tradition, Caesarea Philippi on the foothills of Mt. Hermon was the site of the Lord's Transfiguration (Matt. 16:13, 17:1–9). Anciently, the mountain was covered with cedar trees and inhabited by lions and leopards (Song 4:8). Thomson observed the following after tracking a family of bears on Mt. Hermon: "It is remarkable that bears were common in Palestine, as far south at least as Bethlehem, when David kept his father's sheep 'in the wilderness;' but they have long since disappeared from all parts of the country, excepting the snow-covered summit of Hermon. There, too, they are diminishing in numbers, and will soon become extinct" (Thomson 2: 520).

A1-4 The Upper Golan region, pictured here, is higher in elevation than Lower Golan to the south. Anciently, it was a region of brush, forest, and pastures. Passages in the Bible that refer to the oaks of Bashan (Isa. 2:13; Ezek. 27:6) and to the cattle of Bashan (Amos 4:1; Ezek. 39:18) provide

HAURAN
Unit A1a
1: 300,000

1 Abel	5 Caesarea Philippi	9 Edrei; Deraa	13 Gamala
2 Aphek, Upper ?	6 Capitolias	10 Eietha ?	14 Golan
3 Beth-arbel; Irbid	7 Damascus	11 Enab ?	15 Hazor
4 Beth-shan	8 Dan	12 Gadara	16 Hermon, Mt.

N

Mt. HERMON & GOLAN
UNIT A1b

1 : 200,000

1 Abel	5 Ashtaroth ?	9 Dan	13 Gergesa
2 Ain ?	6 Caesarea Philippi	10 Dium ?	14 Golan
3 Aphek, Lower ?	7 Capernaum	11 Eietha ?	15 Hammath Gader
4 Aphek, Upper ?	8 Chaspho	12 Gamala	16 Hazor

7

N

A1-4   Mt. Hermon & Upper Golan   View: NE

an apt description of the Upper Golan region. Here the fattened animals from Bashan, which included rams, lambs, goats, and bulls, found rich pasture (Ezek. 39:18).

A1-5 The ruins in this picture (lower left) are in the vicinity of ancient Aphek, about 3 miles east of the Sea of Galilee (upper right). Here, the Israelites inflicted heavy casualties on the Arameans (1 Kgs. 20:26–30). With the help of the prophet Elisha (ca. 790 B.C.), Israel was able to defeat the Syrians a second time in the region of Aphek and recover again the Israelite towns (2 Kgs. 13:14–19,25). Below Aphek, and on top of the cone-shaped hill (upper right) overlooking the Sea of Galilee, was Hippus, one of the cities of the Decapolis. Mt. Tabor comes into view at the top of the picture (upper center).

A1-6 The Golan region consists of two subregions: the Upper Golan in the north (see **A1-4**) and the Lower Golan in the south. Lower Golan, pictured here, much more level than Upper Golan, was well suited for farming. Agriculture in this region was successful because: (1) the hills of Galilee are lower, thus allowing the rains to sweep farther inland; and (2) the soil of Lower Golan is a rich volcanic alluvium. The strong bulls of Bashan were used to plow the heavy volcanic soil and prepare it for raising wheat and barley (Ps. 22:12). The Golan region was an important granary of the Roman empire. Wheat and barley were transported across Lower Galilee to the port of Acco/Ptolemais.

BIBLICAL/HISTORICAL REVIEW
Cross references to the Student Map Manual

• Wars of Ahab against Aram: Aphek and Ramoth-gilead
1 Kgs. 20:1–43; 1 Kgs. 22:2–40; 2 Chron. 18; SMM 8–5f,h. Five years before the end of Ahab's reign, Ben-hadad, king of Damascus, attacked Samaria. Ahab was able to break the siege and soundly defeat the Arameans. Ben-hadad returned the following year, but was again defeated by Ahab near Aphek on the Golan (see **A1-5**). In a final battle at Ramoth-gilead, Ahab was killed and his army defeated. As a result, Ben-hadad controlled the northern part of Transjordan.

• Expansion of the Northern Kingdom: Jehoash and Jeroboam II
2 Kgs. 13:10–25; 14:23–29; 15:8–12; Amos; Hosea; SMM 9-1/2e. The battles between Aram/Syria and Samaria that occurred in the days of Ahab continued during the reign of Jehoash, the grandson of Jehu (see

Unit **D1**). The Bible says that Jehoash beat the Syrians three times and that he "recovered the Israelite towns." Jehoash's son, Jeroboam II, extended the borders of the northern kingdom to encompass almost the same area conquered by King David.

• Settlers on Mt. Hermon: The Itureans
Luke 3:1; SMM 12-3b. After his death, Herod's kingdom was divided among three sons, Archelaus, Herod Antipas, and Philip. According to Luke, Philip's part of the kingdom also included the region of Iturea (Mt. Hermon). The ancient historian, Strabo (16.2.18, ca. 63 B.C.–A.D. 24), explains that the Itureans were mountain dwellers who lived on the range that extends into the valley of Lebanon. Their two main centers were Baalbek and Chalcis at the northern end of the valley.

• Campaign of Northern Kings
Gen. 14; SMM 4-3c. Four kings of the north waged war against the kings of Sodom and Gomorrah at the southern end of the Dead Sea. The battle route took the kings of the north through the Golan region, where they "defeated the Rephaites in Ashteroth Karnaim." Ashteroth was the ancient capital of Bashan. When Abraham learned that his nephew Lot was captured in the battle near the Dead Sea, he armed his own men and pursued the kings of the north to Dan at the foot of Mt. Hermon (see **A2-1**). There Abraham "routed them, pursuing them as far as Hobah, north of Damascus."

• The Land that Remains
Josh. 13:1–6; Judg. 3:1–3; SMM 6–1b. The land of Geshur was included among the regions that remained to be possessed by the Israelites. It comprised the western part of Bashan, or what was later called Gaulanitis. Geshur was apparently able to keep its independence even into the reign of King David (see 2 Sam. 13:37–14:24).   ∎

A1-7 (overleaf) This is a second view of Gamala, looking south toward the Lower Golan region (see **A1-2).**

A1-5 Upper Aphek, Apheca (Fiq) & Hippus   View: W

A1-6 Lower Golan: harvest   View: W

A2-1   Dan, Antiochia   View: N

A2-2   Panias, Caesarea Philippi & Mt. Hermon   View: N

A2-3 **Upper Jordan Valley & Golan**   View: E

UPPER JORDAN VALLEY   Unit A2

The Upper Jordan Valley (also called the Huleh Valley) is completely enclosed by higher ground. It is approximately 14 miles long and varies in width from 4 to 6 miles. Until the 1950s it contained a small lake, called Semechonitis by Josephus (1st century A.D.). In modern times the lake was called Huleh, like the valley (see **A2-7**). The valley around the lake was "marsh and fat meadow, with a few mounds and terraces covered by trees" (Smith, 303). The lake and marshes were created when lava formed a dam at the southern end of the valley that impeded the flow of the Jordan River. Thomson remarked that the Huleh plain, including the marsh, lake, and surrounding mountains, was "one of the finest hunting-grounds in Syria, and mainly so because it is not frequented. Panthers and leopards, bears and wolves, jackals, hyenas, and foxes, and many other animals, are found, great and small, while it is the very paradise of the wild-boar and the fleet gazelle." He described the swamp as an impenetrable jungle that not even a wild boar could get through (Thomson 2: 450–454). Thus the landscape of the Upper Jordan Valley was different from that of any other part of Palestine, except possibly the Sharon Plain (see **Unit E1**). The extremely fertile soil and well-watered fields of the valley produced abundant crops of wheat and barley. In biblical times, the Danite spies reported that the Upper Jordan Valley was "a land that lacks nothing whatever" (Judg. 18:10).

In spite of the swamps, the Upper Jordan Valley was a major avenue of communication between Damascus and the Sea of Galilee (see **A2-6**). Its cities were conquered by the armies of Syria and Mesopotamia, who dared not leave Ijon, Dan, and Abel-beth-maacah to threaten important supply lines (1 Kgs. 15:20; 2 Kgs. 15:29). Ben-hadad I, king of Syria, conquered the valley in the days of Baasha, king of Israel (ca. 885 B.C.), as did Tiglath-pileser III, king of Assyria, in the days of Pekah, king of Israel (ca. 734 B.C.). The strategic importance of this region is also hinted at in passages that described Dan as a lion cub leaping from Bashan (Deut. 33:22; see **Unit A1**) and as "a viper along the path, that bites the horse's heels so that its rider tumbles backward" (Gen. 49:17; see **A2-2**).

PHOTO CAPTIONS

A2-1 Tel Dan (center), which covers nearly 50 acres, is 2 miles west of Caesarea Philippi (see **A2-2**). Near the tell is one of the sources of the Jordan River. Dan overlooked the Upper Jordan Valley, and guarded one of the important trade routes between Damascus and Tyre. Before the Israelite conquest, the site was called "Laish" or "Leshem," but it was designated "Dan" after it was captured by the tribe of Dan (Josh. 19:47–48; Judg. 18:27–29). King Jeroboam established a sanctuary at Dan in which he set up a golden calf: "And this thing became a sin; the people went even as far as Dan to worship the one there" (1 Kgs. 12:27–30). The city was conquered by Ben-hadad, king of Syria, early in the 9th century B.C. It was conquered again a century later by the Assyrian king Tiglath-pileser III, who carried away its inhabitants to Assyria (1 Kgs. 15:20; 2 Chron. 16:4; 2 Kgs. 15:29). The biblical expression, "from Dan to Beersheba," indicates Israel's physical extent from north to south (1 Kgs. 4:25). Excavations show that Dan continued into Hellenistic and probably Roman times.

A2-2 Caesarea Philippi guarded the northern end of the Upper Jordan Valley. It was located at the foot of Mt. Hermon (center) near one of the main sources of the Jordan River. It may be the Baal-Gad or Baal-Hermon of Josh. 11:17ff; Judg. 3:3; 1 Chron. 5:23. The Greeks named it Paneas, after the Greek god Pan ("Banias" is an Arabic corruption). In 198 B.C., Antiochus III won a major victory at Paneas that decided the fate of the region and gave him control over Palestine. The name of Paneas was changed to Caesarea by Herod the Great in honor of Caesar Augustus (Jos, *Ant.* 15.10.3; *War* 1.21.3; see Luke 2:1), and then to Caesarea Philippi by Herod's son, Philip (*Ant.* 18.2.1; *War* 2.9.1). Matthew and Mark locate Peter's confession to Jesus here. When Jesus visited this area he asked his disciples, "Who do people say the Son of Man is?" Several suggestions were given: John the Baptist, Elijah, Jeremiah or one of the prophets . Then Peter answered , "You are the Christ, the Son of the living God" (Matt. 16:13–16).

A2-3 The view in this picture is to the east, looking across the Huleh Valley toward the Golan region (see **Unit A1**). There are several volcanic cones on the horizon (upper center), which rise as much as 1,500 feet above the plateau. Today the Upper Jordan Valley is rich in agriculture. Except for the 700-acre Huleh Nature Reserve (see **A2-7**), most of the valley is used for growing fruit, cotton, potatoes, and other vegetables. Fish ponds (center) comprise about 25 percent of all the fish hatcheries in the country.

**UPPER JORDAN VALLEY
UNIT A2
1 : 150,000**

1 Abel-beth-maachah	5 Capernaum	9 Dan, N.	13 Hermon, Mt.
2 Ammud, N.	6 Chastelet castle	10 Daphne	14 Hermon, N.
3 Anafa, T.	7 Chorazin	11 Gamala	15 Hippus
4 Caesarea Philippi	8 Dan	12 Hazor	16 Horshat Tal

17 Huleh Nature Reserve
18 Iyyon, N.
19 Jacob's Daughters, Br.
20 Jordan, R. (Upper)

21 Julias
22 Kedesh
23 Leontes, R.; Litani
24 Metulla

25 Nimrud castle
26 Qiryat Shemona
27 Quneitra
28 Senir, N.; Hasbani

29 Thella
30 Tiberias
31 Volcanic cones
32 Zefat

N

A2-4 Horshat Tal: oak trees

View: SW

A2-4 The Horshat Tal Nature Reserve is a national park, located one and a half miles southwest of Tel Dan (see **A2-1**). The headwaters of the Jordan that rise at Tel Dan flow into the park, which is covered by large oak trees, lawns, and pools. Oak trees, once common in the Holy Land, were often used as landmarks (see Gen. 35:4; Judg. 6:11; 1 Chron. 10:12).

A2-5 This picture shows the Jordan River as it leaves the Huleh Valley on its way to the Sea of Galilee. A bridge of basalt arches was built by the Mamelukes on a natural ford of the river that had been used in ancient times to cross the Upper Jordan Valley. The bridge was named the "Bridge of Jacob's Daughters," after the nuns of a nearby monastery. The Crusaders built Chastellet castle (upper center) in A.D. 1178 to guard this important crossing east of Hazor (see **A2-6**). The distance between the southern end of Lake Huleh (before it was drained) and the Sea of Galilee was about 10 miles. Thomson gave the following description of the river between the lake and the bridge: "The river is about one hundred and thirty feet wide where it issues from the lake, and for a short mile it glides tranquilly onward between green, sloping banks and tall, waving cane towards the bridge of Jacob's daughters" (Thomson 2: 449).

A2-6 Hazor was a large Canaanite and Israelite city. The site consists of a mound (center) covering 26 acres (at the base, 15 acres on top), and the lower part of the city just north of the mound (upper left). Together they cover about 200 acres. Hazor is mentioned in the Execration Texts and other early Egyptian documents and in the Mari archives as a major trade center for caravans traveling to and from Babylon. In the Bible, Hazor is mentioned in connection with the Israelite conquest of northern Canaan and in the story of Deborah and Barak (Josh. 11:10–13; Judg. 4:2). Hazor was also a fortified city of King Solomon (1 Kgs. 9:15).

BIBLICAL/HISTORICAL REVIEW
Cross references to the Student Map Manual

•Tribe of Dan Moves North
Judg. 17–18; Josh. 19:47; SMM 6-4a. The Amorites "confined the Danites to the hill country, not allowing them to come down into the plain" (see Judg. 1:34–35). Unable to take possession of its inheritance in the Shephelah and Coastal Plain, the tribe of Dan moved north to the Canaanite city of Laish . As the Danites passed through Mt. Ephraim, they took the images and priest of Micah. After reaching the Upper Jordan Valley, they conquered Laish, gave the city the name of Dan, and set up a shrine using the idols from the house of Micah. After the division of the kingdom, Jeroboam established a sanctuary at Dan (1 Kgs. 12:28–29).

•Rebellion of Sheba
2 Sam. 20:1–22; SMM 7-7f. Sheba son of Bicri was a Benjamite who led a rebellion against the house of David. David ordered that an army be gathered from among the men of Judah, "or he will find fortified cities and escape from us." The commander of David's army pursued Sheba north to Abel-beth-maachah in the Upper Jordan Valley. To save the city, the people cut off Sheba's head and "threw it to Joab."

•Syrians Invade the Upper Jordan Valley: Ben-hadad I
1 Kgs. 15:16–21; 2 Chron. 16:1–5; SMM 8-5a. Baasha, king of Israel, threatened the southern kingdom of Judah by pushing Israel's southern border to within 5 miles of Jerusalem. Asa, king of Judah, gave silver and gold to Ben-hadad to break his treaty with Israel and enter into an alliance with Judah. Ben-hadad invaded Israel, conquering Ijon, Dan, Abel-beth-maachah, and all Kinnereth "in addition to Naphtali." As a result, Ben-hadad also gained control of the trade routes through the Upper Jordan Valley.

•Jesus of Nazareth: Visit to Caesarea Philippi
Matt. 16:13–20; Mark 8:27–29; SMM 12-4. Jesus traveled ancient roads as he walked from village to village through the Upper Jordan Valley. He would have seen much of the same scenery as that described by 19th century travelers to Palestine, including the animal life, the swamps and papyrus reeds, and the woods that have since disappeared. Caesarea Philippi was the northernmost point in Palestine. At the great spring at Paneas was the grotto of Pan. The inscriptions and cultic niches visible on the cliff face indicate that the worship of Pan was prevalent in this area. Was it this that called forth Jesus' question to his disciples? Caesarea Philippi supports the epithet "Galilee of the Gentiles." ∎

A2-7 (overleaf) The Huleh Nature Reserve is at the southern end of the Upper Jordan Valley and covers an area of approximately 700 acres. It is land set aside to preserve the former near-tropical flora and fauna that existed until the former lake and swamps were drained between 1951 and 1958 (see **A2-3**).

A2-5　Upper Jordan River & Chastelet castle　　　　　　　　　　　　　　　　　　　　　View: S

A2-6　Hazor　　　　　　　　　　　　　　　　　　　　　　　　　　　　　　　　View: N

B1-1 Julias, Bethsaida   View: SW

B1-2 Magdala, Mt. Arbel & Tiberias   View: S

B1-3   Sea of Galilee: fishing boat   View: S

SEA OF GALILEE   Unit B1

The Sea of Galilee's unique geographical location at the junction of the Golan, Galilee and Jordan Valley regions and its position on domestic and foreign trade routes contributed to the economy of the lake region. Merchant caravans from all directions passed along the shores of the lake which measures 13 miles long and 7 miles wide and about 530 feet deep. Market day brought villagers from the surrounding countryside to sell their produce in the town markets (Migdal, Tiberias, Capernaum, Bethsaida, Julias) around the lake.

Several names have been attached to the large fresh water lake. In the Old Testament period it was called the "Sea of Kinneret" (Josh. 12:3; 13:27), perhaps because of its shape (*kinor*: Hebrew for lyre) or because of the nearby village of Kinneret (Jos. 19:35). In later periods the lake was often associated with the adjoining Plain of Gennesaret, i.e. "Water/Lake of Gennesaret" (I Macc. 11:67; *War* 3.10.7; Luke 5:1). Matthew and Mark's gospels knew the lake as the "Sea of Galilee" (Matt. 4:18; 15:29; Mk. 1:16; 7:31). While John's gospel is familiar with this title (John 6:1a), the writer elsewhere associates the lake with the coastal city of Tiberias (John 6:1b; 21:1). The designation, "Sea of Tiberias," is also that commonly found in Rabbinical writings (e.g. *Tosefta. Sukka.* 3:9). Most of the Christian world, however, still uses the name Sea of Galilee because of its association with the ministry of Jesus. Fishermen were some of his earliest disciples. Jesus sometimes preached on the shore of the lake, and when the crowds became too large, he preached from a fishing boat (Matt. 13:2; Luke 5:3). Jesus traveled by boat to towns and villages in the region (Matt. 8:18, 28; 9:1).

The Sea of Galilee is known for its sudden storms (Luke 8:22-25). In rough weather crews need safe harbors, but there are no natural harbors except for a few inlets along the northern shore. As a result of surveys conducted between 1973 and 1986, 13 ancient harbors have been identified, including Gergesa, Hippus, Gadara, Sennabris, Magdala, Gennasar, Tabgha and Capernaum. The extremely low level of the water in the lake in February 1986 led to the excavation of an ancient (first century A.D.) wooden boat at Magdala.

PHOTO CAPTIONS

B1-1 Bethsaida (foreground) was a small fishing village near the northeastern shore of the Sea of Galilee. It was rebuilt by the tetrarch Philip and renamed Julias in honor of Julia the daughter of Augustus. Bethsaida was the birthplace of Peter, Andrew, and Philip (John 1:44; 12:21–22), and the place to which Jesus withdrew when he learned of John the Baptist's death (Luke 9:10). The inhabitants of Capernaum, Chorazin, and Bethsaida were reproached by Jesus for their disbelief (Matt. 11:21–22).

B1-2 Tiberias (upper center) was built by Herod Antipas and inaugurated in 18 A.D. He named it in honor of the emperor Tiberius and made it his chief city. According to Josephus, Herod "built it in the best part of Galilee, at the lake of Gennesareth" (*Ant.* 18.2.3). The foundations of the city were discovered to lie on an ancient cemetary and therefore forbidden for observant Jews as a place of residence. Antipas thus found it necessary to colonize Tiberias by force. The ruins of ancient Magdala (Taricheae) are pictured in the enclosure near the shore (lower left). Here was the home of Mary the Magdalene (Luke 8:2), a follower of Jesus. During the early days of the First Jewish Revolt, the city was an important center of Zealot activity (Jos. Life 59, 72) and later the location of a vigorous land and sea battle with the Romans (*War* 3.10.1-3, 9). There is no record that Jesus ever visited the site; it was considered a Gentile city. After the destruction of Jerusalem, however, it became the chief seat of Jewish learning (see **SMM 13-5b**; **Unit B2**) Both the Mishnah (3rd century A.D.) and the Palestinian Talmud (5th century A.D.) were compiled at Tiberias.

B1-3 The Sea of Galilee is widely associated with the ministry of Jesus. He traveled on and around the lake teaching and doing miracles. According to references in the New Testament most of his ministry was concentrated in the area along the northern shore. No reference is made of a visit by Jesus to Tiberias, and apparently seldom did he journey to the Decapolis region on the eastern shore (Luke 8.26).

B1-4 Tabgha is the traditional location of the multiplication of the loaves and fishes (Matt. 16:13-21; Mark 6:30-44). Its name is derived from the existence of seven warm springs, known in Greek as Heptapegon. The name has been shortened in Arabic to Tabgha. By the shore is the Church of the Primacy, where, by tradition, Peter received the commission from

SEA of GALILEE
UNIT B1
1 : 150,000

1 Aphek, Lower ?
2 Aphek, Upper ?
3 Arbel, Mt.
4 Belvoir castle

5 Beth-shan
6 Beth-yerah
7 Bethsaida ?, Julias
8 Capernaum

9   Chinnereth
10 Chorazin
11 Gadara
12 Gamala

13 Gennesaret, Plain
14 Gergesa
15 Gilboa, Mt.
16 Hammath Gader

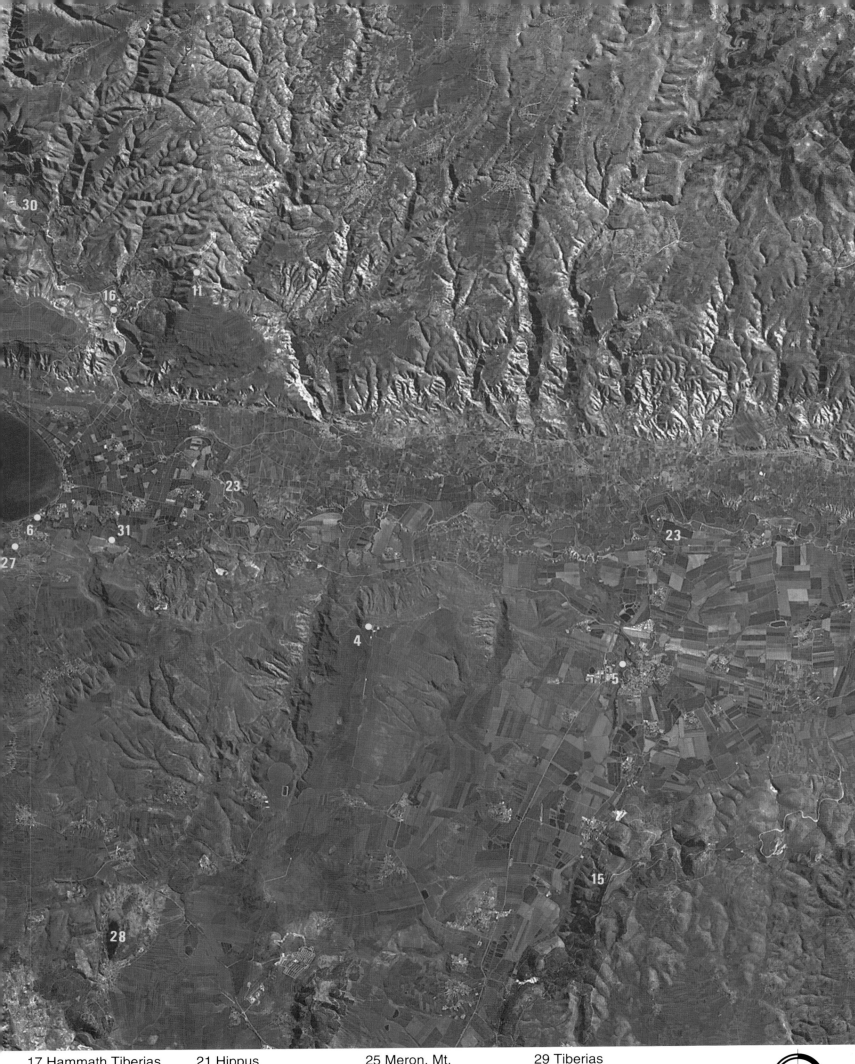

17 Hammath Tiberias	21 Hippus	25 Meron, Mt.	29 Tiberias
18 Hattin, Horns	22 Jordan R. (Upper)	26 Nahal Ammud	30 Yarmuk, R.
19 Hazor	23 Jordan R. (Lower)	27 Sennabris ?	31 Yenoam
20 Heptapegon	24 Magdala	28 Tabor, Mt.	32 Zefat

N

B1-4   Mt. of Beatitudes & Heptapegon (Tabgha)   View: S

through the pass just above the plain (upper right), carrying the commerce and military might of many foreign nations to the plains around the Sea of Galilee. The twin-peaked mountain behind the entrance to the pass is an extinct volcano called the "Horns of Hattin" (upper right; see **B2-2**).

B1-5 Capernaum was a small town on the shore of the lake, inhabited by fishermen, artisans, and farmers. It lay on the Coastal Route and near to the border between the provinces of Galilee and Gaulanitis. After his rejection in Nazareth, Jesus moved the center of his Galilean ministry to Capernaum (Mark 1:21-31; Luke 4:31–38; John 2:12). Here it is recorded that Jesus healed the centurion's servant (Matt. 8:5–13) and performed other miracles. Excavations have uncovered the floor of an earlier basalt building beneath the remains of a limestone synagogue, the latter dated variously between the third and fifth centuries A.D. This early basalt structure may be the synagogue of Caperaum from the time of Jesus.

B1-6 The Jordan River enters the Sea of Galilee through the Plain of Bethsaida, 2 miles east of Capernaum. East of the Jordan is the entry of another river (pictured here), called Nahal Meshushim.

BIBLICAL/HISTORICAL REVIEW
Cross references to the Student Map Manual

- **Egyptian Campaigns in Galilee: Thutmose III and Amenhotep II
  SMM 4-5b,c**. Thutmose III conducted many campaigns through Canaan, primarily against Egypt's chief rival, Mitanni. A major objective of these campaigns was to control the Coastal Route, which linked Lower Galilee and the Upper Jordan Valley (see **Unit B2** and **Unit A2**). A list of Canaanite cities was composed during Thutmose's reign that reflects the main lines of communication along the coast and in the north of Canaan (*ANET*, 234–243). The list provides other detailed information about the land of Canaan. The importance of the Coastal Route is also reflected in several campaigns of Amenhotep II, in which Hazor, Kinnereth, and Shemesh-edom are mentioned (*ANET*, 245–248). All three sites are on this famous international highway.

- **Jesus of Nazareth: Ministry around The Sea of Galilee
  SMM 12-8**. Peter, Andrew, James, and other Apostles were called by Jesus to be "fishers of men" (Matt. 4:18–22; Mark 1:16–20; 2:13–14; Luke 5:1–11); Jesus taught the multitudes from a boat (Mark 3:7–12; Luke 5:1–3); the lake yielded a "large number of fish" (Luke 5:4–11;

John 21:6–8); Jesus stilled the storm (Matt. 8:23–27; Mark 4:35–41; Luke 8:22–25) and walked on the water (Matt. 14:22–33; Mark 6:45–52; John 6:16–21); Jesus taught many parables by the sea (Matt. 13:1–52; Mark 4:1–34; Luke 8:4–18); Jesus healed the multitudes (Matt. 15:29–31; Mark 1:29–45); Jesus ordained Twelve Apostles near the sea (Mark 3:7, 13–19); Jesus appeared in Galilee after the resurrection (Mark 14:28, 16:7; John 21:1–23).

- **First Jewish Revolt against Rome: Vespasian in Lower Galilee
  SMM 12-12c**. To subdue Galilee, Vespasian captured the cities of Diocaesarea (Sepphoris), Jotapata, Tiberias, Taricheae (Migdal), and Gamala. At Taricheae, the revolt was crushed on both land and sea. Here, the number of Jews slain was 6,500. The battle of Gamala is sometimes called the "Masada of the north" (see **A1-2**). The conquest of Gamala and the capture of other minor fortresses meant that all Galilee had fallen into the hands of the Romans. From here the fighting moved south into Judea and against Jerusalem (*War* 4.2.5). ∎

B1-7 (overleaf) The valley leading to the Plain of Gennesaret (see B1-4) was the route of the international highway known as the Coastal Route. Jesus and some of his disciples landed at the Plain of Gennesaret after a severe storm on the lake. Many who were sick were brought to Jesus, "and all who touched him were healed" (Mark 6:53–56).

B1-5 Capernaum   **View: S**

B1-6 Sea of Galilee: entry of Nahal Meshushim   **View: SW**

B2-1   Netofa Valley: Kana, Cana (Kh. Qana) View: N

B2-2   Horns of Hattin: descent to Gennesaret View: NE

B2-3   Bet Kerem Valley: olive trees   View: W

LOWER GALILEE   Unit B2

The regions of Upper and Lower Galilee are distinguished by differences in altitude, climate, and vegetation. The mountains of Lower Galilee are less than 2,000 feet above sea level, whereas those of Upper Galilee attain almost twice that height (see **C1-5**). Upper Galilee is fragmented into isolated hills and deep valleys. Lower Galilee is more open, with flat valleys and gentle inclines. The valleys of Lower Galilee connect the coast with the Jordan Valley as well as with the Sea of Galilee, where the roads tend to converge on the Plain of Gennesaret (see **B2-2**).

Robinson described the mountains of Lower Galilee as "long ridges running from east to west, [rising] one higher than another, until the mountains of Safed [Upper Galilee] overtop them all" (Robinson 3: 190). The slopes of the mountains, which make up just over half the total area of Lower Galilee, were suitable for fruit trees and other types of agriculture. The forest cover of earlier periods provided timber, while the land around the forests was suitable for grazing flocks. According to Josephus (1st century A.D.), "It is thickly covered with towns, and thanks to the natural abundance of the soil, the many villages are so densely populated that the smallest of them has more than fifteen thousand inhabitants" (*War* 3.3.2). What was true of Galilee, in general, applied more specifically to Lower Galilee because of its rich soil and abundant rainfall, and because there was a higher percentage of level ground. Lower Galilee contained some of the best land and busiest towns in Palestine. Settlements grew up along the foothills close to the roads and away from the fertile soil of the valleys (see **B2-1**). These were the settlements that Jesus visited as he "went throughout Galilee, teaching in their synagogues, preaching the good news of the kingdom.

PHOTO CAPTIONS

B2-1 The Netofa Valley (foreground) is often waterlogged in the rainy season because of inadequate drainage. The roads and villages grew up along the edges of the valleys and on the slopes of the hills. Cana of Galilee (Kh. Qana) was such a village, situated on a hilly spur (upper center) about 9 miles north of Nazareth (see **B2-4**). Here Jesus performed his first public miracle by turning water into wine. Cana of Galilee was also the home of Nathanael, the same who inquired of Philip, "Nazareth! Can anything good come from there?"(John 1:46). When Jesus saw Nathanael coming

to meet him, he said: "Here is a true Israelite, in whom there is nothing false." (John 1:47; 21:2). From Cana, Jesus healed the royal official's son who was sick in Capernaum (John 4:46–54; see **B1-5**). Another site identified by some as Cana of Galilee is Kefar Kana (not pictured), 4 miles northeast of Nazareth. A Franciscan Church is built over the traditional spot where it is believed Jesus turned the water into wine. Both the Greek and Roman churches commemorate this event, and the Greek church has a stone jar that is said to have been used in the miracle. Archaeologists, however, identify Cana of Galilee with Khirbet Qana and not with Kefar Kana.

B2-2 The view in this photograph looks across an extinct volcano called the "Horns of Hattin" where, in A.D. 1187, Saladin handed the Crusaders a crushing defeat. Below Mt. Arbel, the narrow valley leading to the Plain of Gennesaret (northwest shore of the Sea of Galilee) was called the "Valley of the Robbers." Rebels occasionally plundered caravans as they traveled up and down this strategic pass. Herod the Great (38 B.C.), for example, gathered a force at the village of Arbela to purge Galilee of the "rebels in the caves" above the pass (*War* 1.16.2-5). This was also the way of the Coastal Route, and the road used by Jesus when he traveled from Nazareth to Capernaum.

B2-3 These olive trees are found in the Bet Kerem Valley which separates Upper and Lower Galilee. In the Bible, the prime importance of the olive tree is reflected by the many ways it was used. It was a symbol of fertility (Ps. 128:3), beauty (Jer. 11:16), and prosperity (Gen. 8:11). It was used for food (Num. 11:8), as fuel for lamps, as a medicine (Luke 10:34), as an anointing oil (1 Sam. 10:1; 2 Kgs. 9:3; Isa. 61:1), in sacrifice (Gen. 28:18; Lev. 2:4), and for making furniture (1 Kgs. 6:23, 31–33).

B2-4 According to Luke, Nazareth was the home of Joseph and Mary, as well as the town in which Jesus "grew in wisdom and stature, and in favor with God and men" (Luke 2:52). Matthew suggests the family moved there from Bethlehem (Matt. 2:22–23). It was a small agricultural village with about 2,000 inhabitants. Although Nazareth itself was small, its position between two branches of the international highway gave it a good view of the ancient world. To the south was the Jezreel Valley, where many events from Israelite history took place. Five miles to the northwest was Sepphoris, the Roman capital of Galilee. The Church of the Annunciation shown here (left center) marks the traditional site of Gabriel's visit

LOWER GALILEE
UNIT B2

1 : 150,000

1 Afula	5 Bet Netofa Valley	9 Chinnereth	13 En-Harod
2 Belvoir castle	6 Beth-haggan	10 Daberath	14 En-dor
3 Bersabe	7 Beth-shan	11 Dothan	15 Gilboa, Mt.
4 Bet Kerem Valley	8 Cana	12 Dothan, Plain	16 Hannathon

N

B2-4   Nazareth   View: S

to Mary (see Luke 1:26–38). It is a modern church, built between 1955 and 1969 on the ruins of a Byzantine and a later Crusader church. The original church was built in the days of Constantine (ca. A.D. 325).

B2-5 Jotapata (bottom center) was situated in the hills above the Netofa Valley near Cana (see **B2-1**). The city was heavily fortified by Josephus in the First Jewish Revolt against Rome. The Roman general Vespasian resorted to a siege of Jotapata after the first assault brought little success. He had his men cut down "all the trees on the mountains that adjoined to the city" to construct earthworks to support the catapults and ballistae (projectile-throwers: 160 in all). A traitor enabled Vespasian's men to enter the city and kill or enslave all its inhabitants. Josephus was taken prisoner by Vespasian after the city was finally conquered in A.D. 67. Josephus was treated well by the Romans after predicting that Vespasian would become the next emperor of Rome (see *War* 3.7.1–36).

B2-6 Mt. Tabor (upper center; see **D1-4**) was where the territories of Issachar, Naphtali, and Zebulun converged (Josh. 19:12, 22, 34). It is not surprising, therefore, that Mt. Tabor was the place where the men of Naphtali and Zebulun gathered to attack the Canaanites in the Jezreel Valley: "So Barak went down from mount Tabor, followed by ten thousand men. At Barak's advance, the Lord routed Sisera and all his chariots and army by the sword" (Judg. 4:6–14). Mt. Tabor is also one of the traditional sites for the transfiguration. On that occasion, Peter, James and John heard a voice say, "This is my Son, whom I love; with him I am well pleased. Listen to him!" (Matt. 17:5). In the background of this picture are the mountains of Gilead.

BIBLICAL/HISTORICAL REVIEW
Cross references to the Student Map Manual

- **Jesus of Nazareth: Ministry in Lower Galilee**
  Mark 6:1–6; John 2:1–11; 4:46–54; Matt. 4:23; 9:35; Mark 1:39; SMM 12-4. After the miracle at Cana, where he turned water into wine (see **B2-1**), Jesus walked from village to village preaching the gospel and "healing every disease and every sickness among the people" (Matt. 4:23). He visited Lower Galilee and the cities around the Sea of Galilee in particular, since settlement was concentrated in these two regions at the time.

- **First Jewish Revolt Against Rome: Vespasian in Lower Galilee**
  SMM 12-12a. The oppressive acts of the Roman procurator Gessius Florus (A.D. 64–66) led to events that began the Jewish-Roman war. The defense of Galilee was entrusted to the Jewish general, Josephus, who would later give us the history of his people (*War* 2.20.4). The task of subduing the revolt was given to the Roman general Vespasian. After emissaries from Sepphoris asked for a Roman garrison (see **B2-4**), Vespasian sent a detachment of 6,000 men to take possession of the city. Josephus and his troops fled to Tiberias and then to Jotapata, where he was captured by Vespasian (see **B2-5**).

- **Movement of the "Sanhedrin" in Galilee**
  SMM 13-5b. After Jerusalem fell in A.D. 70, the Sanhedrin was permanently abolished and replaced by the Beth Din (Court of Judgment). This new "Sanhedrin" is said to have met progressively at Jabneh, Usah, Shefaram, Sepphoris and Tiberias. Though the Talmud regards the Beth Din as continuous with the earlier Sanhedrin, it was markedly different from its predessor and was composed of scribes or rabbinic scholars whose decisions had no real authority and were limited to religious questions. With the presence of the Beth Din at Tiberias at the close of the 2nd century A.D., Tiberias became the center of Jewish life and retained this position until the Arab conquest in the 7th century A.D. ■

> **B2-7** (overleaf) The view in this photograph is across western Lower Galilee toward the mountains of Upper Galilee. In the center is the site of ancient Selame, one of the cities fortified by Josephus in his defense of Galilee during the First Jewish Revolt against Rome.

B2-5   Jotbah, Jotapata   **View: S**

B2-6   Jezreel Valley & Mt. Tabor   **View: SE**

C1-1   Upper Galilee: Central Plateau

View: NW

C1-2   Kedesh of Galilee, Cadasa

View: NE

C1-3   Kedesh of Galilee, Cadasa: Roman temple

View: NW

UPPER GALILEE

Unit C1

As early as the 1st century A.D., Josephus commented that "Galilee consists of two parts, known as Upper and Lower, which are shut in by Phoenicia and Syria" (*War* 3.3.1; see **B2-3** and **C1-7**). The higher altitude of Upper Galilee results in more rainfall and in a dense vegetation that makes much of the region impassable. Rainfall in Upper Galilee is rarely less than 24 inches per year, with parts receiving as much as 32 to 40 inches. Lower Galilee receives only 20 to 24 inches. The days in Upper Galilee are warm and the nights are cool. In winter, the nights can be very cold, and there are a few days of snow every year. The northern sectors of Upper Galilee (Lebanese Galilee) are much more level, with more opportunities for settlement than in the southern sectors of Upper Galilee.

It is evident from archaeological surveys of Upper Galilee that the region was not intensively settled until after the Israelites occupied the land. When Aharoni surveyed Upper Galilee in the 1950s, he discovered 17 sites in the mountains, similar to Israelite settlements in other parts of the country. Settlement in Upper Galilee was relatively stable over the centuries because the lack of main roads kept it safe from invading armies. The campaign of Tiglath-pileser III in 733 B.C. was an important exception (see **C1-2**). The Assyrian army came through the valley of Lebanon (the Beq'a of modern Lebanon), conquering Ijon and Abel-beth-maacah in the Upper Jordan Valley (see **Unit A-2**). From here, part of the army went south to the Jezreel Valley and part went west through Upper Galilee to conquer "all the land of Naphtali" (2 Kgs. 15:29). With this campaign, Tiglath-pileser succeeded in reducing the territory of the kingdom of Israel to the Hill Country of Samaria (see **Unit E2** and **Unit F1**). It again became an important area of Jewish occupation, however, during the Roman-Byzantine periods (63 B.C.—A.D. 640).

PHOTO CAPTIONS

C1-1 In addition to the forests that once covered Upper Galilee (see Introduction), another obstacle to travel is the region's difficult topography; it is fragmented into isolated hills and valleys. This is especially true in the southwest and northeast. The forests, deep valleys, and dense vegetation made Upper Galilee a region of escape, detached from the main events recorded in the Bible. This photograph shows the deep fragmentation of Upper Galilee.

C1-2 Kedesh was one of the great Canaanite cities in Upper Galilee. Its king was defeated by Israel (Josh. 12:22). The ancient site was situated 4 miles west of the Upper Jordan Valley (upper right). In the Bible, Kedesh appears as a city of refuge (Josh. 20:7; 21:32), a Levitical city (1 Chron. 6:76), and as one of the fortified cities of the tribe of Naphtali (Josh. 19:37). When it was conquered by Tiglath-pileser III in 732 B.C., its inhabitants, along with those of many other cities, were deported to other areas of the Assyrian Empire (2 Kgs. 15:29). Upper Galilee was well suited to the small farmer, whose property consisted of a field, a vineyard, and an olive grove. Indeed, the lack of cultivable land in Upper Galilee prevented large-scale agriculture. The best land suitable for cultivation was scattered in patches throughout Upper Galilee, especially in the northwest (Lebanese Galilee) and northeast in the vicinity of Kedesh of Naphtali.

C1-3 Cadasa (Cydasa; Old Testament Kedesh; see **C1-2**) was a Hellenistic city governed by maritime Tyre. Here the Hasmonean Jonathan defeated the army of Demetrius II in 144 B.C. (1 Macc. 11:63–74). Cadasa was also one of the cities that came under attack by Jewish bands after the outbreak of the First Jewish Revolt in A.D. 66 (*War* 2.18.1). Josephus commented that Cadasa "is a strong inland village of the Tyrians, who were always engaged in war with the Galileans. Its large population and the strength of its defenses enabled it to maintain the struggle against the nation" (*War* 4.2.3). The remains of the Roman temple pictured here date to the period of the First Jewish Revolt.

C1-4 This photograph is an excellent general view of Upper Galilee. Robinson described this region as "a high undulating table-land, arable and everywhere tilled, with swelling hills in view all around, covered with shrubs, and trees" (Robinson 3: 370). At the top of the photograph is modern Safed, which lies in proximity to ancient Sepph, one of the Upper Galilean cities fortified by Josephus in the First Jewish Revolt.

C1-5 Mt. Meron (upper right) is 12 miles northwest of the Sea of Galilee. It rises 3,963 feet above sea level and is the highest mountain in Upper Galilee. The mountains in this vicinity are drained by Nahal Ammud, which empties into the Sea of Galilee. The valley proved to be an obstacle to travel, forcing traffic south through the pass below Mt. Arbel (see **B2-2**). Nahal Ammud is also one of the places identified with the "waters of

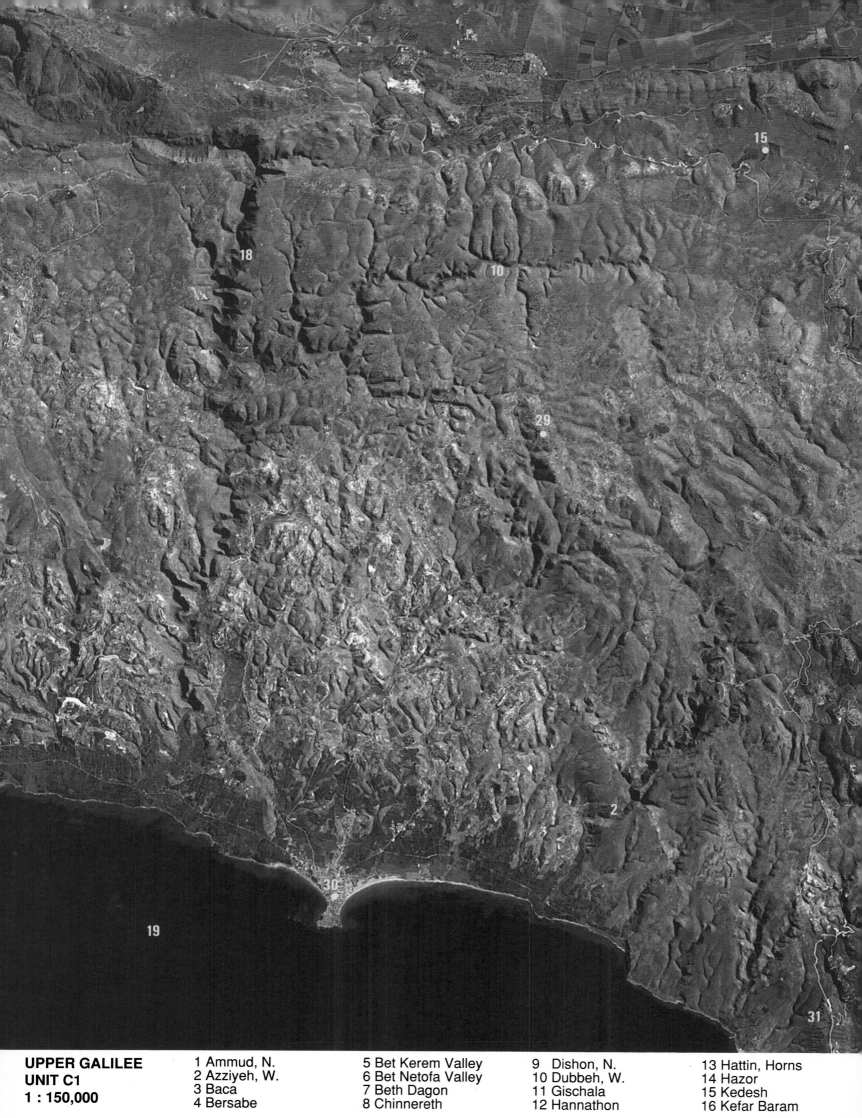

UPPER GALILEE
UNIT C1
1 : 150,000

1 Ammud, N.	5 Bet Kerem Valley	9 Dishon, N.	13 Hattin, Horns
2 Azziyeh, W.	6 Bet Netofa Valley	10 Dubbeh, W.	14 Hazor
3 Baca	7 Beth Dagon	11 Gischala	15 Kedesh
4 Bersabe	8 Chinnereth	12 Hannathon	16 Kefar Baram

17 Kesiv, N.
18 Leontes, R.; Litani
19 Mediterranean Sea
20 Meron

21 Meron, Mt.
22 Montfort castle
23 Rama
24 Rosh Pinna

25 Selame
26 Sepphoris
27 Tekoa ?
28 Tiberias

29 Tibnin
30 Tyre
31 Tyre, Ladder
32 Zefat

N

C1-4   Central Plateau & Sepph (Zefat)

Merom," where a coalition of Canaanite kings came to fight against Israel (Josh. 11:1–15; Baly, pp. 155–156). The synagogue of Kefar Baram (**C1-6**) is seen in the lower center of the photograph.

C1-6 The ancient synagogue of Kefar Baram is typical of synagogues built in Galilee and on the Golan in the 2nd to 6th centuries A.D. They had a rectangular shape with three entrances and a porch on the south side facing Jerusalem. Benches along the walls provided seating for the congregation. Their pavement was of stone slabs, and they had colonnades on the east, west, and north. The Galilean synagogues attest to the flourishing state of Judaism in Upper Galilee during the Roman-Byzantine periods (63 B.C. – A.D. 640).

BIBLICAL/HISTORICAL REVIEW
Cross references to the Student Map Manual

- **Joshua's Campaign in Northern Canaan: Battle of Merom**
  Joshua 11:1–15; cf. Joshua 12:19–23; SMM 5-6. This was an attempt by the Canaanites to defend Upper Galilee from Joshua and the armies of Israel. In the south, the Israelites had already won battles at Jericho and Ai, and against the Amorites and their allies (Josh. 6–10). In the north, Joshua's army struck quickly by the waters of Merom. The battle ended in a victory for Israel.

- **Assyrian Campaign in Galilee: Tiglath-pileser III**
  2 Kgs. 15:29–31; 16:7–20; 2 Chron. 28:20–27; SMM 9-4. Tiglath-pileser III and his two successors changed the balance of power in the ancient Near East, destroying many states, including Israel. Tiglath-pileser campaigned against Philistia, Galilee, Gilead, and Damascus. His second campaign was directed against Israel, where he conquered Upper Galilee and the coastal region of northern Israel.

- **Zenon's Circuit in Ptolemaic Palestine**
  SMM 11-2b. Zenon was a finance officer of the Ptolemaic Empire who traveled throughout the empire in search of goods needed by Egypt. He landed at Strato's Tower on the coast of Palestine, and then traveled to Jerusalem, Jericho, Abila in Transjordan, and into southern Syria. From there he continued to Beth-anath in Upper Galilee, where wine was produced, and then to Cadasa (Kadesh of Naphtali; see **C1-3**). He finally returned to Egypt from Acco/Ptolemais.

- **Jonathan and the Battle of Hazor**
  1 Macc. 11:63–74; SMM 11-8e. After the death of Judas Maccabeus, his brother Jonathan became leader of the Maccabean revolt. In 144 B.C., he met the army of Demetrius, which had camped at Cadasa on the boundary of Galilee (see **C1-3**). Demetrius' commanders kept part of their troops in the hills around Cadasa. While Jonathan was fighting the main force in the plain around Hazor, the remainder of Demetrius' troops came out of hiding and attacked Jonathan from the rear. Many of Jonathan's army panicked and fled, but Jonathan stood his ground, finally defeating the enemy and capturing Cadasa.

- **Jewish Settlement in the North: Aftermath of the Second Jewish Revolt (Bar Kokhba)**
  SMM 13-5a. After the Bar Kokhba Revolt, the Jewish population of Judea was completely uprooted. The name of Jerusalem was changed to Aelia Capitolina; Jews were forbidden to enter the holy city upon penalty of death. Many settlements were established in Upper and Lower Galilee. Galilee became the stronghold of Judaism from the 2nd century onward. ∎

C1-7 (overleaf) Ramah was a fortified town of Naphtali about 20 miles east of Acco (Josh. 19:35–36). The buildings of the modern village appear in the Bet Kerem valley (right center), which separates Upper and Lower Galilee. The hills and valleys south of the Bet Kerem valley belong to Lower Galilee. Through this wide valley ran the main roadway that linked Acco with the Upper Jordan Valley.

C1-5   Kefer Baram & Mt. Meron   **View: S**

C1-6   Kefar Baram: synagogue   **View: SW**

C2-1 Achzib, Ecdippa   View: NE

C2-2 Tel Akko, modern Acco & Bay of Haifa   View: SW

C2-3 Rosh Ha-Niqra   View: NW

PLAIN OF ACCO   Unit C2

The Plain of Acco is bounded by Mt. Carmel to the south and Rosh ha-Niqra to the north (see **C2-3**). The distance between the two is about 23 miles. The city of Acco divides the plain into almost equal parts. North of Acco the plain is 12 miles long and an average of 3 miles wide. It receives more than 24 inches of rainfall and is covered with fertile alluvium that is carried down from the mountains of Upper Galilee (see **C2-5**). South of Acco the plain widens to 6 miles where it first meets the hills of Lower Galilee. Sand dunes once blocked the mouth of the Kishon River (see 1 Kgs. 18:40), which overflowed its banks and caused a wide expanse of marsh land. The swamps caused the routes through Lower Galilee to converge on Acco, which became the natural outlet for both Galilee and Bashan. Wheat from these regions was transported through the Plain of Acco to the Phoenician city of Tyre. The Plain of Acco was controlled by Syrians in the Old Testament era; it was non-Jewish in the Hellenistic-Roman period. Israelites rarely ruled it.

The geographical position of the Plain of Acco made it strategically important to every army waging campaigns in Phoenicia, Syria, and Israel. A branch of the Coastal Route that ran through the plain connected the Phoenician centers of Tyre and Sidon with Megiddo in the Jezreel Valley (see **Unit D1**). From Acco the highway passed between Mt. Carmel and the hills of Lower Galilee near where the Kishon River flowed. As important as the coastal plain was, the Israelites never fully controlled it either in the Old Testament or New Testament periods. In the north, Tyre controlled the territory south to Strato's Tower, and the Philistines (and later the Hellenized population) controlled the southern plain.

PHOTO CAPTIONS

C2-1 The ancient site of Achzib (center, partly covered by modern houses) is 9 miles north of Acco at the mouth of Nahal Keziv (see **C2-6**). It was a harbor town, protected from the sea by rocks and small islands. Achzib is included in a list of unconquered Canaanite cities that were allotted to the tribe of Asher (Josh. 19:29–31; Judg. 1:31–32). During the reign of Hezekiah, king of Judah, the "walled city" of Achzib was conquered by the Assyrian king Sennacherib (701 B.C.), which foreshadowed events that were to follow in Judah and Jerusalem. Much Phoenician pottery was recovered from rock-cut tombs in the city's cemeteries. In New Testament times, Achzib was called Ecdippa by Josephus and in other Greek sources.

C2-2 Acco is mentioned several times in Egyptian documents from the 19th to the 13th century B.C. It was allotted to Asher, but was apparently not incorporated into the Israelite domain until the time of King David (see Judg. 1:31–32). The city was lost to Sennacherib in 701 B.C. In the 4th century B.C., Acco began to expand after Tyre was destroyed by Alexander the Great. By the 3rd century B.C., Acco had grown to twice its size and expanded to the coast. It was now called Ptolemais, after Ptolemy II of Egypt, and was a Hellenistic city. When Paul stopped at Ptolemais on his way to Jerusalem, he greeted the brothers and stayed with them for a day (Acts 21:7). Fulton described trading activities at Acco/Ptolemais: "There is a large trade in the export of grain from the country beyond Jordan, from two to three hundred ship-loads being exported every year. The transport over land is by camels, and long trains of these patient beasts of burden are constantly passing along the road north of Nazareth and near to Sefuriyeh [Sepphoris]. In the time of our Saviour, when the whole country was at its highest point of prosperous activity, 'the multitude of camels' and 'dromedaries of Midian' thronged that same road in greater numbers than now; and thus, even in his childhood at Nazareth, the Saviour must often have beheld the commerce of the great Roman world moving past the quiet and secluded village where He had his home" (Fulton, 502–503). Settlements in the Plain of Acco formed along the coast and eastern foothills to avoid encroaching on the valuable farmland.

C2-3 Rosh ha-Niqra, "the Ladder of Tyre," is a white, steep mountain ridge overlooking the Mediterranean Sea. At the foot of Rosh ha-Niqra the sea has created several subterranean channels or "caves," hence the name which means "head of the cave." The name "Ladder of Tyre" comes from having to climb the range in order to travel from Acco to Tyre, and because the traveler gets his first view of Tyre from the top of the range. Ridgaway called the Ladder of Tyre "a bold, high, and precipitous headland, and well deserving its name.... Here we obtained our first view of modern Tyre, jutting out into the sea" (Ridgaway, p. 603). The crest of the ancient Ladder of Tyre forms the boundary between Israel and Lebanon today.

C2-4 The port of Acco fell into a state of decline as it became unfit for modern shipping. Early in the 20th century, the Turks lifted the ban on building outside the "Old City" walls and construction began on what is

PLAIN of ACCO
UNIT C2
1 : 150,000

1 Acco, Ptolemais	5 Aphek	9 Beth Shearim	13 Carmel, Mt.
2 Achzib	6 Atlit castle	10 Caesarea	14 Crocodilon Polis
3 Afula	7 Bet Kerem Valley	11 Cana	15 Dor
4 Akko, T.	8 Bet Netofa Valley	12 Carmel caves	16 Haifa

17 Hannathon
18 Helkath ?
19 Jezreel
20 Jokneam

21 Jotapata
22 Kesiv, N.
23 Kishon, N.
24 Megiddo

25 Montfort castle
26 Muhraqa
27 Nahariyya
28 Nazareth

29 Sepphoris
30 Shefaram
31 Shimrom
32 Tanninim, N.

N

C2-4 Modern Acco   View: W

called the "New City" to the north (see **C2-7**). Today, Acco serves as an administrative center for most of Western Galilee.

C2-5 To the north of Acco are the remains of an aqueduct built by Ahmad al-Jazzar in A.D. 1780. The original aqueduct was built by the Romans and brought water to Acco from springs in Galilee.

C2-6 In A.D. 1228, the Teutonic Knights built Montfort castle as their central treasury and archives and to control a route across Upper Galilee that connected the Upper Jordan Valley with the northern Plain of Acco (background). It is located on a high peak (center) overlooking Nahal Keziv, about 7½ miles east of Achzib (see **C2-1**). Robinson gave this description of the region: Nahal Keziv is "so deep and precipitous as to be impassable.... The whole prospect was that of a mountainous region; a sea of rocky hills and deep precipitous valleys, mostly wooded; but without many villages" (Robinson [1856], 66).

BIBLICAL/HISTORICAL REVIEW
Cross references to the Student Map Manual

- **Campaigns of Pepi I in the 'Land of the Sand-dwellers'**
  SMM 3-1c. The biography of an Egyptian officer named Weni (or Uni) from the middle of the 24th century B.C. tells of five military campaigns to Canaan, which the Egyptians called "the land of the Sand-Dwellers." On one campaign part of the army traveled by sea, landing at the Plain of Acco north of what was apparently Mt. Carmel, which the Egyptians called the "Nose of the Gazelle's Head." Weni's description of the land tells about local settlement during this period in history. He described villages, fortified towns, orchards, and vineyards (*ANET*, 228).

- **Egyptian Campaign to Southern Phoenicia: Seti I**
  SMM 4-9a. The cities of Phoenicia gained a certain amount of independence during the last half of the 14th century B.C. At the start of Seti's reign, rebellions broke out among the people of Canaan. Seti moved quickly to put down the rebellions and reestablish Egypt's control over Canaan and southern Phoenicia. His campaign demonstrated Egypt's need to control Canaan and the important roadways that led to Phoenicia and Syria. One of his main objectives was to ensure a regular supply of Lebanese cedar wood to Egypt (*ANET*, 254).

- **Trade with Hiram I, King of Tyre: David and Solomon**
  2 Sam. 8:15–18; 1 Chron. 18:14–17; 1 Kgs. 2:12–11:43; 2 Chron. 1–9; SMM 7-1/2c, 7-7e. King David expanded the kingdom of Israel to the point of controlling the overland trade routes across Israel, Jordan, and Syria. Tyre, which dominated seafaring commerce for nearly 300 years, joined forces with Israel so that together they controlled the most important trade routes in the Near East. By controlling much of the trade that passed to Tyre, David and Solomon greatly enriched Israel.

- **Assyrian Campaign to Israel: Shalmaneser III**
  SMM 8-7e. In the 18th year of his reign, Shalmaneser III of Assyria attacked Damascus and the regions of Hauran and Galilee. He marched unopposed through Israel to Mt. Carmel, where he set up a statue of his "royal image" and received tribute from Israel, Tyre, and Sidon. From Mt. Carmel, Shalmaneser demonstrated that he stood between any future alliance of Israel and Tyre that might be formed against him (*ANET*, 280).

- **Sennacherib's campaign along the northern coast of Palestine**
  2 Kgs. 18:13–19:37; Isa. 30, 36–37. SMM 9-6b. After putting down rebellions in Mesopotamia, Sennacherib, king of Assyria, turned his attention toward Palestine (701 B.C.). He advanced along the coast from Tyre to Ashkelon, and then turned against the kingdom of Judah. The following towns were included in Sennacherib's list: Sidon, Zarephath, Mahalab, Usu, Achzib, and Acco. The kings who paid tribute to Sennacherib included the kings of Sidon, Byblos, Ashdod, Ammon, Moab, and Edom (*ANET*, 287–288).

- **Jesus and the Plain of Acco**
  The New Testament says that Jesus visited the region of Tyre (Mark 7:24, 31) or Tyre and Sidon (Math. 15:21). There is the possibility that this may refer to the Upper Galilean hills east of Tyre and Sidon. ∎

> **C2-7** (overleaf) The Old City (center) is enclosed by a wall built by Ahmad al-Jazzar, governor of Acre from A.D. 1775–1804. Al-Jazzar also built the al-Jazzar Mosque (white building with green dome), and three khans or inns (the large enclosures on the east side of the city near to the harbor). Helped by the British fleet under the command of Sir Sidney Smith, Al-Jazzar successfully defended Acre by defeating Napoleon in A.D. 1799. In biblical times this site was called Acco.

C2-5   Plain of Acco & aqueduct   **View: NE**

C2-6   Montfort castle & coastal plain   **View: SW**

D1-1 Megiddo: Canaanite temple

View: E

D1-2 Megiddo

View: NW

D1-3   Jezreel, Esdraelon & Hill of Moreh

View: NE

JEZREEL VALLEY

Unit D1

The Jezreel Valley connects the Mediterranean coast of Palestine with the Jordan Valley and the Sea of Galilee. The valley shares the same name as the city of Jezreel at the foot of Mt. Gilboa (see **D1-3**), where Jezebel and the house of Ahab came to an end (2 Kgs. 9:30–37; 10:1–11). The biblical "valley of Jezreel" is thought by some to have been the eastern section of the valley only, which ran between the cities of Jezreel and Beth-shan (Judg. 6:33; 7:1). West of the city of Jezreel was the great inland plain, or "valley of Megiddo," which separated Mt. Ephraim (Samaria) from Lower Galilee (2 Chron. 35:22; Zech. 12:11). In time the name Jezreel was applied to the whole valley. Esdraelon is the Greek form of the Hebrew Jezreel, and is another name for the valley.

The Jezreel Valley is remembered for the principal branches of the Coastal Route that crossed it in several directions: west to the Plain of Acco (see **Unit C2**), northeast to the Sea of Galilee (see **Unit B1**), east to the Jordan Valley (see **Unit G1** and **Unit G2**), south to the Dothan Valley (see **E2-5**), and southwest to the coast through the Carmel passes (see **Unit D2**). It was at the latter, Megiddo, that Josiah lost his life trying to stop Pharaoh Neco from going north. The Jezreel Valley has been called the battlefield of nations, and prophets predicted that it would be the place where nations would assemble for the final conflict at "the place that in Hebrew is called Armageddon" (Zech. 12:11; Rev. 16:14–21).

PHOTO CAPTIONS

D1-1 This view of the excavation of Tel Megiddo shows the outline of a Canaanite temple (ca. 2500 B.C.) built several hundred years before Abraham made his appearance in the land. The circular structure (upper center) was a sacrificial altar measuring 5 feet high by 25 feet in diameter. The altar was built of small field stones, reminding one of God's instructions to Moses: "Make an altar of earth for me and sacrifice on it your burnt offerings and fellowship offerings, your sheep and goats and your cattle. Wherever I cause my name to be honored, I will come to you and bless you. If you make an altar of stones for me, *do not build it with dressed stones,* for you will defile it if you use a tool on it" (Ex. 20:24–25; italics added). Sacrificial remains, including animal bones, were discovered inside the wall that surrounds the altar. Megiddo is first mentioned in the annals of Pharaoh Thutmose III, who defeated a Canaanite coalition here in 1468 B.C. Because Megiddo strategically controls a key pass on the Coastal Route from the Jezreel Valley to the Mediterranean Coast (see **Unit E1**), Thutmose commented that "capturing Megiddo is as good as capturing a thousand cities." Megiddo was also fortified by King Solomon (1 Kgs. 9:15).

D1-2 The 15-acre Tel Megiddo was extensively excavated between A.D. 1903–1905, 1925–1935, and 1960–1970. The hole near the center of the tell is actually a silo that held some 12,800 bushels of grain. One of the most remarkable features of the ancient city was its water system. Workers dug a stairway 115 feet into the earth (end of path, left side of the tell) and then tunneled horizontally 224 feet to a fresh water spring outside the city walls. When Megiddo came under siege, the tunnel enabled the people to reach the spring without leaving the safety of the city. An outside entrance to the spring could be closed to conceal it from enemies. The altar and palm trees in photograph **D1-1** can also be seen in this photograph. The altar is located just to the left of the shadow on the right side of the tell.

D1-3 This picture was taken from Tel Jezreel, the site of King Ahab's winter palace (9th century B.C.). Here was the location of the vineyard of "Naboth the Jezreelite," whom Jezebel killed because Naboth would not sell or trade his vineyard to King Ahab (1 Kgs. 21). Across the valley is the hill of Moreh (upper center), where Gideon defeated the Midianites with only 300 men. Each man blew his trumpet, broke his jar and shouted, "A sword for the Lord and for Gideon!" Gideon's small army took the Midianites by surprise (Judg. 7). At the foot of the hill of Moreh was Shunem, where the Philistines gathered to fight King Saul (1 Sam. 28:4; 31). Shunem was also the town in which Elisha raised a woman's son from the dead (2 Kgs. 4:8–37). Behind the hill of Moreh is the Nazareth Mountain Range (see **D1-7**).

D1-4 Mt. Tabor rises 1,843 feet above sea level and is the highest mountain in Lower Galilee. Because of its isolation in the plain (see **B2-6**), it was compared in the Bible to Mt. Carmel (Jer. 46:18) and Mt. Hermon (Ps. 89:12), the two most prominent peaks in the Holy Land. In a later period, the prophet Hosea condemned the children of Israel for sacrificing to false gods on Mt. Tabor (Hos. 4:13; 5:1). One tradition places the transfiguration of Jesus here.

JEZREEL VALLEY
UNIT D1
1 : 150,000

1 Afula	5 Bet Netofa Valley	9 Chinnereth	13 En-Harod
2 Belvoir castle	6 Beth-haggan	10 Daberath	14 En-dor
3 Bersabe	7 Beth-shan	11 Dothan	15 Gilboa, Mt.
4 Bet Kerem Valley	8 Cana	12 Dothan, Plain	16 Hannathon

17 Hattin, Horns
18 Jezreel
19 Jotapata
20 Kishon, N.

21 Megiddo
22 Moreh, Hill
23 Nain
24 Nazareth

25 Selame
26 Sepphoris
27 Shimron
28 Shunem

29 Taanach
30 Tabor, Mt.
31 Tiberias
32 Zefat

N

D1-4 Mt. Tabor   View: W

D1-5 The Jezreel Valley is covered with rich alluvial soil. According to Robinson, fields in the Jezreel Valley in 1838 "were covered with the richest crops of wheat and barley" (Robinson [1856], 116). Another early traveler to Palestine, Henry Ridgaway (1876), saw "waving wheat of a ... luxuriance surpassing any grain yet seen, and free from tares and weeds" as he rode toward Dabburiya (Ridgaway, 571). The agriculture in this picture depicts the fruitfulness of the Jezreel Valley.

D1-6 The narrow pass of the Kishon River was protected by Tel Qashish (center), identified with biblical Helkath (Josh. 19:25; see **D2-6**). Before 1930, the Kishon River flowed through a deep bed in marshy ground that became dangerous to those who tried to ford it during the rainy season when its tributaries were swollen with water. Robinson described the area around the Kishon, as so "miry as to be almost impassable." He also indicated that the channel of the Kishon had, in some places, sunk 15 or 20 feet below the level of the plain (Robinson [1856], 116).

BIBLICAL/HISTORICAL REVIEW
Cross references to the Student Map Manual

- **Egyptian Campaign to Jezreel: Thutmose III**
  SMM 4-7. Thutmose III led campaigns into Asia almost every year for 20 years. His first campaign was directed against an alliance of Canaanite kings who gathered at Megiddo in the Jezreel Valley. The alliance, which consisted of more than 100 cities, was led by the kings of Kadesh on the Orontes and Megiddo. The battle was fought on the plain just south of Megiddo and ended in complete victory for the Egyptians.

- **War of Deborah: Israelite Victory in the North**
  Judg. 4–5; cf. Ps. 83:9–10; Josh. 12:19–23; SMM 6-5a. Barak, from Kedesh in Naphtali, was called upon by Deborah to lead an Israelite force against Sisera in the Jezreel Valley. Barak gathered his force of 10,000 men on top of Mt. Tabor and, at Deborah's command, descended to the valley to fight the alliance of Canaanite kings. As the enemy fled, Barak gave chase to the waters of Megiddo, where the Canaanites apparently made a second stand. Completely defeated and retreating, the chariots of Sisera must have become trapped in the marshes that formed around the Kishon at the foot of Mt. Carmel, for "the river Kishon swept them away, the age-old River, the river Kishon."

- **War of Gideon: Midianites and Amalekites**
  Judges 6–8; SMM 6-6b. The Bible describes Gideon as a "mighty warrior," called to save Israel from the Midianites. The Midianites, Amalekites, and other eastern peoples had apparently gathered together in one place by the hill of Moreh in the Jezreel Valley. Gideon gathered his forces on the south side of the valley near the spring of Harod. His original army of 32,000, was reduced to 10,000 when those who were afraid turned back. The Lord further reduced Gideon's force to 300, so that " Israel may not boast against me that her own strength has saved her." Gideon and his small force launched a surprise attack at night and defeated the enemy.

- **House of Jehu: Death of Jezebel and the Omride Dynasty**
  2 Kgs. 8:28–10:31; 2 Chron. 22:1–9; cf. 1 Kgs. 21; SMM 8-7d. During the battle between Israel and Syria at Ramoth-gilead, Jehu was anointed king of Israel by an unnamed prophet sent by Elisha. King Joram (Israel) had returned to Jezreel to recover from wounds received in the battle. Ahaziah, king of Judah, was also in Jezreel. After Jehu was anointed king, he left the battle and rode his chariot to Jezreel, where he slew Joram with an arrow. Ahaziah was wounded and fled to Megiddo, where he died. Jehu entered the city of Jezreel and commanded that Jezebel be thrown from her window to the ground. With the death of Jezebel, daughter of the king of Tyre, the close ties between Israel and Tyre came to an end. ∎

D1-7 (overleaf) This view looks north across the western half of Mt. Tabor toward the Nazareth Mountain Range. At the foot of Mt. Tabor is the modern city of Dabburiya, or biblical Daberath. This was a Levitical city on the border between Issachar and Zebulun (Josh. 19:12).

D1-5   Jezreel, Esdraelon: harvest   **View: SW**

D1-6   Helkath ? (Tel Qashish) & Nahal Kishon   **View: SE**

D2-1   Mt. Carmel & monastery of Elijah   View: SE

D2-2   Dor, Dora   View: N

D2-3   Mt. Carmel (forestation near Bet Oren)   View: S

MT. CARMEL & PLAIN OF DOR   Unit D2

Mt. Carmel is the name of a range of mountains that juts into the Mediterranean Sea, splitting the coast of Palestine into two parts. North of Carmel is the Plain of Acco; to the south are the plains of Dor, Sharon, and Philistia (see **Unit K**). The name *Carmel* means "vineyard of God," which describes this important mountain range well-known for its lush vegetation (see **D2-3** and **D2-4**). It was controlled by Tyre in Old Testament times. Caves in the northern cliffs of Mt Carmel served as homes for prehistoric man.

From ancient times, Mt. Carmel was considered a holy mountain. In Egyptian documents dating from the 18th and 19th dynasties (ca. 1567–1200 B.C.), Mt. Carmel is called *Rosh Kadesh*, or the "Holy Cape." Before his contest with the priests of Baal, Elijah had to repair the altar of the Lord on Mt. Carmel, indicating that the Israelites also worshiped here (1 Kgs. 18:30). Mt. Carmel was also important for military reasons. Three passes led from the Plain of Dor into the Jezreel Valley past either Jokneam, Megiddo, or Taanach. Thutmose III, king of Egypt, advanced on Megiddo through the middle pass, and the Canaanite forces failed to attack (1468 B.C.).

The Plain of Dor is named after the Phoenician city of Dor. It is also called the Carmel Coast and stretches for about 20 miles from the headland of Mt. Carmel to the Crocodile River (Nahal Tanninim). Beyond the Crocodile River, the Plain of Dor meets the Plain of Sharon (see **Unit E1**). The Plain of Dor is very fertile, covered with deep alluvial soil carried down from the slopes of Mt. Carmel (see **D2-5**). The fertile soils, an average annual rainfall of 24 inches, good drainage, and the protection from frost and storm that Mt. Carmel provides make the Plain of Dor a favored region for agriculture.

PHOTO CAPTIONS

D2-1 The monastery of Elijah (upper center) overlooks the western section of the Jezreel Valley (upper left). This is the traditional site of Elijah's contest with the priests of Baal, where "the fire of the Lord fell and burned up the sacrifice," and the people cried, "The Lord, he is God!" (1 Kgs. 18:38–39). Amos' declaration that "the pastures of the shepherds dry up, and the top of Carmel withers" (Amos 1:2) is meaningful because Carmel was quite fertile and as a rain barrier for storms off the sea was

very unlikely to dry up. Amos also alluded to Carmel's dense vegetation when he spoke of it as a place of refuge: "Though they hide themselves on the top of Carmel, there I will hunt them down and seize them" (Amos 9:2–3). Elisha visited Mt. Carmel after he received the mantle of the prophet Elijah by the Jordan River near Jericho, apparently to be alone at the start of his formal ministry (2 Kgs. 2:25). Elisha promised a Shunammite woman that she would have a son. The promise was fulfilled, but the son died. The Shunammite woman knew where to find Elisha on Mt. Carmel. Elisha accompanied the woman back across the Jezreel Valley to Shunem, where Elisha restored her son to life (2 Kgs. 4:25; see **D1-3**).

D2-2 Dor first appears in the Bible as a Canaanite city-state that joined a coalition headed by Jabin, king of Hazor, to fight against Israel (Josh. 11:2–5). The coalition was defeated by Joshua, but the Canaanites continued to occupy Dor (Josh. 12:23; Judg. 1:27). According to the Egyptian tale of Wen-Amon (ca. 1100 B.C.), Dor was also occupied by the Tjeker, one of the groups of Sea Peoples related to the Philistines (*ANET*, 26). In the 10th century B.C., Dor became the center of Solomon's fourth administrative district, which supplied provisions to the royal court one month out of the year (1 Kgs. 4:7–11). In 734 B.C., Tiglath-pileser III conquered Dor and turned it into the capital of the Assyrian province of *Duru*. In 721 B.C., the rest of the Northern Kingdom fell to the Assyrians under Sargon II. Samaria fell after a siege of three years.

D2-3 Because of its elevation (1,750 feet) and proximity to the sea (see Jer. 46:18), Mt. Carmel receives about 32 inches of rain annually and is watered by dew an average of 250 nights out of the year. This abundance of water has produced a dense covering of trees, shrubs, and rich pastures (see Micah 7:14). The Bible describes the beauty and fertility of Mt. Carmel as the "splendor of Carmel" and compares its fertility to the Plain of Sharon, Lebanon, Bashan, and Gilead (Isa. 35:2; Jer. 50:19). The natural features of Mt. Carmel are in part the reason for its special religious significance (see above, Introduction).

D2-4 This photograph looks much like Henry Ridgaway's description of Mt. Carmel in the 19th century: "The whole ridge and sides of the mountain are well wooded and low, [with] stunted oaks, terebinths, acacias, and pines, and several species of creeping vines and low bushes. The mountain is said to be full of wild boars, jackals, hares, partridges,

Mt. CARMEL & DOR
UNIT D2
1 : 150,000

1 Acco, Ptolemais	5 Aphek	9 Beth Shearim	13 Carmel, Mt.
2 Achzib	6 Atlit castle	10 Caesarea	14 Crocodilon Polis
3 Afula	7 Bet Kerem Valley	11 Cana	15 Dor
4 Akko, T.	8 Bet Netofa Valley	12 Carmel caves	16 Haifa

17 Hannathon
18 Helkath ?
19 Jezreel
20 Jokneam

21 Jotapata
22 Kesiv, N.
23 Kishon, N.
24 Megiddo

25 Montfort castle
26 Muhraqa
27 Nahariyya
28 Nazareth

29 Sepphoris
30 Shefaram
31 Shimrom
32 Tanninim, N.

N

D2-4   Mt. Carmel (deep valleys near Bet Oren)   View: NE

quails, and woodcock; but we did not chance to scare up either a wild boar or a bird of any size. Deep ravines, running down to the sea, opened from our pathway, some of them a thousand feet deep" (Ridgaway, 596).

D2-5 The Knights Templar built Atlit castle (lower center) in A.D. 1218 to control the coastal road and as a step toward recovering Jerusalem, which had been lost to Saladin in A.D. 1187. The ancient site, which is 12½ miles south of Haifa, covers nearly 200 acres. The castle withstood several attacks and is said to have been one of the great fortresses of that age. After Acre (Acco) fell in A.D. 1291, Atlit was abandoned to the Mamelukes, who dismantled the castle's defenses.

D2-6 The narrow pass of the Kishon River separates Mt. Carmel (right) from the hills of Lower Galilee (upper left). Through the pass ran one of the branches of the Coastal Route, which connected the Plain of Acco with the Jezreel Valley (upper left; see **Unit D1**). The hills of northwestern Samaria are visible in the distance (upper right). After Elijah won the contest with the prophets of Baal on Mt. Carmel (see **D2-1**), he commanded the people, "Seize the prophets of Baal. Don't let anyone get away!" They seized them, and Elijah had them brought down to the Kishon Valley [visible to the left of the modern highway] and slaughtered there" (1 Kgs. 18:40).

BIBLICAL/HISTORICAL REVIEW
Cross references to the Student Map Manual

- **Egyptian Campaign to Jezreel: Thutmose III**
  SMM 4-7. Of the three routes that lead through Mt. Carmel into the Jezreel Valley, Thutmose decided to take the most direct route through the Aruna pass. At the other end of the pass was Megiddo. Once through, Thutmose discovered that the Canaanites had divided their troops and were waiting in ambush by the northern and southern routes. The Canaanite kings hoped to surprise the Egyptians and then retreat into the valley where they could make a better stand against the Egyptian infantry. Instead, the battle was fought near Megiddo and ended in a complete victory for Egypt.

- **Travels of Wen-Amon: Sea Peoples at the Harbor of Dor**
  SMM 6-1b. Wen-Amon was an Egyptian official in the temple of Amon at Karnak, who was sent to Byblos to acquire lumber for the ceremonial barge of Amon. The events that followed Wen Amon's

arrival at Dor (south of Mt. Carmel; see **D2-2**) demonstrate that Egypt's influence on the coastal cities of Palestine and Phoenicia had declined. Egypt's control over Canaan began to wane during the reign of Rameses III (12th century B.C.).

- **Egyptian Campaign Against Israel: Shishak**
  1 Kgs. 14:25–28,30; 2 Chron. 12:2–12; SMM 8-2c, 8-3b. When Shishak attacked Israel after the division of the kingdom, he seems to have had four objectives: first, to attack the capitals of both Israel and Judah; second, to reduce Jeroboam's hold on the routes through the Jezreel, Beth-shan, and Lower Jordan Valleys; third, to get control of the important international highway, the Coastal Route; and fourth, to break up Judean trade with Arabia.

- **Contest on Mt. Carmel: Elijah and the Priests of Baal**
  1 Kgs. 17–19; SMM 8-1. Because of its special religious significance and because it was the border between Israel and Tyre, Mt. Carmel was chosen as the site for the contest between Elijah and the prophets of Baal (see **D2-1** and **D2-6**). After the prophets of Baal failed, Elijah successfully called down fire from heaven that consumed the entire sacrifice and symbolically defeated the main Canaanite gods.

- **Assyrian Campaign to Israel: Shalmaneser III**
  SMM 8-7e. Shalmaneser, king of Assyria, launched several campaigns into Syria between 849 and 841 B.C. A new dynasty began in Damascus when Hazael revolted against Ben-hadad. In 841 B.C., Shalmaneser defeated Hazael at Mt. Senir but was unable to capture Damascus. The campaign was carried into the regions of Hauran and Galilee, where he marched unopposed to a mountain on the coast of Palestine named "Baal-rosh," which was Mt. Carmel. There he received tribute from Israel, Tyre, and Sidon.   ∎

D2-7 (overleaf) This is another view of the Plain of Dor, including offshore islands and harbors (see **D2-2**).

D2-5   Atlit castle, Mt. Carmel & Plain of Dor   View: NE

D2-6   Mt. Carmel & Nahal Kishon: pass to Jezreel   View: SE

E1-1 Caesarea (Maritima): Roman harbor   View: E

E1-2 Caesarea: Byzantine wall & hippodrome   View: NW

E1-3   Arsuf castle & harbor (Apollonia)   View: S

PLAIN OF SHARON   Unit E1

The Plain of Sharon is about 30 miles long and 10 to 12 miles wide. It extends from Nahal Tanninim (Crocodile River) in the north to the Yarkon River in the south (see **E1-5** and **E1-6**). Nahal Tanninim is 18 miles south of Mt. Carmel and might be considered the boundary between the Plain of Dor and the Plain of Sharon. In Roman times builders dammed the Nahal Tanninim a short distance inland from Crocodiliopolis to produce a huge milling center and a lake on the Plain of Sharon. The Sharon was once covered with large tracts of oak trees; in fact, Isaiah alluded to the trees when he compared the Sharon to the "glory of Lebanon" and the "splendor of Carmel" (Isa. 35:2; Micah 7:14). In the Plain of Sharon many swamps formed where the rivers were blocked from reaching the sea. It has been described as a foreboding wilderness of oaks and marshes. On the fringes of the forest, nearer to the settlements that grew up along the coast and eastern foothills, herds grazed (1 Chron. 27:29) .

The Sharon was vitally important to Egypt and other nations that wanted to control the routes through Canaan. The Coastal Route ran along the eastern edge of the Plain of Sharon by the foothills of Mt. Ephraim until it reached Mt. Carmel. From Mt. Carmel it continued into the Jezreel Valley by way of three passes (see **Unit D2**). The only two places of refuge around Jezreel were on Mt. Carmel and in the Plain of Sharon. The Plain of Sharon, with many hiding places and easy access to the Coastal Route, was an ideal spot from which to launch a revolt against foreign aggressors. Pharaoh Amenhotep II, for example, made raids into the Plain of Sharon to put down a Mitanni-inspired rebellion against Egyptian authority in Canaan (ca. 1429 B.C.).

PHOTO CAPTIONS

E1-1 Caesarea Maritima was built by Herod the Great between 22 and 10 B.C. He made it an important seaport with excellent connections to all parts of the Mediterranean world. Herod named Caesarea in honor of the first Roman emperor, Caesar Augustus. This photograph shows the submerged remains of Herod's harbor, *Sebastos* (the Greek translation of Augustus), looking east. The southern breakwater (1,960 feet long) curves away from the city toward the bottom of the photograph from right to left. The shorter northern breakwater (820 feet) and entrance channel are also visible. Part of the breakwater was formed by pouring concrete

into huge forms to make massive concrete blocks, and by sinking 50x10x9 foot blocks of stone into water up to 120 feet deep. On top of the stone foundation, a wall with towers was constructed to protect the harbor. According to Josephus, Herod, in building Caesarea, "triumphed over nature by constructing there a harbor larger than Piraeus" (harbor of Athens; *War* 1.21.5).

E1-2 Caesarea was the Roman-Byzantine provincial capital for over 600 years. The outline of a hippodrome built in the 2nd century A.D. and measuring 1,500 feet in length is still visible today (right center) in the banana fields east of the Herodian city, but inside the walls of the Byzantine city. An inscription with the name of the Roman procurator, Pontius Pilate, was found in the excavation of the Caesarea theater. Archaeologists have also uncovered public buildings, a theater, an amphitheater, a hippodrome, two aqueducts, a colonnaded street, harbor warehouses, a Mithraeum, a temple dedicated to Caesar, and an extensive sewage system that, according to Josephus, was cleaned out by the surge of the sea. Philip preached and lived in Caesarea (Acts 8:40; 21:8–9); Peter preached here to Cornelius (Acts 10); Paul sailed to and from the harbor (Acts 9:30; 18:22) and spent 2 years here under house arrest. During the time of his confinement, Paul addressed the Roman procurator, Felix, and his successor, Festus, as well as King Agrippa (Acts 25–26). Here Origen, an early church father of the third century, collected a famous library, and Eusebius, archbishop of Caesarea, wrote his Ecclesiastical History a century later.

E1-3 Apollonia is first mentioned in the Hasmonean period (167–63 B.C.). Pompey detached Apollonia from the territory of Judea in 63 B.C.; it was rebuilt by Gabinus, the Roman governor of Syria (57–55 B.C.). Apollonia was a commercial center under the Crusaders, who lost it to Saladin in A.D. 1187. It was recaptured by Richard the Lion-Hearted in A.D. 1191, and finally captured and destroyed by the Mamelukes in A.D. 1265. Ruins from the ancient site (center) overlook the Mediterranean Sea.

E1-4 This is a photograph of Old Jaffa, with its restaurants and small shops for tourists. In antiquity cedar wood from Lebanon was brought "in rafts by sea down to Joppa" to be used in the Temple of Solomon (2 Chron. 2:16). Joppa was not a large port and was poorly protected from the sea, but it was the main harbor of Jerusalem and an important city throughout

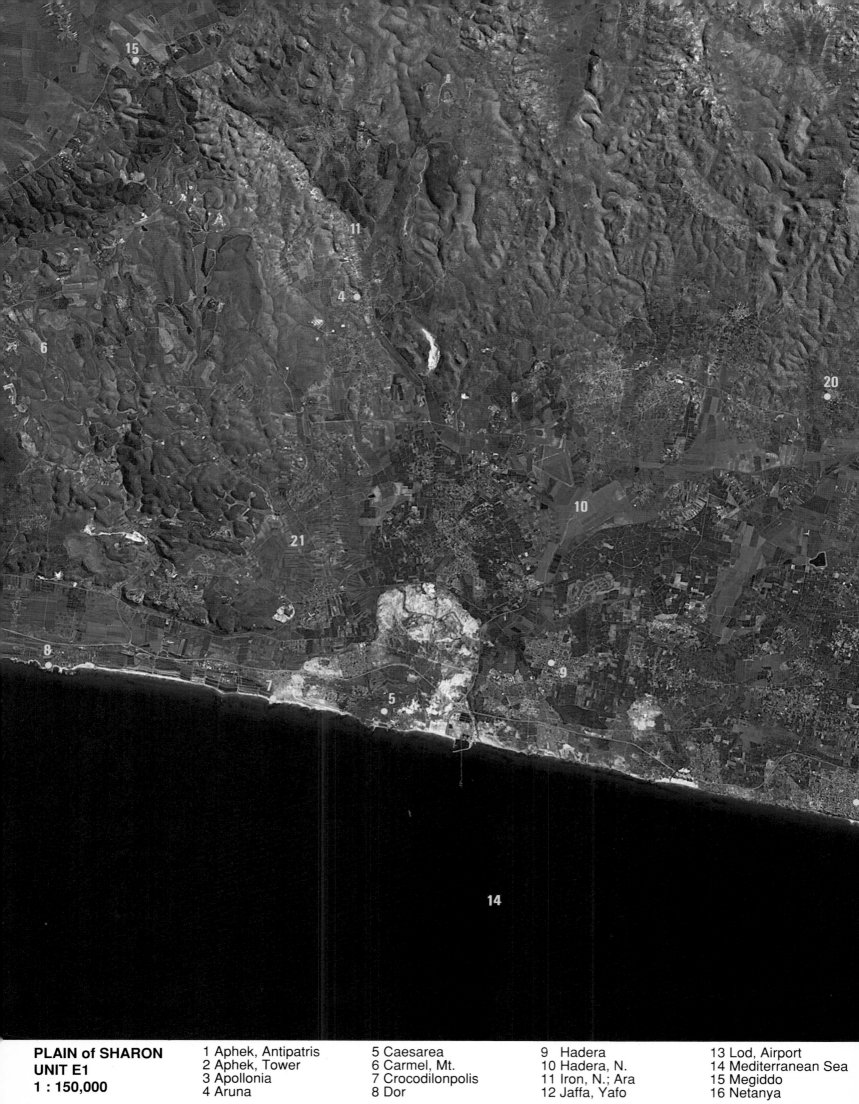

PLAIN of SHARON
UNIT E1
1 : 150,000

1 Aphek, Antipatris	5 Caesarea	9 Hadera	13 Lod, Airport
2 Aphek, Tower	6 Carmel, Mt.	10 Hadera, N.	14 Mediterranean Sea
3 Apollonia	7 Crocodilonpolis	11 Iron, N.; Ara	15 Megiddo
4 Aruna	8 Dor	12 Jaffa, Yafo	16 Netanya

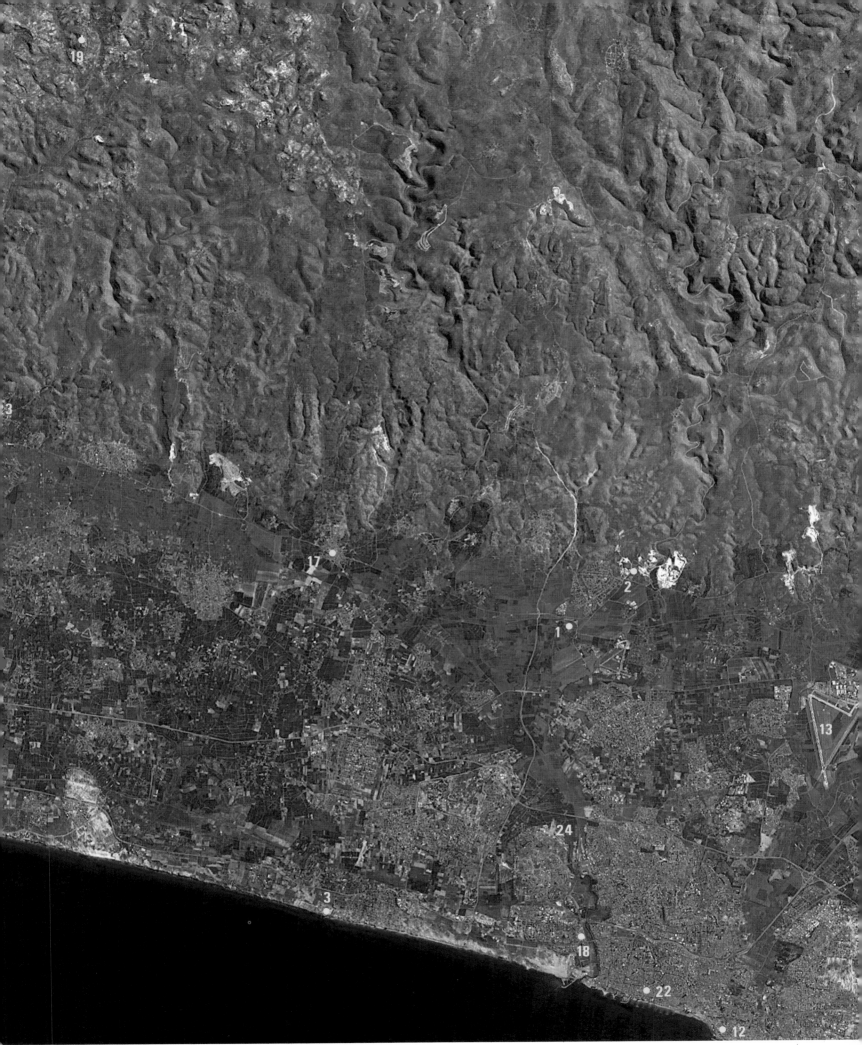

17 Qalqilya
18 Qasila, T.
19 Samaria
20 Socoh

21 Tanninim, N.
22 Tel Aviv
23 Tulkarm
24 Yarqon, N.

N

E1-4   Jaffa: offshore rocks and modern harbor   View: W

most of the biblical period. Instead of going to Nineveh, Jonah tried to run from the presence of the Lord by boarding a ship at Joppa headed for Tarshish (Jonah 1–2). Later, Peter came to Joppa and raised Dorcas from the dead (Acts 9:40). He stayed in Joppa for some time with a tanner named Simon and there had a vision of clean and unclean animals (Acts 9:43; 10). The shore at Jaffa is also the site, in Greek mythology, where Andromeda, chained to a rock in the sea, was freed by Perseus who slew Medusa.

E1-5 The Yarkon River winds its way through the Plain of Sharon toward the Mediterranean Sea. The Yarkon begins near Aphek and was the main obstacle to travel in this part of the plain. Thomson gave this description of the Yarkon: "As we come near I see it is a dark, sullen stream, creeping sluggishly through an impenetrable jungle of reeds and bushes. And here are great black buffaloes buried up to the eyes in its treacherous-looking depths" (Thomson 1: 49).

E1-6 Aphek (Tel Rosh ha'Ayin) was an important station on the Coastal Route that guarded the passageway between the hill country of Samaria and the Yarkon River. It lies near a large spring which is the source of the Yarkon River. Aphek also guarded an access route from the Plain of Sharon into Mt. Ephraim (see Josh. 12:18). The Philistines camped at Aphek before a battle in which they defeated the Israelites and captured the Ark of the Covenant (1 Sam. 4–6). In the New Testament period, Aphek was called Antipatris (Acts 23:31), being renamed by Herod the Great after his father, Antipater. The ruins in this picture are the remains of a large Turkish citadel, which was built on the remains of a Crusader castle. Excavations inside the citadel have found levels of Bronze Age occupation, while streets, shops, and a mausoleum date from the Roman period.

BIBLICAL/HISTORICAL REVIEW
Cross references to the Student Map Manual

- **Egyptian Campaign to the Plain of Sharon: Amenhotep II**
  SMM 4-5c. During the reign of Amenhotep II, Mitanni was at the peak of its expansion and apparently pushed as far south as Chinnereth, on the northwestern shore of Lake Kinnereth (Sea of Galilee). From Chinnereth, Mitanni must have threatened Egypt's position in the Jezreel Valley (see **Unit D1**). Returning from one of his campaigns, Amenhotep captured an emissary of Mitanni in the Plain of Sharon who was apparently trying to incite a rebellion against Egyptian authority in Canaan. Amenhotep made two raids into the forests of

western Sharon. This probably indicates that a rebel base was set up in the protected swamps and forests.

- **Battle of Ebenezer: Ark Lost to the Philistines**
  1 Sam. 4-6; SMM 7-3b,c. There was a constant struggle between the Israelites and the Philistines for control of the roads that led into the hill country from the coastal plain. The battle of Ebenezer was fought on the southern edge of the Plain of Sharon near Aphek (see **E1-6**). Not only did the Israelites lose the battle, they also lost the Ark of the Covenant. As a result of this battle the Philistines were able to extend their influence into the hill country of Judea and Samaria, and north into the Jezreel Valley.

- **King Herod's Port of Caesarea (Maritima)**
  SMM 12-2c. Herod built Caesarea for economic and political reasons, as well as to satisfy his need to be remembered as a great builder. Caesarea was the capital of Roman Judea for over 600 years and is testimony to both the city's strategic location and the building prowess of Herod. Caesarea was built on the former site of Strato's Tower. Herod built many other impressive structures in Damascus, Ashkelon, Samaria, Jericho, the Herodium, Masada and Jerusalem.

- **First Jewish Revolt Against Rome: Revolt at Caesarea**
  SMM 12-11. The oppressive acts of the Roman procurator Gessius Florus (A.D. 64–66) led to events that caused the Jewish-Roman war. In retaliation for the killing of more than 20,000 Jews at Caesarea, the Jewish revolt became general and spread as far as Damascus and Alexandria. The task of defending Galilee was given to Josephus, the future historian. The task of subduing the revolt was given to the Roman general Vespasian. ∎

E1-7 (overleaf) This photograph looks down on the Roman theater and aqueducts of Caesarea. During the Byzantine period, a mile-long cardo was constructed between the city center and the theater. The aqueducts of Caesarea brought water by gravity from springs 12 miles and 4 miles away. The oldest aqueduct was constructed in the Herodian period and is referred to as the "high-level aqueduct."

E1-5   Nahal Yarkon, east of Tel Aviv

E1-6   Aphek, Antipatris & source of Nahal Yarkon   **View: W**

E2-1   Mt. Gerizim, Garizein (Tell er-Ras) & Nablus   View: NW

E2-2   Samaria, Sebaste (Sabastiya): Roman temple   View: S

E2-3 Samaria: Hellenistic tower & Roman theater   View: SW

WESTERN SAMARIA   Unit E2

The mountains of Western Samaria descend upon the Plain of Sharon (see **Unit E1**) in a series of uninterrupted ridges. As George Adam Smith explained, "the whole flank lies in contrast to the precipices and defiles [narrow passes] which run down the west of Judaea; and, whether you ascend by its valleys or by its broad ridges, the way is easy and open" (Smith, 218). The openness of Samaria facilitated the movement of trade and brought increased prosperity to the region. It also brought Samaria into close contact with other cultures, the religious practices of which were condemned by the prophets (Judg. 2:8–13; 8:33–34; 1 Kgs. 18:17–18; Hos. 2:13, 4:13–14, 7:8–9). The roads that brought the merchants also brought the armies. As a result Samaria came under attack numerous times before finally falling to the Assyrians about 125 years before the Babylonians conquered Judea.

The earliest name given to this region was "Mount Ephraim" (Josh. 17:15; 1 Sam. 1:1). The southern part of Mt. Ephraim was occupied by the tribe of Ephraim and the northern part by the half-tribe of Manasseh. After the division of the kingdom (1 Kgs. 12) and the founding of Samaria as the capital of the Northern Kingdom (1 Kgs. 16:24; see **E2-1**), the name Samaria "gradually replaced the name of Ephraim as the general designation for the whole area" (Aharoni, 29).

PHOTO CAPTIONS

E2-1 This picture shows the valley which separates Mt. Gerizim (with trees) from Mt. Ebal (not pictured). The Mediterranean Sea is just visible at the top of the photograph, showing the connection between Samaria and the Coastal Route. Jotham stood on Mt. Gerizim to tell the men of Shechem a parabolic fable in which trees select a thorn bush (Abimelech) instead of a more worthy tree (Judg. 9:7–15). Neapolis (identified with modern Nablus) occupied part of the valley west of ancient Shechem between Mt. Ebal and Mt. Gerizim. It was founded in A.D. 72 by the Roman general Vespasian after the destruction of the Second Temple (Herod's Temple).

E2-2 The steps in this picture lead to the foundations of a temple built by Herod the Great in honor of the Emperor Augustus. The temple measured 105 feet by 72 feet, with a large forecourt that measured 250 feet by 215

feet. Josephus said of the building of the temple: "Now within, and about the middle of it, he built a sacred place..., and adorned it with all sorts of decorations, and therein erected a temple, which was illustrious, on account of both its largeness and beauty: and as to the several parts of the city, he adorned them with decorations of all sorts also; and as to what was necessary to provide for his own security, he made the walls very strong for that purpose, and made it for the greatest part a citadel" (*Ant.* 15.8.5).

E2-3 Samaria, the former capital of the Northern Kingdom, was conquered by the Assyrians between 724 and 721 B.C. The walls of the city were not destroyed, however, and remained in use for a long period of time. The city was partly rebuilt in Hellenistic times, as attested by numerous remains. The large, round tower in this photograph, for example, is from the Hellenistic period; its diameter is 39 feet. The wall to the right of the tower is from the Israelite period. The theater is Roman, and dates to the first part of the 3rd century A.D. Some of the ivories discovered at Samaria belonged to the reign of Ahab, who built a palace inlaid with ivory in Samaria (1 Kgs. 22:39; Amos 3:15; 6:4–6), but the majority were from the reign of Jeroboam II (ca. 785–749 B.C.). Jezebel killed many of the prophets in Samaria (1 Kgs. 18:4, 2 Kgs. 9:7) and with Ahab set up "an altar for Baal in the temple of Baal" (1 Kgs. 16: 31–33). The sin of Samaria was a frequent theme of the prophets, who predicted the city's destruction (Isa. 9:8–24; Jer. 23:13; Ezek. 23:1–4; Hosea 7; Amos 3:12; Micah 1:6). Samaria was rebuilt by Herod the Great in 25 B.C. and renamed Sebaste (Greek for Augustus). New structures included a temple dedicated to Augustus, a theater, a stadium, and a 2½ mile circuit wall around the city (see **E2-2** and **E2-3**). From the New Testament, we learn that "Philip went down to a city in Samaria, and proclaimed the Christ there. When the crowds heard Philip and saw the miraculous signs he did, they all paid close attention to what he said. ... So there was great joy in that city" (Acts 8:5–17).

E2-4 This view shows an important pass between the Dothan and Jezreel Valleys. From Shechem the main north-south route through Judea and Samaria branched in two directions (see **Unit F1**). The western branch passed by Samaria, Dothan, and Beth-haggan before entering the Jezreel Valley. Thus the Dothan Valley was a crossroads of north-south traffic coming from the direction of Shechem and of east-west traffic coming up from the western coast of Palestine. Beth-haggan, identified with modern

WESTERN SAMARIA
UNIT E2

1 : 150,000

1 Aphek, Antipatris	5 Caesarea	9 Dothan, Plain	13 Hadera
2 Aphek, Tower	6 Crocodilon Polis	10 Ebal, Mt.	14 Ibleam
3 Aruna	7 Dor	11 Garizein	15 Iron, N.; Ara
4 Beth-haggan	8 Dothan	12 Gerizim, Mt.	16 Jezreel

10

21

11

12

18

20

22

23

24

19

2

1

N

E2-4   Beth-haggan, Ginae (Genin) & pass to Samaria

View: S

Jenin, was the town toward which Ahaziah fled in an attempt to escape from Jehu. According to tradition, this was also the town in which Jesus healed ten lepers (Luke 17:11–19).

E2-5 Dothan lies in a valley about 10 miles north of Samaria. This fertile valley separates the Carmel range from the hills of Samaria. From ancient times travelers have passed this way from the Jezreel Valley to the Plain of Sharon. Joseph was in the Dothan Valley when a caravan of Ishmaelites and Midianites came from Gilead, and he was sold to the merchants who were on their way to Egypt (Gen. 37:17, 25, 28). Elisha was in Dothan. when he was surrounded by the Syrian army. When Elisha awoke in the morning and saw the army, he said to his servant, "Don't be afraid. Those who are with us are more than those who are with them." The servant looked and saw the hills full of horses and chariots of fire all around Elisha. At Elisha's request, the Lord struck the Syrians with blindness. Elisha then led the Syrians to Samaria (2 Kgs. 6:13–23). Thutmose III (1480 B.C.) includes Dothan in the list of cities he conquered.

E2-6 This picture connects with **E2-4** and **E2-5** to show the pass between the valleys of Jezreel and Dothan. **E2-4** shows the beginning of the pass near Beth-haggan and the Jezreel Valley, while **E2-5** shows the Dothan Valley which connects to the Plain of Sharon. The mound in the center of this picture is the site of ancient Ibleam, now Khirbet Bil'ameh. Ibleam is approximately 10 miles southeast of Megiddo on the road from Beth-shan. As Ahaziah, king of Judah, fled from Jehu along this route, "Jehu chased him, shouting [to his men], 'Kill him too!' They wounded him in his chariot on the way up to Gur near Ibleam, but he escaped to Megiddo and died there" (2 Kgs. 9:27).

BIBLICAL/HISTORICAL REVIEW
Cross references to the Student Map Manual

- **Amarna Age: King Labayu of Shechem (ca. 1400 B.C.)**
  SMM 4-8. The Amarna Age was a time of peace among Egypt, Hatti and Mitanni, when Egypt did not become involved in the local affairs of Canaan unless those affairs interfered with the interests of Pharaoh. Canaan was being ruled by numerous kings who controlled small areas of the country. Labayu, king of Shechem, for example, ruled over Samaria but tried to expand his domain into the Jezreel Valley. When Pharaoh learned of it, he ordered Labayu to come to Egypt to give an accounting of his deeds. Labayu was finally captured by the kings of Acco and Megiddo, but escaped and was killed as he fled across Jezreel toward Shechem.

- **House of Omri: Strengthening Ties with Phoenicia**
  1 Kgs. 16:24–35; SMM 8-5b,c. Samaria was the third and final capital of the Northern Kingdom. Its builder was Omri, who established important ties with Tyre, which he protected by the marriage of his son, Ahab, to the princess Jezebel. The association with Tyre brought prosperity and wealth but had dire consequences for the religion of Israel.

- **Samaria Ostraca**
  SMM 8-8b. The Samaria ostraca were found in the excavations of the city of Samaria. They consist of receipts for wine and oil during the reign of one and possibly two of the kings from the dynasty of Jehu. The ostraca also contain the names of clans and clan holdings known to us from the Bible. Most important, however, are the place names that indicate the existence of many more Israelite settlements in Mt. Ephraim than we know from the Bible.

- **Fall of Samaria: Campaigns of Tiglath-pileser III, Shalmaneser V, and Sargon II**
  2 Kgs. 17; 18:9–12; SMM 9-4, 9-5. After the death of Tiglath-pileser III, Hoshea rebelled against Assyria which controlled all the region of the Northern Kingdom except Mt. Ephraim. In 724 B.C., Shalmaneser V came against Samaria and besieged the city for three years. By 722 B.C., Sargon II had turned Samaria into an Assyrian province called *Samerina*.

E2-7 (overleaf) Early in the 9th century B.C., Omri built Samaria on top of a hill (upper center) rising 300 feet above the valley floor (see 1 Kgs. 16:24). The site is surrounded on three sides by steep slopes and fertile valleys. It was strategically located near major roadways that led north to Megiddo and the Jezreel Valley, south to Jerusalem, west to the Plain of Sharon, and east to Shechem and the Jordan Valley.

92

2-5   Dothan & Plain of Dothan: descent to Sharon   View: W

2-6   Ibleam, Belemoth: pass to Plain of Dothan   View: SW

F1-1 Wadi Beidan: ascent to Shechem   **View: SW**

F1-2 Shechem (Tell Balata): excavations   **View: SW**

-3   Mt. Gerizim & Mt. Ebal: sunrise

View: NW

ASTERN SAMARIA

Unit F1

lestine is divided into four parallel zones comprising the coastal plain, central hill country, the Jordan Rift, and the eastern hill country of nsjordan. Thus, the main lines of communication in antiquity gener- y ran in a north-south direction. The valleys of Samaria were important ause they facilitated east-west travel across the central hill country. e main route crossed Western Samaria through the valley of Shechem d Eastern Samaria through the Wadi Faria (see **E2-1** and **F1-5**). echem was at the crossroads of this main route and the north-south road the hill country spine (see **F1-3**). A series of valleys north of Wadi Faria scend from Shechem to Beth-shan at the eastern end of the Jezreel Valley.

cause of its valleys, Samaria was more open to invasion than was Judea he south. Samaria's cities were also more difficult to defend, situated they were on the lower slopes of hills or on the edges of valleys. though Samaria looks like one continuous mountain range from a tance, it is more or less separate groups of hills, with easy access to its iter. An important exception is the mountain region south of Wadi ria that extends to the Jericho-Jerusalem road. This region is similar to Judean Hill Country (see **Unit J1**).

PHOTO CAPTIONS

-1 The main east-west route through the central hill country left echem by way of Wadi Beidan to join the Wadi Faria (see **F1-5**). The ad in this picture runs alongside the Wadi Beidan, descending from echem. It was the route most likely taken by both Abraham and Jacob arrive at Shechem (see Gen 12; 33). The top of Mt. Gerizim is visible he distance (upper right), with trees covering its eastern slope. Eastern maria does not have the broad valleys and rounded hills of Western maria (see **Unit E2**). Less rainfall in Eastern Samaria has also produced sher forms of landscape. All this had an effect on settlement, which s restricted mainly to the small basins along the western edge of the ountains. These settlements included towns such as Shiloh (see **F1-4**) d Arumah (Judg. 9:41).

-2 First settled in the Chalcolithic period, Shechem was prominent in Canaanite or MBII Age (1850–1550 B.C.). This view of the excavation Tell Balata, the site of ancient Shechem, shows the northern gate of the

city (lower right), the temple-fortress (center) with *massabah* (sacred stone pillar) and wall. The temple-fortress was a large building measuring 68 by 84 feet with walls that were 17 feet thick. The stone pillar may be similar to one set up by Joshua as a witness that the children of Israel were put under covenant to serve and obey God: "And Joshua recorded these things in the Book of the Law of God. Then he took a large stone and set it up there under the oak near the holy place of the LORD. 'See!' he said to all the people. 'This stone will be a witness against us'" (Josh. 24:21–27).

F1-3 The twin heights of Mt. Gerizim (upper left) and Mt. Ebal (upper right) are separated by the Shechem pass (see **E2-1**). After the conquest of Jericho and Ai, Joshua brought the tribes of Israel to this spot and "read all the words of the law—the blessings [from Mt. Gerizim] and the curses [from Mt. Ebal]" (Josh. 8:30–35; Deut. 27:1–8). Shechem, which was between the mountains in the valley, was the natural focus of the Samaria region. Here the main east-west road met the north-south road coming from Jerusalem. After the death of Solomon, Rehoboam went to Shechem to be made king. The kingdom under David was founded on a voluntary union between the tribes of Israel (2 Sam. 5:1–3). Rehoboam went to Shechem as a concession to the northern tribes and to prevent anything from upsetting the existing state of affairs. Rehoboam unwisely told the people, "My father laid on you a heavy yoke; I will make it even heavier. My father scourged you with whips; I will scourge you with scorpions" (1 Kgs. 12:1–24). This act marked the division of the kingdom and the beginning of nearly constant struggle between the kings of Israel and Judah (1 Kgs. 15:6,16). Jeroboam led the rebellion and made Shechem his capital (1 Kgs. 12:25–33). In New Testament times, Jesus sometimes traveled through Samaria on his way between Judea and Galilee. On one occasion he came to Sychar near Shechem and there rested by Jacob's well in the shadow of Mt. Gerizim, the Samarian holy mountain. While his disciples were in the city buying food, Jesus spoke to "a Samaritan woman" and declared that he was indeed the Messiah for whom the people were looking (John 4:3–42).

F1-4 The site of Shiloh (left center) was the administrative and religious center of Israel after the tribes settled in Canaan. The tabernacle was set up in Shiloh, which was also the seat of the priesthood (Josh. 18:1; 21:1–2). Here Samuel was brought by his mother, Hannah, and turned over to Eli as fulfillment of her vow to the Lord. Shiloh was apparently destroyed by

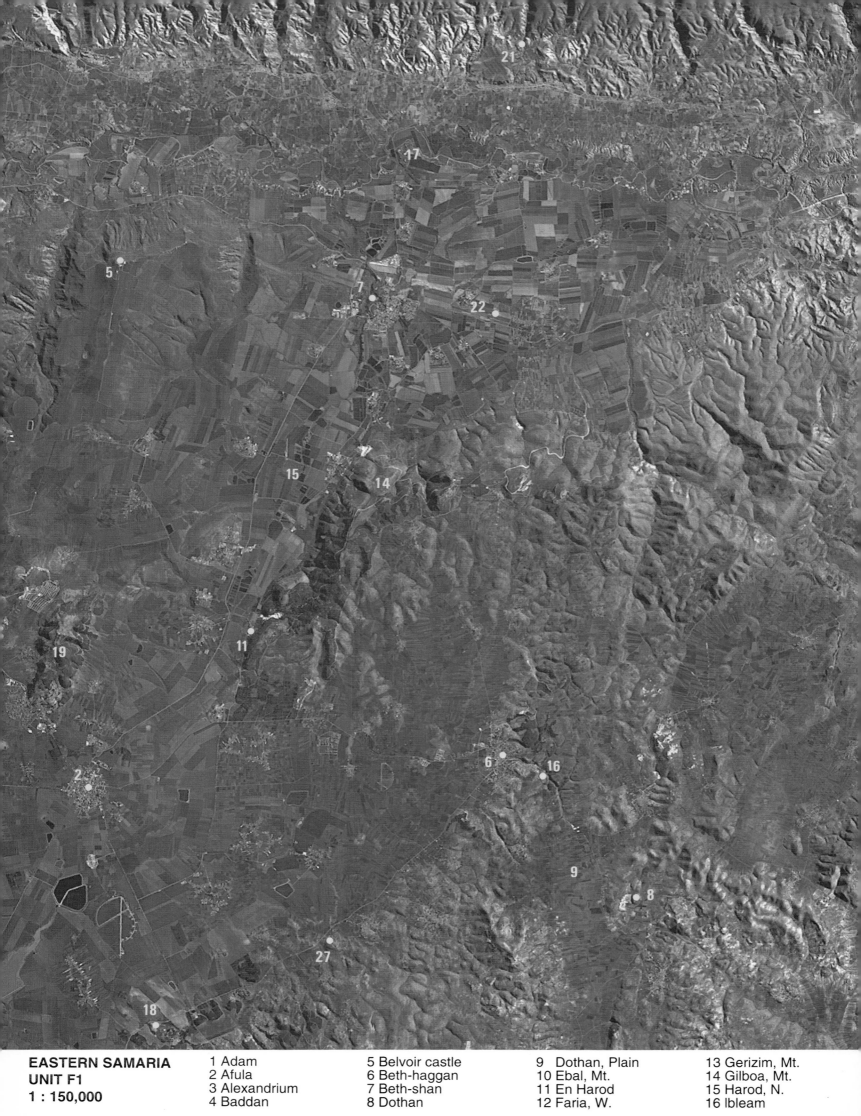

EASTERN SAMARIA
UNIT F1

1 : 150,000

1 Adam	5 Belvoir castle	9 Dothan, Plain	13 Gerizim, Mt.
2 Afula	6 Beth-haggan	10 Ebal, Mt.	14 Gilboa, Mt.
3 Alexandrium	7 Beth-shan	11 En Harod	15 Harod, N.
4 Baddan	8 Dothan	12 Faria, W.	16 Ibleam

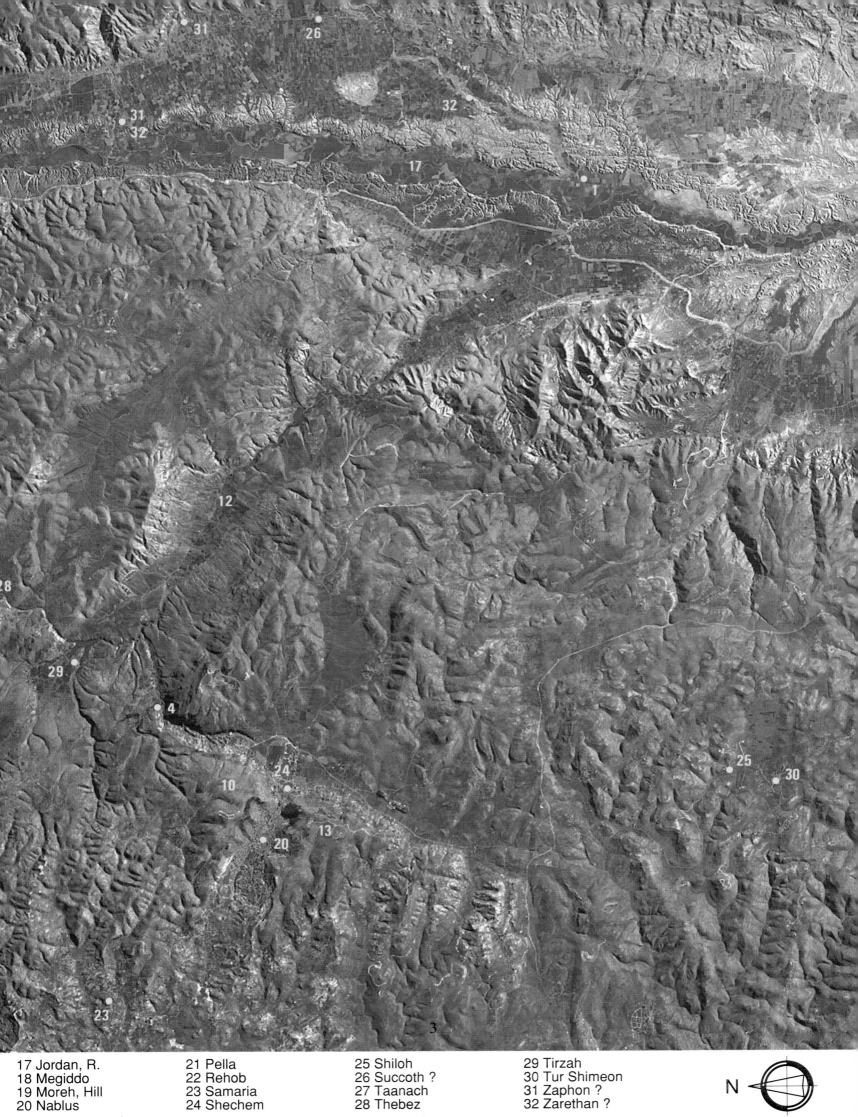

17 Jordan, R.   21 Pella   25 Shiloh   29 Tirzah
18 Megiddo   22 Rehob   26 Succoth ?   30 Tur Shimeon
19 Moreh, Hill   23 Samaria   27 Taanach   31 Zaphon ?
20 Nablus   24 Shechem   28 Thebez   32 Zarethan ?

N

F1-4   Shiloh, Silo   **View: W**

the Philistines after the Ark of the Covenant was lost in the battle at Ebenezer (1 Sam. 4; Jer. 7:12–14; 26: 6–9; see **E1-3**). Although barren today, much of this region was covered with large trees in antiquity.

F1-5 The site of ancient Tirzah (lower right) is situated at the western end of the Wadi Faria, 7 miles northeast of Shechem. After Shechem, Tirzah was the capital of the northern kingdom for 40 years until Omri moved the capital to Samaria (1 Kgs. 14:12,17; 1 Kgs. 16:23-24). The Wadi Faria was the probable route used by Abraham as he "traveled through the land as far as the site of the great tree of Moreh at Shechem" (Gen. 12:6; see **F1-1**). Jacob also must have come this way after he separated from Esau in the mountains of Gilead (upper center; Gen. 33). The city of Adam was located at the eastern entrance to Wadi Faria near a main crossing of the Jordan River. Near there the waters of the Jordan backed up, allowing the children of Israel to cross the Jordan River near Jericho (Josh. 3:16; see **Unit G2**).

F1-6 The Lebonah Valley is on "the road that goes from Bethel to Shechem" a little north of Shiloh (Judg. 21:19; see **F1-4**). The modern village of Lubban (center) was built on the side of the hill away from the good farming land. After the Hasmonean family revolted at Modein in 164 B.C., the governor of Samaria, Apollonius, took action against the Jews, gathering Gentiles and "a large force from Samaria to fight against Israel." Judah the Hasmonean "went out to meet him" (1 Macc. 3:11), apparently in the Lebonah Valley.

BIBLICAL/HISTORICAL REVIEW
Cross references to the Student Map Manual

- **Way of the Patriarchs: Abraham and Jacob**
  Gen. 12, 34–35; SMM 4-3a, 4-4b. The ridge route through Mt. Ephraim and Judea was used by Abraham and Jacob as they traveled between Shechem and Bethel (the region north of Jerusalem), and between Bethel and the Negev. For that reason the route is sometimes referred to as the "Way of the Patriarchs."

- **Kingdom of Abimelech**
  Judg. 8:30–9:57; SMM 6-7b. Abimelech was the son of Gideon, who defeated the Midianites and freed Israel (Judg. 6–7). After his father's death, Abimelech attempted to establish a kingship through inheritance.

He set up his capital at Arumah on the mountaintop southwest of Shechem. After an internal rebellion he razed Shechem. Abimelech tried to extend his influence over other Canaanite cities, but was killed in an attempt to conquer the city of Thebez. He reigned only three years.

- **Division of the Kingdom: King Rehoboam**
  1 Kgs. 11:26–12:24; 1 Chron. 10:1–11:4; SMM 8-2a. After the death of Solomon, all the Israelites went to Shechem to make Rehoboam king. Rehoboam was arrogant and refused to lighten the repressive measures of his father Solomon. This attitude led to the division of the country and marked the end of the united monarchy established by King David (see **F1-3**).

- **Tirzah: Capital of the Northern Kingdom**
  1 Kgs. 16:1–23; SMM 8-4f. After Baasha (Israel) destroyed the house of Jeroboam (1 Kgs. 15:21,33), he reigned in Tirzah for 24 years. His son Elah ruled 2 years and then was killed by Zimri, who ruled only 7 days before the city was captured by Omri. When he saw the city was taken, Zimri set fire to the palace and perished in the flames. After ruling 6 years in Tirzah, Omri moved the capital of the northern kingdom to Samaria.

- **Jesus of Nazareth: Journey through Samaria**
  John 4:1–43; SMM 12-6. Traveling through Samaria, Jesus came to Jacob's well at Sychar. This town was near Shechem at the northern end of the Michmethath Valley. Here he asked a Samaritan woman for a drink. In the conversation that followed, Jesus announced that he was the Messiah for whom the Samaritans were waiting and that salvation came through him. ∎

F1-7 (overleaf) This photograph looks across the top of Mt. Gerizim to Mt. Ebal (see **E2-1** and **F1-3**). The Samaritans built a temple on Mt. Gerizim in the 4th century B.C. This temple was desecrated by Antiochus IV, who then dedicated it to "Zeus the Friend of Strangers" (2 Macc. 6:2). In 128 B.C., John Hyrcanus destroyed the temple completely. Hadrian, in the 2nd century A.D., erected a temple to Zeus on the site. The Samaritans celebrate the feasts of Passover, Pentecost and Tebernacles on Mt. Gerizim each year.

F1-5   Tirzah, Aenon ? & Wadi Faria   View: SE

F1-6   Lebonah: terracing & olive trees   View: W

F2-1   Gibeon, Gabaon: Roman road   View:

F2-2   Lower Beth-horon: ascent to Plain of Gibeon   View:

F2-3 Olive trees, terraces & watch tower   View: S

SOUTHERN SAMARIA   Unit F2

Southern Samaria lays claim to more recorded biblical events than any other region of the Holy Land. At its heart is a small plateau north of Jerusalem in the territory allotted to the tribe of Benjamin. This plateau is only a few miles north of Jerusalem and was the meeting place of north-south and east-west traffic. According to George Adam Smith, it was "debatable land across which... the most accessible frontier of Judaea fluctuated; and therefore became the site of more fortresses, sieges, forays, battles, and massacres than perhaps any other part of the country" (Smith, 198).

Before the division of the Israelite kingdom, the territory of Benjamin was considered part of the northern tribes. It was, for example, the southern-most region of Solomon's twelve districts, which did not include Judah. After the division of the monarchy, control of the Central Benjamin Plateau was critical to the kings of both the Northern and Southern Kingdoms. According to the Bible, "there was continual warfare between Rehoboam [of Judah] and Jeroboam [of Israel]" (1 Kgs. 14:30). The border between Israel and Judah changed from time to time according to the strength of their respective kings. Rehoboam's son, Abijah, succeeded in pushing the disputed border into the northern part of the territory of Benjamin. King Baasha later recovered the land, but "there was war between Asa [king of Judah] and Baasha king of Israel throughout their reigns" (2 Chron. 13; 1 Kgs. 15:16–17; see **F2-4**). All this points to the strategic importance of controlling the routes through Southern Samaria.

PHOTO CAPTIONS

F2-1 This picture looks across the southern half of the Benjamin plateau toward the site of ancient Gibeon (upper right), located about 5 miles northwest of Jerusalem. The Gibeonites resorted to a ruse and quickly made peace with Israel after hearing what Joshua had done to Jericho and Ai (see Josh. 9). When the five kings of the Amorites heard that Gibeon had "made a treaty of peace with Israel," they were alarmed because "Gibeon was an important city, like one of the royal cities; it was larger than Ai, and all its men were good fighters." The Amorites attacked Gibeon (Josh. 10); when Joshua heard of it, he came to Gibeon's defense: "The Lord threw them into confusion before Israel, who defeated them in a great victory at Gibeon. Israel pursued them along the road going up to

Beth Horon" (see **F2-2**). Gibeon was "the most important high place" where Solomon offered sacrifice and where he received a "discerning heart," enabling him to govern the people of Israel. Here, in Gibeon "the Lord appeared to Solomon during the night in a dream" (1 Kgs. 3:4–15).

F2-2 The modern road in this picture follows the Beth Horon route into Central Benjamin. This was the main road from the Shephelah to Jerusalem in antiquity as well. The deeply eroded hills on either side of the road made it difficult for east-west traffic except along this ridge route, which connected the Valley of Aijalon with Gibeon and the Central Benjamin Plateau. The Canaanites retreated along this route after their defeat at Gibeon (Josh. 10:10–11; see **F2-1**), and the Philistines after their defeat at Mizpah (1 Sam. 7:5–12). The Philistines retreated along this route before Jonathan and Saul and before King David (1 Sam. 13:15–18; 14:31). Because of its strategic importance, Beth Horon was one of the sites fortified by Solomon (1 Kgs. 9:17). In the fifth year of the reign of Rehoboam, Shishak king of Egypt attacked Jerusalem (2 Chron. 12:2–4). The city list of Shishak reveals that his army came up by way of Beth Horon, attacked Jerusalem, and then turned north against Israel. In A.D. 66, the Romans tried to invade Jerusalem via Beth Horon, but suffered a miserable defeat at the hands of the Jews (*War* 2.19.2).

F2-3 This is a typical view of terrace agriculture, complete with watch-tower. A large percentage of the central hill country is covered with man-made terraces. Gathering the stones was back-breaking work. Many hours were required to clear even the smallest area. Watchtowers, like this one, often consisted of two levels: a ground level to provide temporary living quarters, and a top level surrounded by a low wall from which the farmer could watch his crop and prevent it from being stolen.

F2-4 Michmash (center) is situated opposite Geba about 7 miles north of Jerusalem. Here the Israelites defeated the Philistines and broke their power in the hill country (1 Sam. 13,14). Numerous battles between the kings of Israel and Judah demonstrate the strategic importance of this region as a crossroads of the hill country (see 1 Kgs. 15:6,16). A northern attack on Jerusalem by the Assyrians was suggested by Isaiah, who included a description of the pass (center) from Michmash to Geba: "they store supplies at Michmash. They go over the *pass*, and say, 'We will camp overnight at Geba'" (Isa. 10:28–29; italics added). The "pass" crosses the

SOUTHERN SAMARIA
UNIT F2
1 : 150,000

1 Ai	5 Beth-horon, Upper
2 Alexandrium	6 Bethany
3 Baal Hazor	7 Bethel
4 Beth-horon, Lower	8 Birzaith

9 Dead Sea	13 Gerizim, Mt.
10 Ebal, Mt.	14 Gibeah (of Saul)
11 Faria, W.	15 Gibeon
12 Geba	16 Gophna

17 Jericho (ancient)   21 Michmash   25 Qumran, Kh.   29 Shillo, N.
18 Jericho (modern)   22 Mizpah   26 Rama(h)   30 Shiloh
19 Jerusalem   23 Nablus   27 Ramallah   31 Suweinit, W.
20 Lebonah   24 Qilt, W.   28 Samaria   32 Tirzah

N

F2-4   Michmash, Machmas & Wadi Suweinit

View: SE

Wadi Suweinit. George Adam Smith called this and the Beth Horon route (see **F2-2**) the real route across Southern Samaria—"the line up Wadi es-Suweinit, across the plateau south of Bethel, and down Aijalon [the valley below Beth-horon]. This was a real pass across the range" (Smith, 172).

F2-5 Bethel (center) was near the spot where Abraham set up his second altar of worship in Canaan (see **F2-6**). Here he separated from Lot because "the land could not support them, while they stayed together" (Gen. 13:6–12). Years later, Jacob stopped at Bethel on his way to Padan-aram and saw in a vision a stairway reaching to heaven (Gen. 28). When Jacob returned to Bethel, "God appeared to him again and blessed him" (Gen. 35:9). After the division of the monarchy, Jeroboam set up a golden calf in Bethel (1 Kgs. 12:25–33), an act denounced by the prophets (Jer. 48:13; Hosea 10:15; Amos 3:14, 5:5).

F2-6 This view of the excavation of Et-Tel, identified as biblical Ai, shows the remains of a temple, citadel and Bronze Age wall (upper center), and an Iron Age village (right center). At the time of Joshua, Ai may have been a military outpost for the city of Bethel, for Joshua's spies reported that "only a few men are there" (Josh. 7:3; see **F2-7**). There is no archaeological evidence that the site was occupied at the time of the conquest by Joshua.

BIBLICAL/HISTORICAL REVIEW
Cross references to the Student Map Manual

- **Conquest of Canaan: Joshua and the Battle of Ai**
  Joshua 7–8; SMM 5-3c. After his victory at Jericho, Joshua advanced on the towns in the hill country. His first objective was Ai, identified with Et-Tell 12 miles west of Jericho and just 9 miles north of Jerusalem (see **F2-6**). Ai was at the junction of two natural routes between Jericho and the hill country, and was part of the hill country's first line of defense against an attack from the Jordan Valley. The Israelites made two attacks on Ai. In the first, they were defeated by the men of Ai who "struck them down on the slopes" between Ai and Jericho. In the second attack, Joshua was able to defeat the men of Ai by stratagem. The story of Joshua and the battle of Ai is valued not only for its historical significance, but also for the detailed geographical information that it provides.

- **Philistine Penetration: Jonathan and the Battle of Michmash**
  1 Sam. 13–14; SMM 7-4d. In the 11th century B.C., the Philistines began to expand into the hill country of Canaan. By the time Saul was anointed king, the Philistines had placed a garrison at Geba on the eastern side of the Central Benjamin Plateau (see **F2-4**). Their objective was to control the east-west routes connecting the coastal plain with the Jordan Valley, and at the same time place a wedge between the tribes of Ephraim and Judah. Saul's son, Jonathan, attacked the Philistine outpost at Geba. The Philistines established a camp at Michmash where there was space for a large concentration of troops. Jonathan then attacked the Philistines at Michmash, killing about 20 of them and causing panic in the Philistine army. "The Israelites who had hidden in the hill country" joined in the battle, and Israel was victorious.

- **Israel-Judah Border Disputes: Conflict in Benjamin**
  1 Kgs. 15: 1–8, 16-22; 2 Chr. 13; SMM 8-4b. After the problems at Shechem and the division of the united monarchy, there was continual fighting between the kings of Israel and Judah (see above, Introduction). At the center of the dispute was the Central Benjamin Plateau, which controlled the northern approaches to Jerusalem, and the routes on either side of the hill country that led to the plateau. Baasha king of Israel attempted to fortify Ramah, but Asa king of Judah hired Ben-Hadad king of Aram to break his treaty with Baasha. Ben-Hadad attacked the northern cities of Israel, and Baasha withdrew. Asa then fortified Geba and Mizpah with the stones and timber Baasha was using at Ramah. ∎

F2-7 (overleaf) A view of Et-Tell (center), with the Jordan Valley and the Dead Sea visible in the upper left-hand corner. The wilderness spreads across the top of the photograph.

F2-5 Bethel (Beitin)

View: N

F2-6 Ai (Kh. et-Tell): excavations

View: W

G1-1 Beth-shan Valley: Mt. Gilboa & Rehob, Roob   View: NW

G1-2 Belvoir castle   View: N

G1-3   River Jordan & entry of River Yarmuk   View: E

LOWER JORDAN VALLEY (North)   Unit G1

The Lower Jordan Valley is divided into two zones by a narrowing of the valley approximately 25 miles south of the Sea of Galilee. Here, for nearly 13 miles, the valley is only 2 miles wide. Just north of the narrowing, the Jordan widens to 7 miles where it joins the Beth-shan Valley (see **G1-1**) but narrows again to 4 miles near the Sea of Galilee. The northern zone receives the most rainfall and has more streams and rivers. The most important of these (besides the Jordan itself) are the Yarmuk River and the Harod River, the latter running near Beth-shan (see **G1-7**). At the Harod spring, situated at the foot of Mt. Gilboa, Gideon camped before going against the Midianites. Here the 300 men who drank the water in a specific way were chosen to be the army God used to defeat the Midianites (Judg. 7; see **D1-3**).

The Jordan River runs in too deep a channel for its waters to have been exploited by primitive methods of irrigation. Settlements were mostly limited to areas in which irrigation by gravity flow was possible (see Gen. 13.10); nevertheless, the valley's potential for lucrative irrigative farming made it a prized possession. The Jordan Valley constituted a frontier and was difficult to defend against desert marauders. These "eastern peoples" invaded settled communities when the local authorities were unable to control their movement, as in the days of Gideon (see Judg. 6:33). Ridgaway made the same observation in 1876: "The invasions of Palestine from the wandering Bedawin of the East have been frequent, and even modern eyes have looked upon the warlike Beni Sawkis and their allies encamped on this very spot, reveling ... on the rich spoils of this and adjacent valleys" (Ridgaway, 560). As there were no bridges in antiquity, natural fords linked the regions on either side of the river that were at first allotted to Reuben and Gad, and to half the tribe of Manasseh (Josh. 13:29–31; 17:7–10).

PHOTO CAPTIONS

G1-1 At the top of this picture are Mt. Gilboa (upper left), the Hill of Moreh (upper center; see **D1-3**), and Mt. Tabor (upper right; see **D1-4**). When David learned that Saul and Jonathan had been killed in a battle with the Philistines, he lamented, "Your glory, O Israel lies slain on your heights. How the mighty have fallen! ... O mountains of Gilboa, may you have neither dew nor rain,... For there the shield of the mighty was defiled... How the mighty have fallen in battle! Jonathan lies slain on your heights" (2 Sam. 1:17–25). The principal city in this part of the valley in antiquity was Rehob (center), situated $3^{1}/_{2}$ miles south of Beth-shan. Rehob is frequently mentioned in Egyptian sources from the 15th to the 12th centuries B.C. Seti I (ca. 1303–1290 B.C.), for example, sent an expedition to the Beth-shan Valley to put down a rebellion and protect Rehob (*ANET*, 253).

G1-2 The Crusader fortress of Belvoir was built in the 12th century A.D. by the order of the Knights Hospitaler. It was one of the few strong points that was able to resist the Muslim forces, until it was finally captured by Saladin in A.D. 1189. The fortress commanded a lengthy stretch of the Jordan River, which was once the frontier between Crusader and Muslim territories. "Belvoir held out for eighteen months more—as any well-manned fortress on that height could not help doing—but to what purpose? The Christian banner at Belvoir waved a mere signal, remote, ineffectual above the Arab flood that speedily covered the land. The mistake was to neglect Bethshan. When the Crusaders left Bethshan to its fate, they sealed their own" (Smith, 237; see **G1-5**).

G1-3 This view is of the Jordan Valley just below the Sea of Galilee (left center). It also shows the Jordan River, which meanders for about 200 miles, entirely below sea level, between the Sea of Galilee and the Dead Sea. The direct distance is only 65 miles. "To those who look down from the hills along any stretch of the valley, this Zor [trough of the river], as it is called, trails and winds like an enormous green serpent" (Smith, 312). In the Hebrew Old Testament the Zor is called the "pride of the Jordan." The Zor was used by the prophets as a symbol of trouble and danger (Jer. 12:5; 50:44). The Yarmuk Valley (center) was the boundary between the territories of Golan (left center) and Gilead (right center; see **Unit A1** and **Unit N**).

G1-4 Between the Sea of Galilee and the Dead Sea, the Jordan River drops an average of 9 feet per mile, or a total of almost 600 feet. According to George Adam Smith, writing in 1897, "the river itself is from 90 to 100 feet broad.... The depth varies from 3 feet at some fords to as much as 10 or 12. ...near the Lake of Galilee the fall is over 40 feet a mile, and this impetus given to a large volume of water, down a channel in which it cannot sprawl and few rocks retard, induces a great rapidity" (Smith, 313). Because a large volume of water is now taken from the Jordan River for irrigation, the river's appearance is quite different from what it was in ancient times.

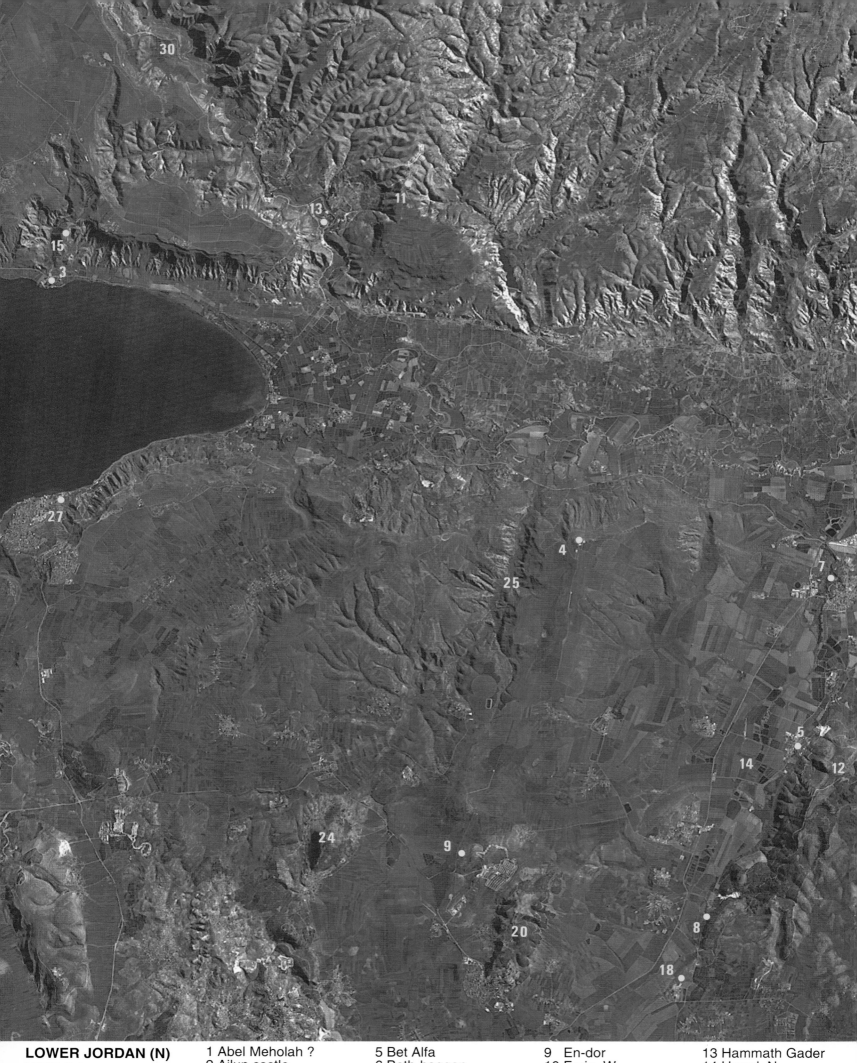

LOWER JORDAN (N)
UNIT G1
1 : 150,000

1 Abel Meholah ?	5 Bet Alfa	9 En-dor	13 Hammath Gader
2 Ajlun castle	6 Beth-haggan	10 Faria, W.	14 Harod, N.
3 Aphek, Lower ?	7 Beth-shan	11 Gadara	15 Hippus
4 Belvoir castle	8 En Harod	12 Gilboa, Mt.	16 Jabbok, R.; Zarqa

17 Jabesh Gilead
18 Jezreel
19 Jordan, R.
20 Moreh, Hill

21 Pella
22 Rehob
23 Succoth ?
24 Tabor, Mt.

25 Tavor, N.
26 Thebez
27 Tiberias
28 Tirzah

29 Yabis, W.
30 Yarmuk, R.
31 Zaphon ?
32 Zarethan ?

N

G1-4 River Jordan View: W

G1-5 In a well-watered, fertile region of strategic importance, about 15 miles south of the Sea of Galilee, lies the site of Beth-shan. Identified with Tell el-Husn, it stood at the junction of the road running the length of the Jordan Valley, the road to the Jezreel Valley, and the main highway that crossed the Jordan at the fords south of the Sea of Galilee. It was settled almost continuously from the Chalcolithic period to modern times. Six Egyptian temples have been discovered at Beth-shan, ranging from the 14th to the 11th centuries B.C. Beth-shan is also mentioned in Egyptian documents from the time of Thutmose III (15th century B.C.) to that of Rameses III (12th century B.C.). The Philistines controlled the city in the time of Saul; it is assumed to have fallen to the Israelites during the reign of David.

G1-6 About 250 yards south of Tell el-Husn (Beth-shan) is one of the best preserved Roman theaters in Palestine. Elaborately decorated, it had a seating capacity of some 8,000. It is similar to one built by Herod the Great at Caesarea on the coast of the Mediterranean (see **E1-7**). In addition to this magnificent theater, archaeologists have uncovered public buildings, columns, streets, baths and other ruins from the Roman and Byzantine periods. During the New Testament period, Beth-shan (now called Scythopolis) was the chief city of the Decapolis and the only city of the Decapolis west of the Jordan River. Scythopolis was specially devoted to Dionysus, the god of wine and ecstasy. Jesus may have passed Beth-shan on his way north to Cana from the south (John 1:28; 2:1).

BIBLICAL/HISTORICAL REVIEW
Cross references to the Student Map Manual

- **Egyptian Campaign to the Jordan Valley: Seti I (1303 B.C.)**
  SMM 4-9a. After the Hittites conquered the kingdom of Mitanni, it became necessary for Egypt to restore full authority over Canaan. The campaign of Seti I (ca. 1303–1290 B.C.), first pharaoh of the 19th dynasty, shows the extent to which Egyptian authority had weakened in Canaan during the Amarna Age (see **Unit E2**). The campaign is described in great detail on a stele from the first year of Seti I, discovered in the excavations of Beth-shan. Seti's campaign was mainly directed against the Phoenician coast, with his objective being to restore the regular supply of wood from the mountains of Lebanon to Egypt (see **Unit C2**). When the army reached the Jezreel Valley,

however, several units were sent to deal with the insurrection in the Beth-shan region. Seti's armies were able to smash the rebellion in one day.

- **War of Gideon Against the Midianites**
  Judg. 6–8; SMM 6-6b. Gideon is described as a "mighty warrior," called to save Israel from the Midianites. The Midianites, Amalekites, and "eastern peoples" had apparently gathered in one place by the hill of Moreh in the eastern Jezreel Valley. Gideon gathered his forces on the south side of the valley near the spring of Harod. The Lord gave Gideon a test to reduce his force from 10,000 to 300, "in order that Israel may not boast against me that her own strength has saved her." Gideon and his small force of 300 launched a surprise night attack that left the enemy confused and fighting among themselves. The battle ended in Gilead (see **Unit N**), where "Midian was subdued before the Israelites and did not raise its head again ."

- **Philistine Victory in the North: Death of Saul (ca. 1005 B.C.)**
  1 Sam. 28–29, 31; 1 Chron. 10; SMM 7-4h. Wanting to control the Jezreel Valley and cut off the tribes of Galilee from those of Mt. Ephraim, the Philistines gathered a large force at Shunem in the Jezreel Valley (see **D1-3**). Saul deployed his army on Mt. Gilboa opposite the Philistines. The next day the Philistines fought against Israel; the Israelites fled before them, and many fell slain on mount Gilboa. Saul and three of his sons also were killed, and their bodies were hung by the Philistines on the wall of Beth-shan. The men of Jabesh-gilead rescued the bodies and took them to Jabesh where they burned them. The Philistines had undisputed control of the great valley. ∎

G1-7 (overleaf) General view of the Tell el-Husn (lower center) (see **G1-5**). The view is to the northeast. The Jordan Valley is to the right.

G1-5 Beth-shan, Scythopolis: tell & Roman theater **View: SW**

G1-6 Beth-shan, Scythopolis: Roman theater **View: SE**

G2-1 Jericho (Tell es-Sultan) & fountain of Elisha View: S

G2-2 Naaran, Neara: synagogue <inline style="float:right">View: N</inline>

LOWER JORDAN VALLEY (South)   Unit G2

The Jordan Valley consists of three types of landscape. The first is the main floor of the valley, called the *Ghor* in Arabic. The Ghor consists of cultivated fields and pasture lands watered by springs or by tributaries of the Jordan River. The water was brought to the fields by canals or aqueducts. The second is the uncultivable badlands, a desolate strip devoid of vegetation, consisting of roughly eroded ridges and peaks. It separates the Ghor from the "pride of Jordan" (called the *Zor* in Arabic), "a deeper, narrower bed—perhaps 150 feet deeper, and from 200 yards to a mile broad" (Smith, 312). It is through the Zor that the Jordan winds its way to the Dead Sea (see **G1-3**). "The pride of the Jordan or the glory of Jordan is its luxuriant thickets and cane-brakes, in olden times the chosen lair of the lion, whence he came up (Jer. 49:19; 50:44) in search of prey, and over the desolation of which he roared (Zech. 11:3)" (Barrows, 148–149).

There were few towns in the Jordan Valley, but some sites show ancient occupation. Jericho has structures dating to before 8,000 B.C. The reasons for few settlements are the heat, the wild beasts (i.e., lions, wild boars, etc.), and the frequent raids of desert marauders. Nevertheless, the valley was important for travel (especially the side east of the Jordan River; see **G2-3**), as a "border and barrier," and because it was associated with four of Israel's greatest prophets: Elijah, Elisha, John the Baptist, and Jesus (Smith, 315–320).

PHOTO CAPTIONS

G2-1 The mound in this picture is Tell es-Sultan, the site of Old Testament Jericho, which is about 2 miles north of New Testament Jericho (see **G2-6**) and 6 miles north of the Dead Sea. At an elevation of 800 feet below sea level, it is the lowest city on the surface of the earth. Jericho is considered to be the oldest walled city in the world. What appears to be the effects of erosion is the result of three major excavations that began in 1907. A pre-pottery Neolithic tower was found in an excellent state of preservation. Joshua's Jericho was part of this same site. The biblical account of the battle is described in Joshua 6. God commanded Joshua to have the people march around the city once for six days. On the seventh day, "when the people gave a loud shout, the wall collapsed;…and they took the city" (Josh. 6:20). 'Ein es-Sultan, the "fountain of Elisha" is across the street from the small building at the south end of the mound. It

is one of the largest fresh water springs in all Palestine. This is the traditional spot where Elisha healed the waters of Jericho (see **G2-4**).

G2-2 The structure in this picture marks the site of biblical Naaran, which is identified with Ein Duyk (see **G2-7**). The structure was built to protect the mosaic pavement of a 6th century synagogue. In biblical times, Naaran was a town in the Jordan Valley on "the border of the children of Ephraim" (Josh. 16:7; 1 Chron. 7:28). Naaran was called Neara by Josephus, who said that Archaelaus, son of Herod the Great, "diverted half the water with which the village of Neara used to be watered, and drew off that water into the plain, to water those palm-trees which he had there planted" (*Ant.*17.13.1). Archaelaus offended the Jews by interfering in the high priesthood and in other matters. For this, and for what Josephus calls "barbarous and tyrannical usage" of the people, the principal men of Judea and Samaria denounced Archaelaus before Caesar. Caesar responded by banishing Archaelaus to Gaul in A.D. 6. The dry river bed below Naaran is the outgoing of the Wadi Makkuk. Still visible are the remains of an aqueduct from the 7th century A.D.

G2-3 Wadi Faria joins the Jordan near the ford at Adam, the place where the Jordan River was stopped, enabling the children of Israel to cross over on dry ground (see Josh. 3:16; **F1-5**). From this point to the oasis of Jericho, the west side of the Jordan Valley, is a virtual desert. In biblical times, people would most often have traveled along the eastern side of the Jordan Valley through Perea, where there were many more towns and water. This was the route taken by Jesus on his last journey to Jerusalem. On top of the cone-shaped mountain (center) was a fortress built by Alexander Jannaeus, called Alexandrium. It was rebuilt by Herod the Great in 38 B.C. Here, Herod buried his mother-in-law, his wife Mariamne (whom he had killed in 30 B.C.), and two sons (whom he ordered strangled in 7 B.C.).

G2-4 The mountain in this picture marks the beginning of the Judean Wilderness (see **Unit H2**), which stands in sharp contrast to the verdancy of Jericho (foreground). In Elisha's day (9th century B.C.), the men of Jericho complained, "the water is bad and the land is unproductive." Elisha healed the waters of Jericho, saying to the people, "This is what the Lord says: 'I have healed this water. Never again will it cause death or make the land unproductive.'" (2 Kgs. 2:18–22; see **G2-1**).

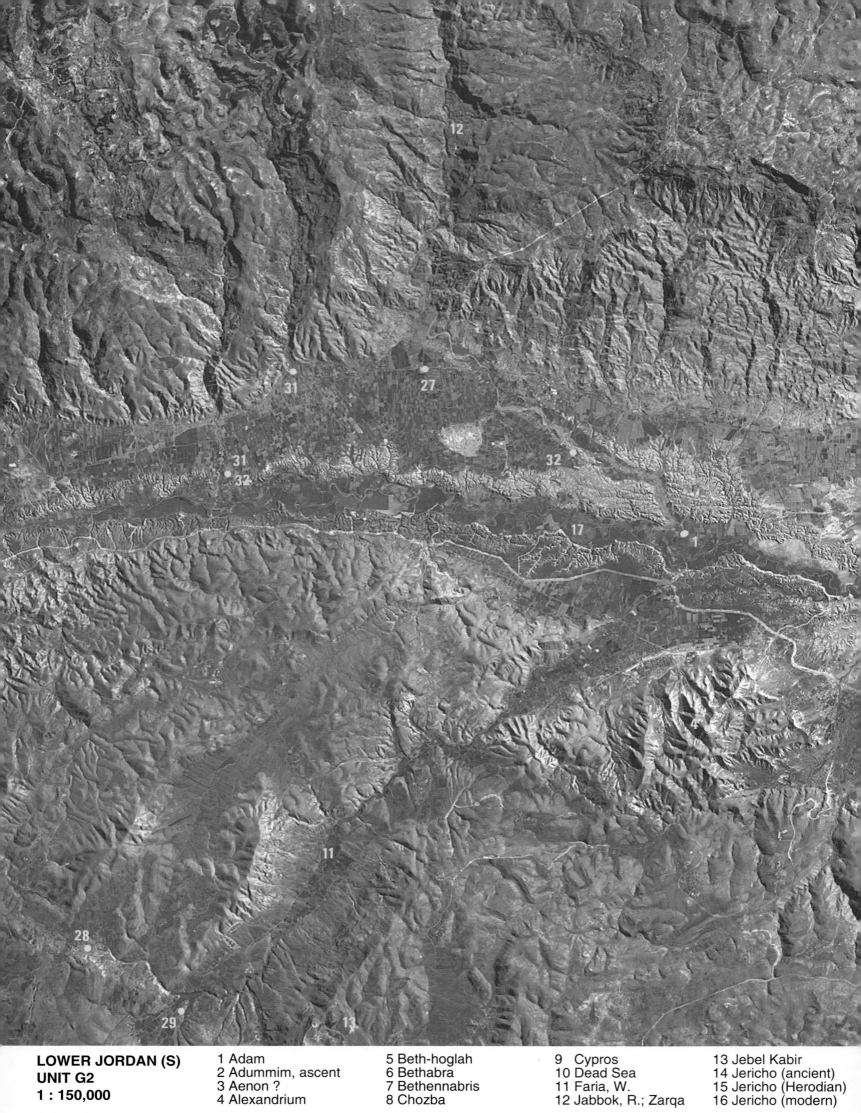

LOWER JORDAN (S)
UNIT G2
1 : 150,000

1 Adam	5 Beth-hoglah	9 Cypros	13 Jebel Kabir
2 Adummim, ascent	6 Bethabra	10 Dead Sea	14 Jericho (ancient)
3 Aenon ?	7 Bethennabris	11 Faria, W.	15 Jericho (Herodian)
4 Alexandrium	8 Chozba	12 Jabbok, R.; Zarqa	16 Jericho (modern)

17 Jordaan, R.   21 Nebo, Mt.   25 Shuieb, W.   29 Tirzah
18 Julias, Livias   22 Phasaelis   26 Siyagha   30 Tyre, Tyrus
19 Muhallik, W.   23 Qilt, W.   27 Succoth ?   31 Zaphon ?
20 Neara   24 Qumran, Kh.   28 Thebez   32 Zarethan ?

N

G2-4   Jericho oasis & Mt. of Temptation   View: W

G2-5 Ancient Cypros (bottom center) was originally a Hasmonean fort built above Jericho to guard the road to Jerusalem. Herod the Great renamed the fort Cypros after his mother. The winter palaces of Herod situated at the mouth of Wadi Qilt are visible in the distance (right center; see **G2-6**), as well as the oasis of Jericho (top right).

G2-6 New Testament Jericho was built up by Herod the Great and served as his winter capital. The ruins, called Tulul Abu el-Alayiq (lower center), are on the western edge of the Jordan Valley. The city was constructed on both sides of the Wadi Qilt, and included civic buildings, villas, parks, and pools. Jesus was entertained near here by the tax collector Zacchaeus in what likely would have been one of the finest houses in the city (Luke 19:1–10). After telling the parable of the nobleman who went into a far country, Jesus left the house of Zacchaeus, "going up to Jerusalem" (Luke 19:28). Inasmuch as the Wadi Qilt paralleled the main road to Jerusalem, Jesus must have passed through New Testament Jericho a number of times on his way to and from Jerusalem (see Matt. 20:29–34; Mark 10:46–52; Luke 18:35–43). Jericho was given to Cleopatra of Egypt by Mark Antony (*War* 1, 18, 5).

BIBLICAL/HISTORICAL REVIEW
Cross references to the Student Map Manual

- **Conquest of Canaan: The Battle of Jericho**
  Josh. 2–6; SMM 5-4. Archaeological evidence indicates that a number of towns were destroyed at the end of the Late Bronze Age or 13th century B.C. Most scholars take this to mean that the Israelite conquest took place at that time. Jericho, however, is problematic, in that we know very little about it from the Late Bronze Age. Significant quantities of Late Bronze pottery have not been found in the area, and there is no confirmation of a city wall. The Late Bronze inhabitants may have reused the fortifications of the Middle Bronze Period, as they did in other parts of the country, but there is no way of knowing for sure. For the moment, there is not enough physical evidence to shed light on the battle of Jericho.

- **Roman Intervention: Pompey's Campaign in Palestine**
  SMM 11-12a. After the death of queen Alexandra in 64 B.C., civil war broke out between her sons Hyrcanus II and Aristobulus II. Hyrcanus II was backed by the Idumean Antipater (father of Herod the Great).

The Roman general Pompey ordered a truce and commanded both men to appear before him. He decided in favor of the weaker Hyrcanus and made him ruler over the Jews. Aristobulus fled to the Alexandrium where he held up for a time before finally surrendering to Pompey (see **G2-3**). From the Alexandrium, Pompey marched to Jericho where he learned that some of Aristobulus' followers had taken control of Jerusalem. Pompey next invaded the Temple Mount in Jerusalem. During the early reign of Herod, Jericho was given by Antony to Queen Cleopatra of Egypt as her personal property. She leased it to Herod. Octavian restored the city to Judean rule in 30 B.C., and Herod built a winter palace there.

- **Jesus of Nazareth: Ministry in the Jordan Valley**
  Matt. 3:13–17; SMM 12-4. When Jesus came to John to be baptized in the Jordan River, John said to the Master: "I need to be baptized by you, and do you come to me?" Jesus replied, "Let it be so now; it is proper for us to do this to fulfill all righteousness."   ■

G2-7 (overleaf) South of the "narrowing" (see **Unit G1**) the Jordan Valley widens first to 8 miles and then to 14 miles near the oasis of Jericho (upper center) and northern end of the Dead Sea (upper right). Across the Jordan from Jericho are the mountains of Moab and the "plains of Moab" (upper left), where the children of Israel camped "across from Jericho" (Num. 22:1; 26:3). The men of Jericho searched for Joshua's spies along the road that led from Jericho to "the fords" of the Jordan (dark line, upper left; Josh. 2:1–7). The spies were concealed by Rahab, who warned: "Go to the hills [right center], so the pursuers will not find you" (Josh. 2:16). In the mountains above Jericho, there are small caves and many other hiding places. The site of Old Testament Jericho is above and to the right of a Palestinian refugee camp, just below the oasis of Jericho. The square structure on top of the cone shaped hill (upper right) is the highest point of what is called the "Mount of Temptation," the traditional site of Christ's temptation (Matt. 4:1–2; see **G2-4**).

G2-5   Cypros, Threx ? & Jericho oasis

View: NE

G2-6   Cypros, Threx ? & Roman road to Jerusalem

View: W

H1-1   Dead Sea & Ein Feshka

H1-2   Kh. Qumran: excavations

H1-3   Wadi Nar: entry to the Dead Sea

View: E

DEAD SEA & LISAN

Unit H1

The Dead Sea is 1,300 feet below sea level and is the lowest spot on the earth (above water). Its 50-mile length is divided into unequal parts by the Lisan Peninsula. At the peninsula, the sea narrows from 10 miles to only about 2 miles. In ancient times, the Lisan was used to cross the Dead Sea. The length of the Dead Sea varies due to the constant evaporation. The northern section of the Dead Sea is about 35 miles long and is nearly 1,300 feet deep at its deepest point. The southern section has all but dried up, and large artificial pools have been created to extract potash that is used in fertilizers and soaps. In biblical times, the Dead Sea was valued for its salt and bitumen which sometimes floated to the surface. The mineral concentration of the Dead Sea is 25 to 30 percent, or 10 times greater than that of the oceans. The biblical name for the Dead Sea was "Salt Sea" (Gen. 14:3; Josh. 15:2), or the "Sea of the Arabah" (Deut. 3:17; Josh. 3:16). The Romans called it *Lacus Asphaltitis*.

The oppressive heat and lack of vegetation give the Dead Sea region a feeling of desolation. Still, there is a prophecy that water will flow from the Temple toward the eastern region and "down into the Arabah, where it enters the Sea. When it empties into the Sea, the water there becomes fresh. Swarms of living creatures will live wherever the river flows. There will be large numbers of fish, because this water flows there and makes the salt water fresh; so where the river flows everything will live....Fruit trees of all kinds will grow on both banks of the river....Their fruit will serve for food and their leaves for healing" (Ezek. 47:1–12).

PHOTO CAPTIONS

H1-1 Most of the springs along the shore of the Dead Sea are saline. Two exceptions are the fresh water springs of Ein Feshka at the northern end of the western shore of the Dead Sea and En-gedi in the center. The springs of Ein Feshka are in the canyon (center) just south of Qumran. The caves in this and other canyons along the western shore of the Dead Sea were dwelling places to various sects around the time of Jesus who wanted to avoid contact with civilization. Many of the Dead Sea scrolls were hidden in these caves only to be discovered in the 20th century. The fresh water spring of En-gedi is in Nahal Arugot, 20 miles south of Qumran (see **H1-2**) and 10 miles north of Masada (see **H1-5**). Nahal Arugot is a canyon similar to the one pictured here, where waterfalls emerge from underground

springs that fill a number of pools with cool water. The region west of En-gedi was called the "Desert of En-gedi " (1 Sam. 24:1). Here, David sought refuge from King Saul. The "strongholds at En-gedi" were the camps at the top of the mountains overlooking Nahal Arugot (1 Sam. 23:29; 24:22). David spared Saul's life when the king went into a cave at En-gedi (1 Sam. 24).

H1-2 This photograph shows the excavations of Qumran, where the main occupation was between 150 B.C. and A.D. 68. The people who lived here carefully planned the complex of buildings to include communal facilities, a water system, a library, and a large cemetery. Pliny (1st century A.D.) described a sect called Essenes, who lived in isolation in a region west of the Dead Sea. The community of Qumran is generally identified with the Essenes. This identity is now challenged by modern archaeologists. The region was made famous by the chance discovery of the Dead Sea Scrolls in 1947, many of which were discovered in caves just south of Qumran (upper left; see **H1-7**). Similar discoveries were made in other caves in 1952 and 1956. In addition to many secular works—such as the Hodayot, the Manual of Discipline, the War Scroll, and the Temple Scroll—all the books of the Hebrew Bible except Esther are represented in the Dead Sea Scrolls. A copy of the complete scroll of Isaiah is now displayed in the Shrine of the Book Museum in Jerusalem. The sectarian scrolls of this community have enlarged our understanding of the variety of perspectives in early Judaism. The ages of the scrolls range from the 3rd century B.C. to A.D. 68, but most are from the 1st century B.C.

H1-3 The "brook Kidron" (see 2 Sam. 15:23; John 18:1) runs from north of Jerusalem (east of the Temple mount and west of the Mount of Olives) through the Judean Wilderness to the Dead Sea. "So barren and blistered, so furnace-like does it become as it drops below the level of the sea, that it takes the name of Wadi en-Nar, or the Fire Wady. At last its dreary course brings it to the precipices above the Dead Sea" (Smith, 328–329). David crossed the Kidron Valley in his flight from Jerusalem during the revolt by Absalom (2 Sam. 15:23).

H1-4 These cliffs and the wilderness behind them were a natural defense for the hill country of Judah (view is 10 miles south of Qumran; see **H1-2**). "Except at En-gedi, the west range [of the Dead Sea] is bare, unbroken, menacing; and there are few places in the world where the sun beats with

DEAD SEA & LISAN
UNIT H1
1 : 220,000

1 Adummim, ascent	5 Callirhoe	9 En-gedi	13 Jericho (modern)
2 Arnon, R.; Mujib	6 David, N.	10 Esbus	14 Jerusalem
3 Arugot, N.	7 Dibon	11 Herodium	15 Kir-hareseth; Kerak
4 Bethlehem	8 En Boqeq	12 Hyrcania	16 Lemba

17 Lisan Peninsula
18 Machaerus
19 Madaba
20 Mar Saba

21 Masada
22 Mezad Zohar
23 Mishmar, N.
24 Nebo, Mt.

25 Qumran, Kh.
26 Rabbath Moab
27 Sdom, Mt.
28 Tekoa

29 Zarqa Main, W.
30 Zeelim, N.
31 Zered, R., Hasa
32 Zoar

N

H1-4 Western shore below Mizpe Shalem   View: N

so fierce a heat. Beyond this rocky barrier stretches Jeshimon, ...the wilderness of Judaea" (Smith, 324; see **Unit H2** and **H1-1**).

H1-5 Rising above the Lisan peninsula to the east are the mountains of Moab, and in the haze to the south is the beginning of the Wadi Arabah (upper right; see **Unit M** and **Unit N**). This picture is particularly important because the southern end of the Dead Sea no longer looks like this. A passable ford from the south-western point of the Lisan enabled Herod the Great to escape the Parthians in 40 B.C. after he left his family in the fortress of Masada (right center). It is thought that Masada was the "stronghold" or the wilderness base of David while he was trying to evade King Saul (1 Sam. 22:4–5). Still visible from the 1st century A.D. are the remains of a siege-wall that the Romans built around Masada to prevent anyone from escaping (center to lower center), Roman camps (square structures), and a man-made earthen ramp (right center). The Romans were able to breach the wall with the aid of an iron battering-ram on the first of May, A.D. 73.

H1-6 The site of ancient Callirhoe ("Fair flowing springs") is located on the eastern shore of the Dead Sea, directly across from Mizpeh Shalem (see **H1-4**). Mentioned by Josephus, Pliny, and Jerome, as well as in rabbinical literature, Callirhoe was known for its hot springs. Herod the Great came here in hopes of recovering from various physical disorders described by Josephus (*War* 1.33.5). Zereth-shahar was part of the inheritance allocated by Moses to the tribe of Reuben (Josh. 13:19).

BIBLICAL/HISTORICAL REVIEW
Cross references to the Student Map Manual

- **Campaign of Northern Kings: Abraham rescues Lot**
  Gen. 14; SMM 4-3c. According to the account in Gen. 14, there was war between four kings of the north and five kings from the valley of the Dead Sea. G. A. Smith argued that the cities of the plain—Sodom, Gomorrah, Admah, Zeboiim and Bela (Zoar)—were north of the Dead Sea. His reasons for doing so were that Abraham and Lot viewed these cities from near Bethel (Gen. 13:10) and they would not be visible if they were at the southern end, and the "Circle" of the Jordan fits the northern end better (Smith, 505–506). But Gen. 13:10 speaks of the whole plain of the Jordan; Lot was interested in the pasture land, not the cities. The Valley of Siddim may originally have been a fertile plain watered by the five streams which today flow from the east and

the southeast into this part of the Dead Sea. Archaeological evidence points to a devastating natural catastrophe that struck this area ca. 2,000 B.C. All but Zoar were destroyed by the Lord because of their wickedness (Gen. 19:24–29).

- **David in the Wilderness: Flight from Saul (ca. 1000 B.C.)**
  1 Sam. 18–26; SMM 7-5d. As the rivalry grew between David and King Saul, David sought refuge in the Judean Wilderness as well as in the caves and strong points that overlook the Dead Sea. Even after David saved the inhabitants of Keilah (Shephelah of Judah; see **Unit K**) from the Philistines, "Saul called up all his forces for battle, to go down to Keilah to besiege David and his men." Warned by the Lord that the people of Keilah would deliver him into Saul's hands, David fled and "stayed in the desert strongholds" (see **H1-1**). Saul chased David even into this desolate region, but "God did not give David into his hands."

- **First Jewish Revolt Against Rome: Masada (A.D. 73)**
  SMM 12-13m. George Adam Smith gave this description of Masada: "[Masada] is isolated, precipitous on every side and inaccessible except in two places, where winding paths ... may be followed by men in single file. On the west this stronghold falls only some 400 feet upon a promontory that connects it with the range behind. Everywhere else it shows at least 1300 feet of cliff, but seaward as much as 1700" (Smith, 329). Masada was the last stronghold of the Jews in the First Jewish Revolt against Rome (see **H1-5**). Jerusalem had fallen three years earlier in A.D. 70. As their final act of defiance, nearly 1,000 men, women, and children of Masada took their own lives rather than fall into Roman hands. ∎

H1-7 (overleaf) Khirbet Qumran (upper center) is 7 miles south of Jericho and a mile west of the Dead Sea. The site, which some would identify with the biblical "City of Salt" (Josh. 15:62), was occupied mainly during the Greco-Roman period (ca. 150 B.C.–A.D. 68). Some scholars feel that John the Baptist was influenced by "Qumran" theology, and may even have been a member. But if he was, he left the sect, and his attitude toward the Jewish leadership was a call to repentance; their's was a total repudiation.

H1-5   Masada & Lisan Peninsula   View: SE

H1-6   Zereth-shahar ?, Callirhoe   View: N

H2-1   Judean Wildernes: Nebi Musa   **View: SE**

H2-2   Pharathon & Wadi Suweinit   **View: SW**

H2-3 Judean Wilderness   View: NW

JUDEAN WILDERNESS   Unit H2

West of the Dead Sea is the Judean Wilderness. Not considered a "true desert," its barren appearance is mainly due to the fact that it is on the leeward side of the Judean Hill Country where it receives very little rainfall. (The leeward side is away from the wind.) As the moist air coming off the Mediterranean Sea rises against the western side of the central mountain range, it cools and condenses, forming droplets of water that fall as rain. As air descends the eastern side of the central mountains, the air warms and expands. Thus, the Judean Wilderness is said to be in the rain-shadow. Rainfall decreases from about 16 inches annually near the top of the wilderness to only 6 inches at Jericho, and to 2 inches at the southern end of the Dead Sea.

The wilderness region was a frontier zone that had to be crossed before attacking the hill country from the east. Most of the passes between Jericho and the southern end of the Dead Sea were too narrow and crooked to carry a road of any significance. And because ancient travelers had to cross a waterless desert for up to 8 hours, it was necessary and important that a journey begin from one of the few well-watered spots on the eastern edge of the wilderness region nearer the Dead Sea. Such a spot was En-gedi on the western shore of the Dead Sea. Aharoni summed up the effect the Judean Wilderness has had on the Judean Hill Country and the role the wilderness has played in the history of the Holy Land: "Thanks to this frightful wilderness the mountains of Judah are a rather *isolated* and *closed country*: the desert not only serves as an impassable guardian from the east, it also prevents a west-east passage through Judah" (Aharoni, 30; italics added).

PHOTO CAPTIONS

H2-1 The view in this photograph is to the southeast, looking across the Judean Wilderness toward the Dead Sea and Moab (upper left). In the foreground (right) is the site of Nebi Musa, where, according to a late Muslim tradition, the prophet Moses is buried. The site, which is about 1 mile south of the Jerusalem-Jericho road and about 5 miles southwest of Jericho, was originally chosen because of its strategic location on one of the roads between Jericho and the Judean Hill Country. The present building was built in 1265 by the Mameluke sultan, Baybars. According to Stanley, the site is so sacred to Muslims that "its entrance is rigidly barred against unbelievers, and its votaries [devotees] are so numerous, that the authorities of Jerusalem have ... fixed the days of the pilgrimage thither at the same time as the Greek Easter; so that at the very moment when Jerusalem might, it was feared, be in danger of a surprise from the influx of Christian pilgrims, a body of Mussulman pilgrims might be on the spot to defend the Holy City" (Stanley, 302). This practice was discontinued in 1947.

H2-2 This view is to the west toward Jerusalem and the Judean Hill Country, looking across the site of Pharathon (lower center) and the Wadi Suweinit. Pharathon was one in a chain of fortresses that once surrounded Jerusalem. They were used by the Seleucid general Bacchides (160 to 155 B.C.) to guard Judea against the Hasmonean forces that had gathered in the wilderness south of Tekoa. The Wadi Suweinit was part of "a real pass across the range" that crossed the plateau north of Jerusalem and went down the western side of the hill country to Aijalon. "Not only did Israel by it first come up from the Jordan on to the tableland, and by it sweep down towards the sea, but it was in all ages a regular route for trade" (Smith, 172–173).

H2-3 This picture was taken about midway between Jerusalem and Jericho. The view is to the northwest. At the top of the picture, just below the clouds, one can see the top of Mt. Ephraim (see 1 Sam. 1:1). At the start of Jesus' formal ministry, he retired to the wilderness. "After fasting forty days and forty nights, the tempter came to him and said, 'If you are the Son of God, tell these stones to become bread.' Jesus answered, 'It is written: "Man does not live on bread alone, but on every word that comes from the mouth of God"'" (see Matt. 4:1–11). John the Baptist also came into the wilderness of Judea, saying to the people, "Repent, for the kingdom of heaven is near" (Matt. 3:1–2).

H2-4 Umm Qatafa in the Wadi Khareitun is one of the most important prehistoric caves discovered in the Holy Land. Archaeologists discovered hearths with traces of burning, which are thought to be "the earliest testimony to the use of fire in the Middle East" (Aharoni [1982], 14). Caves such as this one were places of refuge for people who fled from the Romans in the First and Second Jewish Revolts (A.D. 66–73 and A.D. 132–135).

**JUDEAN WILDERNESS
UNIT H2**

1 : 150,000

17 Jerusalem
18 Khareitun, W.
19 Mar Saba
20 Michmash

21 Muhallik, W.
22 Murabbaat cave
23 Nar, W., Kidron
24 Netopha (h)

25 Pharathon
26 Qilt, W.
27 Qumran, Kh.
28 Ramallah

29 Remmon
30 Suweinit, W.
31 Tekoa
32 Umm Qatafa cave

N

H2-4   Wadi Khareitun: cave Umm Qatafa   View: NW

H2-5 The Herodium (upper center) was built by Herod the Great in about 23 B.C., and was the place in which he was finally buried by his own order. It is located 2¹/₂ miles southeast of Bethlehem on the edge of the wilderness and the Judean Hill Country. The Upper Herodium was a palace-like fortress constructed on top of a cone-shaped mountain. The Lower Herodium was directly north and connected to the fortress. It was used by Herod as a summer residence and elaborately decorated (see **J1-2**). The Wadi Khareitun is in the foreground (see **H2-4**).

H2-6 The Monastery of Mar Saba (lower center) stands in the canyon of Nahal Kidron (right center), about 7 miles east of Bethlehem. The Kidron begins a mile north of Jerusalem's Temple Mount and descends through the wilderness 20 miles to the Dead Sea. Mar Saba was founded by Saint Sabas in A.D. 483 and was the center of Palestinian monasticism. St. John of Damascus came to the Mar Saba monastery in the 7th century. He was the last of the Eastern fathers and a great hymnographer. The mountain-like appearance of the wilderness is due to the steep descent, the highly erosive chalky soil, and the imperviousness of the bedrock, which turns rainfall into a sudden rush of erosive runoff. Except for a few small settlements and forts, the Judean Wilderness did not have any permanent settlements of consequence (see **H2-1**, **H2-2**, and **H2-5**).

BIBLICAL/HISTORICAL REVIEW
Cross references to the Student Map Manual

- **Attack from En-gedi: Moab and Ammon**
  2 Chron. 20; SMM 8-6e. Because of physical obstacles in the east, most invasions of Judah came from the north. One exception was the invasion of the Ammonites and Moabites, who attempted to cross the wilderness via the pass at En-gedi, 28 miles south of Jericho on the western shore of the Dead Sea. Jehoshaphat, king of Judah, led his army into the wilderness of Tekoa about 5 miles south of Bethlehem. There he encouraged his troops with a call to believe in the Lord and to follow his prophets: "As they set out, Jehoshaphat stood and said, 'Listen to me, Judah, and people of Jerusalem! Have faith in the Lord your God and you will be upheld; have faith in his prophets and you will be successful.'"

- **Parthian Invasion: Herod's Flight to Idumea**
  SMM 11-13c. At the time of the Parthian invasion in 40 B.C., Herod the Great fled through the Judean Wilderness to escape his pursuers (see **H2-5**). He sought refuge for his family in the fortress of Masada (see **H1-5**). From Masada Herod made his way to Rome where the Roman Senate appointed him king of the Jews in ca. 40 B.C.

- **Parable of the Good Samaritan**
  Luke 10: 25–37. The parable of the good Samaritan reflects the kind of calamity that could have happened to anyone traveling between Jerusalem and Jericho. First, a certain man "was going *down* from Jerusalem to Jericho, when he fell into the hands of robbers" (italics added). Others came that way, including a Priest, a Levite, and a Samaritan. Only the Samaritan had compassion on the injured man and took care of him. After doing all he could, the Samaritan took the man to an inn and paid for his continued care. Jesus asked, "Which of these three do you think was a neighbor to the man who fell into the hands of robbers?" The expert in the law replied,"The one who had mercy on him." Jesus told him,"Go and do likewise."

- **Second Jewish Revolt Against Rome: Judean Desert Caves**
  SMM 13-4. The supporters of Bar Kokhba hid in caves in the canyons that descend to the Dead Sea. Coins, letters, and other artifacts shed new light on this important period of Jewish History. Unable to assault the caves directly, the Romans set up camps above the caves to prevent the Jews from escaping. Most of them perished within the caves. ∎

H2-7 (overleaf) Hyrcania was one of Herod the Great's principle fortresses. After Herod captured the fortress in about 32 B.C., opponents of his kingdom "were brought to the citadel Hyrcania, both openly and secretly, and were there put to death" (*Ant.* 15.10.4). Herod had his son Antipater executed and ordered that his own body be buried in Hyrcania (*War* 1.33.7). Herod died 5 days later (see **J1-2**).

H2-5   Wadi Khareitun & Herodium View: N

H2-6   Mar Saba monastery & Wadi Nar View: SE

I-1   **Jerusalem: Old City**   **View: SE**

I-2   **Jerusalem: Ophel & Dome of Rock**   **View: N**

I-3   **Wadi Nar (N. Kidron) & Mt. of Olives**   **View: NW**

JERUSALEM

Jerusalem is located in the Judean Hill Country about 2500 feet above sea level. It is 16 miles due west of the northern end of the Dead Sea (see I-1) and 38 miles east of the Mediterranean Sea (see I-3). In ancient times, it was called Jebus and Salem (Ps. 76:2), the city in which Abraham paid tithes to Melchizedek (Gen. 14:18–20). Jerusalem is sometimes called the "City of Peace" (the author of Hebrews identified Melchizedek as the "King of Salem, which is, King of peace" [Heb. 7:2]), yet more wars probably have been fought at its gates than at those of any other city in the world. After David captured it from the Jebusites in about 1000 B.C., Jerusalem was also called the "city of David" and the "fortress of Zion" (2 Sam. 5:6–7).

The natural strength of Jerusalem was provided by the hills that surround the city on every side and the fact that the site of Jerusalem was easily defensible on three sides. Jerusalem was first built on the eastern spur, the Ophel, but was later expanded to the north and west. Except on the north, the city is naturally defended by the Hinnom and Kidron valleys. The prophets understood that Israel could not fight the armies of Egypt and Mesopotamia using those countries' methods of warfare. Chariots and armies fought well on the plains but were less effective on the rocky hillsides of Judea, where organized bands hiding among the hills and in caves could spring unexpectedly upon their enemies. This type of warfare worked well for David and Judas Maccabeus, but it required a unified nation committed to the cause for which the people were fighting. Most of the time, however, the Israelites fought like other nations, just as they had a king "such as all the other nations have" (1 Sam. 8:5). Isaiah warned them that they should stay home and trust in their natural defenses: "Woe to those who go down to Egypt for help, who rely on horses, who trust in the multitude of their chariots and in the great strength of their horsemen, but do not look to the Holy One of Israel, nor seek help from the Lord!" (Isa. 31:1).

Jerusalem fell to the Babylonians and the Romans. Both powers employed siege warfare. The Assyrians perfected the use of battering rams and other engines for use against fortified cities; the Babylonians were heirs to the Assyrians. The Romans were even more effective in their siege warfare with the use of the catapult, crossbow, ballista, onager, assult tower and the circumvolution wall.

PHOTO CAPTIONS

I-1 The Temple Mount was the site of the temples of Solomon, Zerubbabel, and Herod. After 37 B.C., the city was completely transformed as a result of the building program of Herod the Great. He strengthened the existing walls and built a second wall to include more of the area west of the Temple Mount. Herod also fortified the Citadel, a fortress north of the Temple Mount that he renamed Antonia after Mark Antony. Today, the Temple Mount is a holy place to Muslims, who believe that Muhammad ascended to heaven from this spot. The Dome of the Rock was built between A.D. 687 and 691, and is decorated with beautiful Persian tiles. The silver-domed (now lead) el-Aksa mosque was built between A.D. 709 and 715. The present wall of Jerusalem's Old City was built in A.D. 1542 during the reign of Sultan Suleiman. Inside the southern gate, called Dung Gate, is the Western Wall of the Temple Mount (center). East of the Temple Mount is the Kidron Valley and the Mount of Olives, and in the background is the Judean Wilderness. The Dead Sea is visible at the top of the picture (upper right).

I-2 At the time of King David, the area of Jerusalem was relatively small. It was located on the hill south of the Temple Mount (center) between the Tyropoeon and Kidron Valleys, opposite the village of Silwan today (right center). The city's principal water source was the Gihon spring, below and outside the city walls in the Kidron Valley. Solomon was anointed king at this spring. Hezekiah, king of Judah, brought the water inside the city by having a tunnel cut (2 Chron. 32:2–4,30). The end of the tunnel and the Pool of Siloam are located at the southern end of the City of David where the Tyropoeon and Kidron Valleys meet to form a "V" (lower right; see John 9:7–11). Solomon expanded the city to the north, building "his palace and the temple of the Lord, and the wall around Jerusalem. " (1 Kgs. 3:1; 6–7).

I-3 East of the Temple Mount is the Mount of Olives. It was the place of many biblical events and has a place in the prophesied events of the last days (Zech. 14:4–5). The road from Jericho crossed the Mt. of Olives to the Kidron Valley. On the western side of the Mount was the Garden of Gethsemane where Jesus prayed before he was taken before the Jewish leaders and Pontius Pilate (Matt. 26:39). The northern part of the Mount was called Mt. Scopus (Lookout point. Scopus comes from a Greek word meaning "to watch"). The legions of the Roman general Titus camped here before the destruction of Jerusalem in A.D. 70. The southern part of the Mount of Olives was called the Mount of Offense, where Solomon built "a high place for Chemosh the detestable god of Moab" (1 Kgs. 11:7). The Mediterranean Sea is visible in the distance (top left).

BIBLICAL/HISTORICAL REVIEW
Cross references to the Student Map Manual

- **Josh. 10:1–39; SMM 5-5b,c.** Joshua defeated the kings of Jerusalem, Hebron, Jarmuth, Lachish, and Debir.

- **2 Sam. 5:6–16; 1 Chron. 11:4–7.** David captured the Jebusite city, called Jebus, and made it his capital.

- **1 Kgs. 6–9.** A description of Solomon's building projects in Jerusalem, including the temple and his own palace.

- **2 Kgs. 24–25; 2 Chron. 36:15–21; Jer. 39:9–14; SMM 9-7c,d.** Nebuchadnezzar, king of Babylon, captured Jerusalem in 605 and again in 586 B.C.

- **Ezra 3:8–13; 4:23–24; 5:15; 6:15–18; Haggai.** Jews built the temple of Zerubbabel after the Babylonian captivity.

- **Luke 2:22–39.** Jesus was brought to Jerusalem as a baby.

- **Luke 2:41–50.** At age 12, Jesus was found "in the temple courts, sitting among the teachers, listening to them and asking them questions."

- **Matt. 26:36–56; Mark 14:32–49; Luke 22:39–53; John 18:1–13.** Jesus prayed in the Garden of Gethsemane, was betrayed, and arrested.

- **Matt. 27:32–56; Mark 15:21–41; Luke 23:26–46; John 19:16–37.** Jesus was crucified to "save his people from their sins."

- **Matt. 27:57–66; Mark 15:42–47; Luke 23:50–56; John 19:41–42.** Jesus was buried in the tomb of Joseph of Arimathaea.

- **Matt. 28:1–15; Mark 16:1–11; Luke 24:1–12; John 20:1–18.** Jesus was resurrected, and was seen by Mary Magdalene.

- **John 20:4.** Peter and John discover the empty tomb.

I-4 (pp. 150–151) A 6th century A.D. mosaic of the Holy Land was discovered in 1884 during the construction of a new Greek Orthodox church in Medeba (Jordan). This detail of Jerusalem shows two colonnaded streets, twenty-one towers (the big tower on the south is probably the Tower of David), six gates, the Church of the Holy Sepulcher, other churches and monasteries, and other details.

JERUSALEM
UNIT I

1 : 75,000

1 Ai	10 Bethther	9 Bethlehem	13 Geba
2 Anathoth	4 Beth-hacc(h)erem ?	7 Beth-zechariah	14 Gibeah (of Saul)
8 Bethany	5 Beth-horon, Lower	11 Emmaus; Mozah	15 Gibeon
3 Bethel	6 Beth-horon, Upper	12 Emmaus; Qubeibe	16 Jerusalem

17 Kiriath-jearim
23 Michmash
18 Mizpah
19 Nabi Samwil

20 Rama(h)
21 Ramallah
22 Refaim, N.
24 Tekoa

N

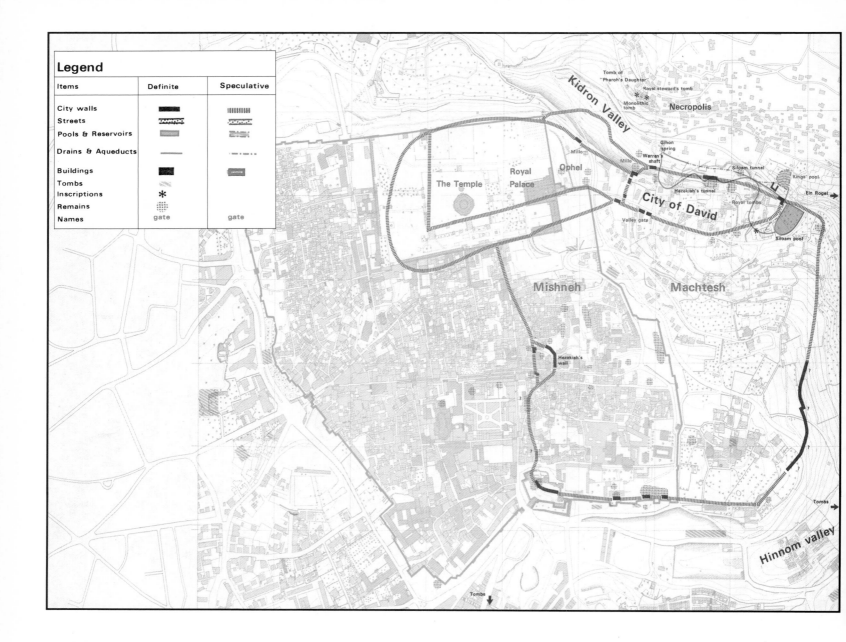

Jerusalem in the First Temple Period

The "City of David" consisted of a relatively small area south of the Temple Mount (see I-2). It was protected by the Kidron Valley to the east, the Tyropoeon Valley to the west, and the Hinnom Valley to the south. The valleys were deeper anciently than they are today. Solomon extended the city northward to include the area of the Temple Mount. Here he built the First Temple in which the Ark of the Covenant was placed (see 2 Sam. 7:1–13; 1 Kgs. 6, 8). He connected the City of David with the Temple Mount by filling in the narrow neck of land that separated the two. Solomon also built a wall north and west of the Temple Mount to protect the city from invasion. The walls west of David's City that encompass the western hill region, or upper city, represent the expansion of Jerusalem from the 8th century B.C. until its destruction by the Babylonians in 587 B.C.

The conquest of Jerusalem by David is described in 2 Sam. 5:6–9, although not many details are given. It has been suggested that David's men were able to enter the city through a water installation known today as Warren's shaft (after Charles Warren who discovered it in 1867). The shaft would have allowed the inhabitants of Jerusalem to bring water into the city without having to go outside the city's walls. A much more extensive system was built by King Hezekiah in the latter part of the 8th century B.C. that brought water from outside the city, from the Gihon

spring, through a sinuous tunnel ca. 1750 feet long, although the distance in a straight line is only 1050 feet . The tunnel varies in height from 3½ to 11 feet . The water coming through the tunnel emptied into the pool of Siloam just south of the City of David (see John 9:1–7). An inscription, found in 1880 in the wall near the lower entrance, reads in part: "And when the tunnel was driven through, the quarrymen hewed (the rock), each man toward his fellow, axe against axe; and the water flowed from the spring toward the reservoir for 1,200 cubits, and the height of the rock above the head(s) of the quarrymen was 100 cubits" (ANET, 321). In addition to building the tunnel, Hezekiah fortified the walls of Jerusalem (see "Hezekiah's Wall" above; Isa. 22:8–11), and other cities of Judah.

The following passages relate to the building of Hezekiah's Tunnel: "[Hezekiah] made the pool and the tunnel by which he brought water into the city" (2 Kgs. 20:20).

"When Hezekiah saw that Sennacherib had come and that he intended to make war on Jerusalem, he consulted with his officials and his military staff about blocking off the water from the springs outside the city, and they helped him. A large force of men assembled, and they blocked all the springs and the stream that flowed through the land. 'Why should the kings of Assyria come and find plenty of water?' they said" (2 Chron. 32:2–4).

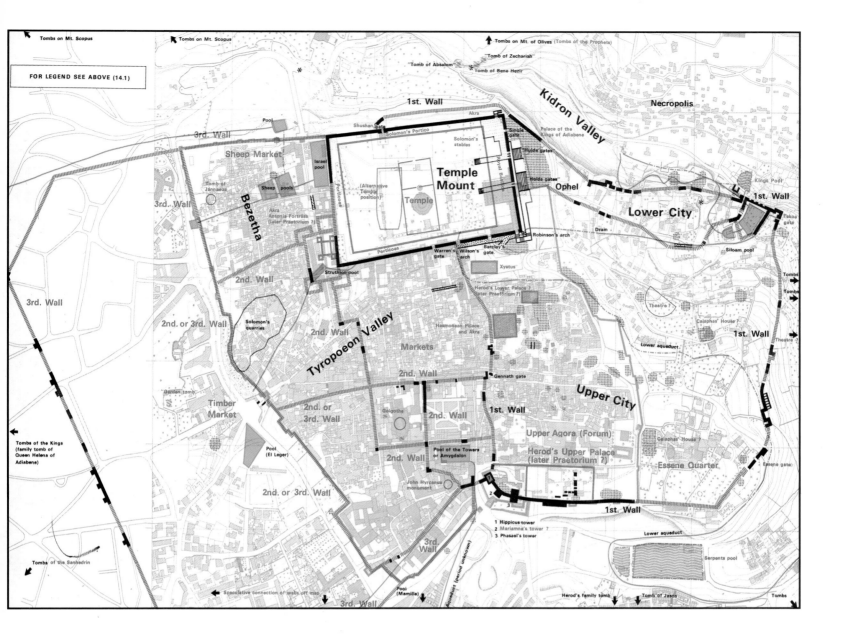

Jerusalem in the Second Temple Period

In 538 B.C., after the fall of Babylon, Cyrus, king of Persia, allowed the Jewish exiles to return to Jerusalem and rebuild the temple (Ezra 1). About a century later, Nehemiah, a Jew who held the office of "cupbearer" at the court of Artaxerxes, received a royal commission authorizing him to rebuild the walls of Jerusalem (Neh. 2–6). From that time, throughout the Hellenistic period (333–63 B.C.), Jerusalem grew in importance as the political and religious center of the Jews. The Jews returning from captivity built the Second Temple, called the temple of Zerubbabel (Ezra 3:8–13; 4:23–24; 5:15; 6:15–18; Haggai). In the years that followed, the city expanded again to the western hill which had been abandoned since the Babylonian siege of Jerusalem. In the center of the Upper City, was the *agora*, or upper market place.

Jerusalem was completely transformed after the Romans conquered the city in 63 B.C. This was mostly due to the building program of Herod the Great, who was appointed king of Judea in 40 B.C. Herod strengthened the existing walls of the city and built a second wall to include more of the area immediately west of the Temple Mount. Herod also fortified the citadel north of the Temple Mount, which he renamed Antonia after Mark Antony. Flagstones dating to the time of the Roman emperor Hadrian (A.D. 117–138) can still be seen in the area of the Antonia, as well as the symbols of a game that were scratched probably by Roman soldiers into

the surface of some of the stones. Another of Herod's projects was to build a new administrative and defensive center (which included a beautiful palace) at the western side of the Upper City. According to Josephus it had "two very spacious and beautiful buildings with which the Temple itself could not be compared" (*War* 1.21.1). Attached to Herod's palace in the north was a citadel with three large towers which Herod named after his brother, Phasael; his friend, Hippicus; and his wife, Mariamne (Herod had Mariamne executed because he suspected her of adultery). Some of the original stones used to build the tower named after Phasael can be seen in the Citadel today.

One of Herod's projects was the restoration of the temple in Jerusalem. In reply to Jesus' statement, "Destroy this temple, and I will raise it again in three days," the Jews replied, : "It has taken forty-six years to build this temple, and you are going to raise it in three days?" (John 2:20–21.) To accommodate the large crowds that gathered in Jerusalem, Herod doubled the area of the Temple Mount by means of huge supporting walls. This project required the changing of the course of the Tyropoeon Valley (to the west of the Temple Mount) and a smaller valley to the north. Josephus said in reference to Herod's building program in Jerusalem: "The expenditure involved was tremendous and the result was magnificent beyond compare" (*War* 1.21.1).

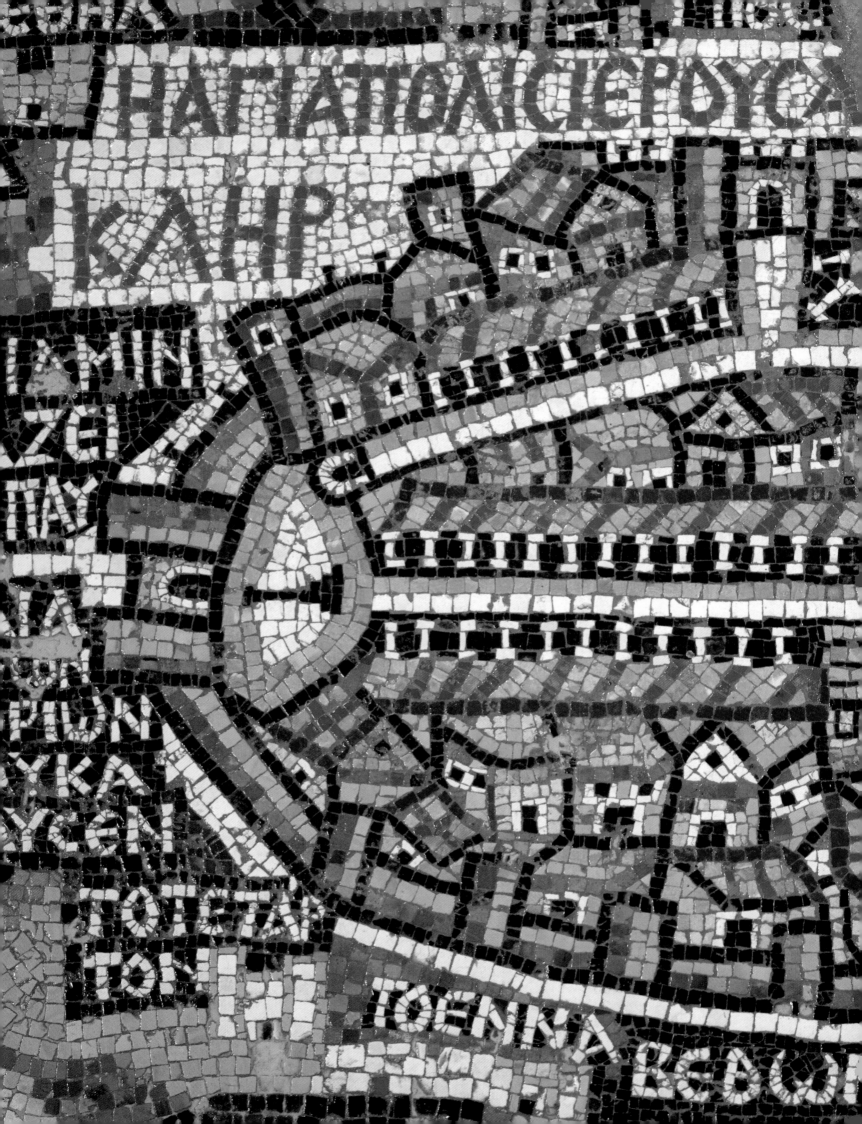

J1-1   Bethlehem: "Shepherds' Field"

View: W

J1-2   Herodium

View: NE

J1-3　Nahal Refaim: terracing　　　　　　　　　　　　　　　　　　　　　　View: NW

JUDEAN HILL COUNTRY　　　　　　　　　　Unit J1

The Judean Hill Country is a mountainous region between the Judean Shephelah on the west (see **Unit J2**) and the Judean Wilderness on the east (see **Unit H2**). The crest extends for about 50 miles without interruption, and is from 9 to 15 miles wide. The main north-south highway ran along the crest to connect the cities of Jerusalem, Bethlehem, Beth-zur, and Hebron. The natural center of the Judean Mountains is at Hebron, where the mountains "form the highest continuous area of Palestine" (Karmon, 329). Jerusalem is located in the northern part of Judea near the Benjamin territory, which in antiquity was a buffer zone between the northern and southern tribes of Israel (see **Unit I**).

The Hill Country is guarded on the west by steep slopes and narrow valleys (see **F2-2** and **J1-4**) and on the east by the Judean Wilderness (see **H2-5**). Because the Canaanites were largely successful in keeping the Israelites out of the plains and the valleys (see Josh. 17:16–18; Judg. 1:34), the Israelites had to become economically self-sufficient by mastering terrace agriculture. It has been estimated that 56 percent of the Judean Hill Country is covered with man-made terraces (see Isaiah 7:25; **J1-3).**

PHOTO CAPTIONS

J1-1 Bethlehem is only 5 miles south of Jerusalem. The fields in this picture provided the setting for the story of Ruth and Boaz who became the great-grandparents of David, king of Israel (Ruth 4:17). Micah prophesied that Bethlehem would be the birthplace of the Messiah, "But you, Bethlehem Ephrathah, though you are small among the clans of Judah, out of you will come for me one who will be ruler over Israel" (Micah 5:2; see Matt. 2:4–6; John 7:42). This picture also illustrates the setting for "shepherds living out in the fields nearby, keeping watch over their flocks at night," and of an angel standing above the shepherds saying, "Today in the town of David a Savior has been born to you; he is Christ the Lord" (Luke 2:8–12). "Judaea offers as good ground as there is in the East for observing the grandeur of the shepherd's character.... On some high moor, across which at night hyenas howl, when you meet him, sleepless, far-sighted, weather-beaten, armed, leaning on his staff, and looking out over his scattered sheep, every one on his heart, you understand why the shepherd of Judaea sprang to the front in his people's history; why they gave his name to their king, and made him

the symbol of Providence; why Christ took him as the type of self-sacrifice" (Smith, 210).

J1-2 The Herodium (lower right) was built by Herod the Great on the site where he overcame his Jewish pursuers while escaping to Masada at the time of the Parthian invasion in 40 B.C. (*War* 1.13.8). By Herod's own order, he was buried here with great pomp and ceremony. "Everything was done by Archelaus to add to the magnificence of the ceremony; he brought forth all the royal ornaments to be carried in procession in honor of the deceased. The bier was of solid gold, studded with precious stones and draped with the richest purple embroidered with various colors. On it lay the body wrapped in a crimson robe, with a diadem resting on the head, and above that a golden crown and the sceptre by the right hand" (*War* 1.33.9). The fortress is 7 miles south of Jerusalem and $2^1/_2$ miles southeast of Bethlehem.

J1-3 Nahal Refaim begins southwest of Jerusalem. It is called the "Valley of Rephaim" in the Bible and is mentioned as part of the boundary between Judah and Benjamin (Josh. 15:8; 18:16). It was the scene of two of David's victories over the Philistines, who advanced from the coast to "spread out in the valley of Rephaim" within easy reach of Jerusalem (2 Sam. 5:18–25). David asked the Lord if he should attack the Philistines and whether or not the Lord would hand the Philistines over to him. The Lord said, "Go, for I will surely hand the Philistines over to you." In the next battle with the Philistines, the Lord told David to circle around behind the Philistine army, apparently to cut off their retreat. David's men routed the Philistines, causing them to run north and down the road leading past Beth-horon through the Aijalon Valley, "all the way from Gibeon to Gezer" (2 Sam. 5:18–25; see **F2-1**, **F2-2**, and **F2-3**). Note the terracing used to increase the amount of arable land.

J1-4 This is Nahal Sorek, which begins in northern Jerusalem and continues westward to the Mediterranean Sea. The tributaries of Nahal Sorek do not meet in the mountains, but in the Shephelah west of the mountains (see **Unit J2**). This means there are more continuous ridges, which in ancient times served as routes into the Hill Country. Today there is a railway line (center) that ascends the Hill Country along Nahal Sorek to Jerusalem. The Sorek Valley was the home of Delilah (Judg. 16:4) and the scene of events from the life of Samson (see **J2-4**).

JUDEAN HILL COUNTRY
UNIT J1
1 : 150,000

1 Adora	5 Beth-shemesh	9 Bethlehem	13 Debir
2 Anathoth	6 Beth-zechariah	10 Bethther	14 Ekron
3 Beth-hacc(h)erem ?	7 Beth-zur	11 Betogabris	15 Emmaus, Colonia
4 Beth-horon, Upper	8 Bethany	12 Carmel	16 Emmaus, Nicopolis

17 Eshtemoa
18 Gath
19 Gezer
20 Gibeah (of Saul)

21 Guvrin, N.
22 Hebron
23 Jerusalem
24 Kiriath-jearim

25 Mamre
26 Maon
27 Mizpah
28 Refaim, N.

29 Sorek, N.
30 Suseya, Kh.
31 Tekoa
32 Ziph

N

J1-4   Nahal Sorek: forestation   View: W

J1-5 This photograph looks down on the Church of the Nativity (building with gabled roof that forms a cross), which was built over the traditional site of the birth of Jesus. Justin Martyr already spoke of the stable as a cave. According to St. Jerome, it is "the earth's most sacred spot." The original church was built in A.D. 326 by the emperor Constantine. The present church was built during the reign of the emperor Justinian (A.D. 527–65), and then restored by the Crusaders in the 12th century A.D. The building with the long red roof is the Franciscan Church of St. Catherine.

J1-6 Hebron is considered a holy place to three religions: Judaism, Christianity, and Islam. It is mentioned many times in the Old Testament, especially in connection with the patriarchs Abraham, Isaac, and Jacob. The mosque of Abraham (center) is supported by a magnificent wall of hewn stones that measure up to 23 feet in length. The style of stonecutting is characteristic of Herod the Great. Beneath the mosque is the Cave of Machpelah which Abraham purchased from Ephron the Hittite for 400 silver shekels. The cave was the burial place of Abraham, Sarah, Isaac, Rebekah, Jacob, and Leah. Jacob commanded his sons not to bury him in Egypt, but with his fathers in the cave of Machpelah (see Gen. 23; 25:7–11; 47:28–31; 49:29–31; 50:13). David was anointed king over the house of Judah when he was only 30 years old. In Hebron he reigned over Judah for seven years and six months, and in Jerusalem he reigned over all Israel and Judah thirty-three years" (2 Sam. 2:1–4, 10–11; 5:1–5).

BIBLICAL/HISTORICAL REVIEW
Cross references to the Student Map Manual

• **Spies in Canaan: Joshua and Caleb (13th century B.C.)**
Num. 13; Deut. 1:22–39; SMM 5-2c. Moses sent twelve spies to search the land of Canaan. All agreed that the land "does flow with milk and honey!" Ten of the spies were of the opinion, "We can't attack those people; they are stronger than we are." Joshua and Caleb, on the other hand, said, "We should go up and take possession of the land, for we can certainly do it."

• **Conquest of Jerusalem: David Defends the Hill Country (ca. 1000 B.C.)**
2 Sam. 5:5–25; 1 Chron. 11:4–9; 14:1–16; SMM 7-7b,c. David conquered Jebusite Jerusalem and made it his capital. By this action he accomplished two objectives: (1) he eliminated the Jebusites and, at the same time, established his capital in a neutral area between the northern and southern tribes; and (2) he made Jerusalem royal property by right of

conquest. The Jebusites are reported to have said, "You will not get in here; even the blind and the lame can ward you off." This may be boastful confidence, but it may also refer to some sort of religious or magical stratagem to prevent an attack. David promised that whoever led the attack would become commander-in-chief. Joab earned this distinction. How the city was captured is a matter of debate. The word translated "water shaft" can just as easily be taken as "scaling hooks" or a weapon of some kind. After the capture of Jerusalem, David crushed two attempts by the Philistines to invade the Hill Country (see **J1-3**).

• **Defense of Judah: The Fortifications of Rehoboam (ca. 925 B.C.)**
2 Chron. 11:5–23; SMM 8-4a. The placement of Rehoboam's fortifications suggests that he meant to hold only the heart of his kingdom. The western fortifications defined the border of Philistia (see **Unit K**), while the southern fortifications did not include the Negev or the hill country south of Ziph and Adoraim. Rehoboam did not build any fortresses in the north, which suggests that he hoped someday to reunite Judah with the northern tribes.

• **Egyptian Campaign in the Days of Rehoboam: Shishak (ca. 924 B.C.)**
King Solomon controlled the trade routes running between the Euphrates River and the brook of Egypt (Wadi el-Arish), including the important Coastal Route and the King's Highway. Egypt also desired to control these routes. In the 5th year of Rehoboam's reign, Pharaoh Shishak invaded the Negev, the Southern Kingdom of Judah, and the Northern Kingdom of Israel; his purpose was to gain control of the international trade routes. ■

J1-7 (overleaf) This photograph shows olive trees and terracing around Bethlehem today. David was tending his father's sheep in the hills near Bethlehem (upper left) when he killed the lion and the bear. From Bethlehem David went to Saul's army in the valley of Elah and slew Goliath with a stone from his sling (1 Sam. 17:12–58; **J2-1**).

J1-5   Bethlehem: basilica of the Nativity   **View: SW**

J1-6   Hebron: mosque of Abraham   **View: NW**

J2-1 Valley of Elah

J2-2 Azekah: towards Beth-Shemesh

J2-3   Azekah & Valley of Elah

View: NW

JUDEAN SHEPHELAH

Unit J2

Even though the word "Shephelah" is recognized today as the name of a specific region in the Holy Land, it is translated as "foothills" (NIV), "lowland/s" (NKJ; JB), and "vale," "low plains," and "low country" (KJV) (2 Chron. 1:15; 9:27; 26:10). It was "a famous theatre of the history of Palestine—debatable ground between Israel and the Philistines, the Maccabees and the Syrians, Saladin and the Crusaders" (Smith, 143).

The Shephelah is a region of low hills between the Coastal Plain and the Judean Hill Country. A narrow north-south valley separates the Shephelah from the hill country (see **J2-7**), and several cross valleys connect both the north-south valley and the hill country with the Coastal Plain (see **J2-2**). The number of fortified cities that stood at the entrances to these valleys (Azekah, Socoh, Adullum, Zorah, Aijalon, Mareshah and Lachish) indicates how important they were to the Kingdom of Judah. For the Philistines and other invaders (such as the Egyptians, Assyrians, and Babylonians), conquering the cities of the Shephelah was the first step toward conquering Judea. The Assyrian king Sennacherib invaded Judah in 701 B.C. Before attacking Beth-zur, Bethlehem (see **J1-1**), and Jerusalem (see **Unit I**), he conquered the coastal cities and the cities of the Shephelah. Sennacherib's inscription of the campaign mentions the capture of many cities in Judah. Some of these cities are mentioned by the prophets Isaiah (Isa. 10:28–32) and Micah (Micah 1:10–16). The Shephelah was a valued part of the kingdom of Judah in the days of Uzziah (ca. 811 B.C.; see 2 Chron. 26:10). It was lost during the reign of his grandson, Ahaz (ca. 742 B.C.), when the Philistines invaded and occupied the cities of the Shephelah. (2 Chron. 28:18). The struggle between Philistines and Israelites for control of the Shephelah accounts for much of this region's history.

PHOTO CAPTIONS

J2-1 The Valley of Elah is one of several which transverse the Shephelah. The valley in this picture was the scene of the battle between David and Goliath. Just west of the valley was the Philistine city of Gath, home of Goliath (see K-4). The eastern end of the valley led to the hill country and Bethlehem, which was in the heart of Judah only 5 miles south of Jerusalem. It was critical that the army of King Saul win the battle to keep the Philistines out of the Hill Country. David, who came from Bethlehem, accepted the challenge of Goliath, and with a stone from a sling, "he struck

the Philistine on the forehead" and killed him (1 Sam. 17:45–50). Encouraged by David's victory, the Israelite army rose up and chased the Philistines to the gates of Ekron (see **K-7**).

J2-2 The view in this photograph looks across the site of ancient Azekah, which guarded the western entrance to the Valley of Elah. The view is to the northeast toward the Sorek Valley just visible at the top of the photograph (see **J2-4**). Azekah was one of the fortified cities of Rehoboam, son and successor of King Solomon (2 Chron. 11:9). It was also one of the last cities to fall before Nebuchadnezzar when his army attacked Judah in 588 B.C. (Jer. 34:7; see **K-5**).

J2-3 The mound of Azekah (upper left) dominates the entrance to the Elah Valley. In the battle between David and Goliath, according to the Bible, the Philistines pitched camp "between Socoh and Azekah," while Saul's army camped "in the Valley of Elah" (1 Sam. 17:1–2) In fact, both of the armies were in the valley. Socoh is not pictured, but is just beyond the left edge of this photograph. The brook or dry stream bed out of which David chose "five smooth stones" to use against Goliath, runs the length of the valley to the Coastal Plain. After David defeated Goliath, the Philistine army retreated toward Azekah, heading for the Coastal Plain just west of the valley's entrance (1 Sam. 17:52; see J2-2).

J2-4 Ancient Timnah (center) was situated at the western entrance to the Sorek Valley. Samson married a young Philistine woman from Timnah, and it was here that Samson killed a young lion with his bare hands (Judg. 14). He later "fell in love with a woman in the Valley of Sorek whose name was Delilah" (Judg. 16:4). The Ark of the Covenant passed near Timnah when it was returned by Philistines to Beth-shemesh at the eastern end of the Sorek Valley (1 Sam. 5–6).

J2-5 Bet Guvrin (foreground) was one of the principal cities of the Shephelah during the period of the Second Temple (see **Unit I**). It [Betabris] is mentioned by Josephus as one of "two villages in the very middle of Idumea" captured by the Romans in A.D. 68 (*War* 4.8.1). In the late Roman period (A.D. 200), Bet Guvrin was granted the privileges of a Roman city and renamed Eleutheropolis ("city of the free"). From here, Eusebius (4th century A.D.) measured distances in the region which were recorded in his *Onomasticon*.

JUDEAN SHEPHELAH
UNIT J2
1 : 150,000

1 Adullam	5 Azekah	9 Beth-shemesh	13 Elah, Valley
2 Aijalon, Valley	6 Bet Guvrin	10 Beth-zur	14 Emmaus, Colonia
3 Aphek, Antipatris	7 Beth-horon, Lower	11 Betogabris	15 Emmaus, Nicopolis
4 Ayyalon, N.	8 Beth-horon, Upper	12 Ekron	16 Eshtaol

17 Gath　　　　　21 Jabneel, Jamnia　　　25 Lod, Lydda　　　29 Sorek, N.
18 Gezer　　　　　22 Jaffa, Yafo　　　　　26 Modiin　　　　　30 Tel Aviv
19 Guvrin, N.　　　23 Kiriath-jearim　　　27 Shillo, N.　　　31 Timnah
20 Hebron　　　　　24 Lachish　　　　　　28 Socoh　　　　　32 Zorah

N

J2-4   Timnah & Nahal Sorek   View: E

J2-6 This picture shows some of the agriculture in the Shephelah today. In biblical times, the Shephelah was well-known for its production of grain and for having sufficient area to graze large herds. Uzziah, king of Judah, "had much livestock in the foothills and in the plain" (2 Chron. 26:10). The Shephelah was also well-known for its olive, sycamore, and fig trees (1 Kgs. 10:27; 1 Chron. 27:28; 2 Chron. 1:15; 9:27).

BIBLICAL/HISTORICAL REVIEW
Cross references to the Student Map Manual

- **Conquest of Canaan: Battle of Gibeon**
  Josh. 10:1–15; SMM 5-5a, b. After the Gibeonites deceived Joshua into making a league with them, they came under attack by the kings of Jerusalem, Hebron, Jarmuth, Lachish, and Eglon. These kings feared Gibeon as a city greater than Ai which the Israelites had already destroyed. Joshua came to the Gibeonites' defense, and chased the Amorite kings down the descent of Beth-horon toward Azekah in the Shephelah (see **F2-2** and **J2-2**).

- **Tribe of Dan Moves North**
  Judg. 1:34–35; 17–18; Josh. 19:47; SMM 6-4a. The cities assigned to the tribe of Dan extended from the Shephelah across the southern Coastal Plain (Philistia). Their assignment was essential to control international traffic along the Coastal Route. Because the men of Dan were not able to take possession of their inheritance in this very important and strategic area, they migrated north to the Upper Jordan Valley, where they conquered Laish near Mt. Hermon (see **Unit A2**).

- **Battle Between David and Goliath**
  1 Sam. 17; SMM 7-5c. David was from Bethlehem of Judah, where he watched the flocks of his father, Jesse. From Bethlehem a road descended to the Shephelah, where Saul and the army of Israel gathered to fight the Philistines in the Valley of Elah. The Philistines, who already held Azekah at the western end of the valley, camped between Azekah and Socoh. Goliath was a giant Philistine who challenged any Israelite to personal combat. David accepted Goliath's challenge and faced the Philistine with only his sling and five smooth stones. The sling is considered a long-range and powerful weapon, as is evident in the Assyrian reliefs showing methods of warfare; it is equivalent to artillery in the modern army. The tribe of Benjamin had 700 chosen men who "could sling a stone at a hair and not miss" (Judg.

20:16). Goliath was armed with several weapons: javelin, spear and sword. The javelin (used to throw) was on his back; his spear (used to thrust) was in his hand. David was able to use his sling before Goliath was close enough to effectively use his weapons.

- **Babylonian Campaign Against Judah: Nebuchadnezzar**
  2 Kgs. 24:17–25:21; 2 Chron. 36:11–21; Jer. 21; 24; 27–34; 37:1–39; 51:59–52:30; SMM 9-7d. Zedekiah was a puppet king, placed on the throne of Judah by King Nebuchadnezzar after the Babylonian monarch conquered Judah in 598 B.C. Zedekiah disregarded repeated warnings by the prophet Jeremiah and rebelled against the Babylonians a second time, which brought about the destruction of Jerusalem in 587 B.C. As a consequence, the Babylonians slew Zedekiah's sons before his eyes, blinded him, and took him to Babylon. The Babylonian reprisal against the cities of Judah was without pity. The last cities to fall, before Jerusalem was taken, were Lachish and Azekah. ∎

J2-7 (overleaf) The view in this photograph is to the southeast, across the site of Adullam (center), which lies along a southern extension of the Elah Valley (see **J2-1**). From here, two roads ascended the Judean Hill Country (background) toward Beth-zur and Hebron. Adullam was one of the Canaanite cities defeated by Joshua and assigned to the Shephelah district of Judah (see Josh. 12:8; 15:33). David and a group of his followers hid from King Saul in a cave near Adullam (1 Sam. 22:1–2). Adullam was also one of the cities fortified by Rehoboam before the invasion of Shishak (2 Chron. 11:7).

J2-5   Bet Guvrin & Betogabris, Eleutheropolis   View: SE

J2-6   Shephelah: general terrain

K-1   Ashdod, Azotus & coastal sand dunes   View: NW

K-2   Gaza: Crusader church of St. John (mosque)   View: E

K-3   Nahal Shiqma: exit to Mediterranean Sea

View: NE

COASTAL PLAIN (Philistia)

Unit K

Palestine, or *Palestina*, was the Greco-Roman name for Philistia, the country or land of the Philistines (See Isa. 14:29; Ex. 13:17; 1 Kgs. 4:21). The Philistines were one of the tribes of sea peoples that settled on the coast of Canaan about the time the Israelites penetrated the hill country. In time the Philistines gave their name to the whole land of Canaan. The southern Coastal Plain is south of the Plain of Sharon (see **Unit E1**) and corresponds to the territory that was once controlled by the Philistines. Its five main cities were Gaza, Ashkelon, Ashdod, Ekron, and Gath. Except for the sand dunes and marshes nearer the Mediterranean shore, there were no natural obstacles to movement through the southern Coastal Plain, which consists of wide, level areas good for growing wheat and barley (see Judg. 15:5). As the Philistines tried to expand northward and eastward, they encountered the tribes of Israel. The result was a fierce conflict that lasted for centuries.

Free movement through the coastal regions was as important to the empires of Egypt and Mesopotamia as it was to the people of Israel and to the Philistines. This was the region that most concerned everyone because it was part of the great trunk route called the Coastal Route. According to Smith, "It is really not the whole of Palestine which deserves that name of The Bridge between Asia and Africa, but this level and open coastland along which the embassies and armies of the two continents passed to and fro, not troubling themselves, unless provoked, with the barren, awkward highlands to the east" (Smith, 117).

PHOTO CAPTIONS

K-1 Even though Ashdod (center) was allotted to the tribe of Judah, it was not captured at the time of the Israelite conquest of Canaan (Josh. 13:1–3; 15:46–47). Ashdod, one of the 5 Philistine cities, was located 2½ miles from the Mediterranean Sea. After the Philistines captured the Ark of the Covenant near Aphek, they took it to Ashdod and placed it in the temple of Dagon. The next morning Dagon was fallen on his face before the Ark of the Covenant. The next day he was fallen down and his head and hands were broken off. After a plague broke out ("the LORD's hand was heavy upon the people"), the Philistines moved the Ark of the Covenant to Gath, then to Ekron (1 Sam. 5:1–12; 6:17; see **K-4**). Ashdod was later captured by Uzziah, king of Judah (ca. 783–742 B.C.; 2 Chron. 26:6), but he lost it

a few years later to King Sargon II of Assyria (713 B.C.; Isa. 20:1). In the New Testament period, Philip came to Ashdod (then called Azotus) after baptizing the Ethiopian eunuch (Acts 8:26–40).

K-2 Gaza is 22 miles south of Ashdod and 3 miles from the coast. After it was captured by Thutmose III (ca. 1469 B.C.), Gaza became an Egyptian administrative center and the main Egyptian base in Canaan, as indicated by the el-Amarna letters and Taanach tablets. At that time, Canaan was the official name for Palestine and Syria under Egyptian authority. According to contemporary Egyptian documents, the borders of Canaan were then almost identical to the biblical borders of "the land of Canaan" at the time of the Israelite conquest (Aharoni, 69). In the period of the judges, Samson carried the city gates of Gaza toward Hebron—40 miles away in the Judean Hill Country (see **Unit J1**). In Gaza he was imprisoned and blinded, and there he met his death (Judg. 16). Gaza was captured by Tiglath-pileser III (ca. 734 B.C.), king of Assyria, and then by Hezekiah, king of Judah, in his anti-Assyrian revolt a few years later (2 Kgs. 18:8–9). Gaza was a center of Hellenistic culture in the Byzantine era. Procopius of Gaza (ca. A.D. 465–528) was an outstanding Christian rhetorician and commentator. After the Arab conquest it became an important center of Muslim culture.

K-3 This photograph shows the southern Coastal Plain south of Ashkelon, which is just outside the upper right-hand corner of the picture. Nahal Shiqma (center) drains the entire region between Ashkelon and Gaza and east to the Judean Hill Country. This photograph also shows the sharp contrast between the sand dunes that form along the coast and the wide, level areas where wheat and barley were grown. Philistia stretched from the "River of Egypt" (*Nahal* of Egypt in Hebrew, or the Wadi el-Arish) northward to the southern edge of the Plain of Sharon (see **Unit E1**). The Coastal Route ran just east of the sand dunes to connect Gaza, Ashdod, and Joppa with Aphek, where it joined a branch that ran along the foothills.

K-4 Gath (center) was one of the 5 Philistine cities. It is mentioned twice in connection with stories that involved the Ark of the Covenant (see 1 Sam. 4–6; 2 Sam. 6) and was the home of Goliath, whom David slew in the valley of Elah (1 Sam. 17:4, 23). Later, David fled to Gath to escape King Saul. David was befriended by King Achish and dwelt in Gath 16 months with 600 of his mighty men. When Saul learned that David had

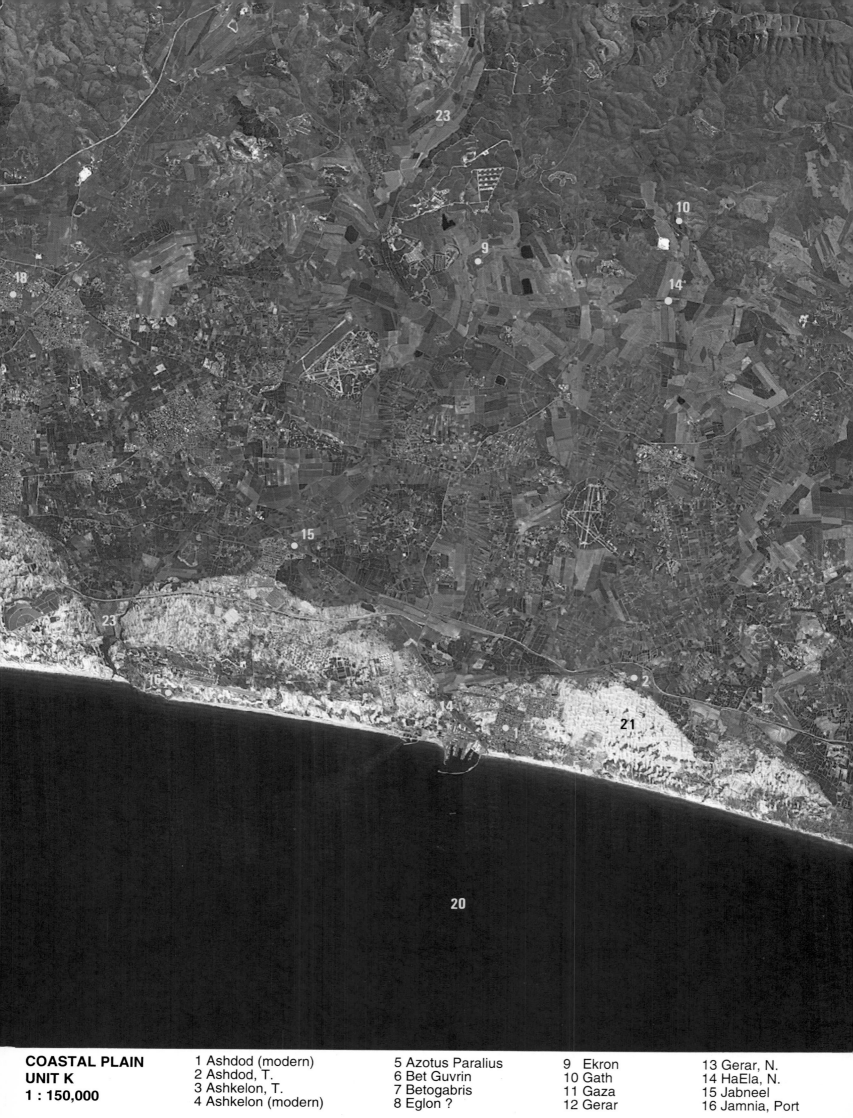

COASTAL PLAIN
UNIT K
1 : 150,000

1 Ashdod (modern)	5 Azotus Paralius	9 Ekron	13 Gerar, N.
2 Ashdod, T.	6 Bet Guvrin	10 Gath	14 HaEla, N.
3 Ashkelon, T.	7 Betogabris	11 Gaza	15 Jabneel
4 Ashkelon (modern)	8 Eglon ?	12 Gerar	16 Jamnia, Port

17 Lachish
18 Lod, Lydda
19 Mareshah
20 Mediterranean Sea

21 Sand dunes
22 Shiqma, N.
23 Sorek, N.
24 Ziklag ?

N

K-4   Gath, Saphitha (Tel Zafit)   View: E

gone to Gath, he quit searching for him (1 Sam. 27:1–12). At the time of
Absalom's rebellion against David, there were 600 men from Gath, together
with Kerethites and Pelethites, who made up David's personal bodyguard
(2 Sam. 15:18; see 2 Sam. 21:20–22). Gath was conquered by Hazael, king
of Syria, during the reign of King Joash of Judah (ca. 800–785 B.C.). It was
recaptured by King Uzziah (ca. 783–742 B.C.; 2 Chron. 26:6). Gath was
one of the cities destroyed by Sargon II, king of Assyria, in 712 B.C.

K-5 Lachish is opposite Ashkelon on the edge of the Judean Shephelah
(see **Unit J2**), 30 miles southwest of Jerusalem. Lachish appears in
Egyptian and Assyrian records, as well as in the Bible. Joshua captured
Lachish and killed its king (Josh. 10:1–32). King Rehoboam fortified the
city (2 Chron. 11:5–12), and King Amaziah fled to Lachish for refuge
during a palace revolt in Jerusalem, "but they sent men after him to
Lachish and killed him there" (2 Kgs. 14:17–20). Lachish was later
conquered by Sennacherib, king of Assyria, in 701 B.C. (2 Kgs. 18:13) and
was one of the last cities left standing while King Nebuchadnezzar of
Babylon laid siege to Jerusalem in 587 B.C. (Jer. 34:7; see **J2-2**). Lachish
letter number 4, discovered in the excavation of Lachish, says, "And let
(my lord) know that we are watching for the signals of Lachish, according
to all the indications which my lord hath given, for we cannot see Azekah"
(*ANET*, 213).

K-6 Ashkelon is mentioned in Egyptian documents dating from the 20th
century B.C. In 1280 B.C., Rameses II crushed a revolt in Ashkelon, which
is depicted on the walls of the Temple at Karnak in Upper Egypt.
Ashkelon is mentioned in the famous "Israel Stele" of Merneptah, who
captured Ashkelon in approximately 1220 B.C. It is also mentioned in
connection with the stories of Samson in the Shephelah (Judg. 14:19; **see
Unit J2**). Ashkelon was conquered by the Assyrians in 734 B.C. Soon
thereafter its citizens revolted due to the encouragement of Hezekiah,
king of Judah (ca. 725 B.C.). Ashkelon was conquered again by the
Assyrians in 701 B.C., when Sennacherib attacked Judah. Ashkelon was
finally destroyed by the Babylonian king Nebuchadnezzar in 609 B.C. (Jer.
47:5–7; Zeph. 2:4–7). In Roman times Ashkelon was an independent city,
and Herod the Great built a large basilica there. The city maintained its
status in the Byzantine period.

BIBLICAL/HISTORICAL REVIEW
Cross references to the Student Map Manual

- **Sale of Joseph into Egypt**
  Gen. 37–47; SMM 4-4c. Joseph went to Shechem to see whether all
  was well with his brothers and with the flocks, but he finally found
  them in Dothan. Because of jealousy, the brothers took Joseph and
  sold him to merchants on their way to Egypt. The caravan traveled the
  Coastal Route, and it would have passed Gaza. In Egypt, Joseph
  interpreted the dream of Pharaoh and was put in charge of the whole
  land of Egypt. In later years, Joseph saved his family from famine.

- **Samson and the Philistines**
  Judg. 13–16; SMM 6-4b. The background to the Samson stories is
  the struggle between Israelites and Philistines. Much of the story takes
  place in the northern Shephelah (see **Unit J2**). An angel appeared to
  Samson's mother and promised that she would give birth to a son who
  would "begin the deliverance of Israel from the hands of the Philistines." Samson went to Ashkelon, killed 30 men, and took their clothes
  to pay his debt for his "riddle" wager. Samson is noted for his great
  strength, but he was weak in moral character and did little to actually
  release Israel from bondage to the Philistines.

- **Assyrian Campaign Against Philistia and Judah: Sennacherib**
  **2 Kgs. 18:13–19:37; 2 Chron. 32:1, 9–22; Isa. 30, 36–37; Micah
  1:10–16; SMM 9-6b.** In response to a revolt led by king Hezekiah of
  Judah, Sennacherib, king of Assyria, campaigned along the coast and
  in the Shephelah of Judah (see **Unit J2**). The coastal cities fell quickly,
  and Sennacherib turned his full force against Judah, conquering many
  cities. Jerusalem was saved when an angel put to death 185,000
  Assyrian soldiers, causing Sennacherib to return to Nineveh.   ■

> **K-7** (overleaf) The view in this photograph is to the east across the site
> of ancient Ekron, Tel Miqne (center), and the northern half of the
> southern Coastal Plain. In the background are the regions of the
> Shephelah (see **Unit J2**) and Judean Hill Country (see **Unit J1**). Ekron
> was only about 22 miles west of Jerusalem, and was the northernmost
> city of the Philistine Pentapolis. It was only 3½ miles west of Timnah,
> which guarded the western entrance to the Sorek Valley in the
> Shephelah (see **J2-4**). The Ark of the Covenant was in Ekron before
> the Philistines sent it back to Israel (1 Sam. 5:10–11).

K-5   Lachish   **View: SE**

K-6   Ashkelon, Ascalon   **View: N**

L-1   Kadesh-barnea: oasis

View: NE

L-2   Nahal Gerar & Gerar, Gerara

View: SE

L-3   Karka(a) ? (Ein Quseima): oasis   View: S

NEGEV   Unit L

The Bible tells us that when Abraham departed from the Bethel region he traveled toward the "Negev" (Gen. 12:8–10). The Bible also records that "Abram went up from Egypt to the Negev" (Gen. 13:1.) These passages show that "Negev" (sometimes translated "south") was a geographical area. "The Negev proper is the strip of about 30 miles between the 300- and 100-mm lines, with Beer-sheba in the centre" (Aharoni, 26). Beersheba has an average annual rainfall of 8 inches. Although famine was common in the Negev, it was possible in wet years to grow a good crop, as Isaac did when he "planted crops in that land and the same year reaped a hundredfold" (Gen. 26:12). Settlement was hindered by the lack of water, however, as well as by marauding desert nomads like the Amalekites (see 1 Sam. 30). The main cities grew up along the river beds, where there was sufficient ground water to sustain the community.

The Negev's chief importance was its roads. Solomon, for example, enriched the coffers of Israel by controlling the trade that passed through the Negev from Arabia, Sinai, and Egypt. The Queen of Sheba came to Solomon with "camels carrying spices, large quantities of gold, and precious stones" (2 Chron. 9:1). Indeed, "all the kings of Arabia…brought gold and silver to Solomon" (2 Chron. 9:14). Uzziah, king of Judah, rebuilt Elath and "built towers in the desert" for the purpose of guarding these important trade routes (2 Kgs. 14:22; 2 Chron. 26:10). When Hagar fled from Sarah, an angel of the Lord found her "near a spring in the desert; it was the spring that is beside the road to Shur" (Gen. 16:7; Shur apparently was a line of fortifications on the Egyptian frontier—the Israelites went into the "Desert of Shur" after they crossed the Red Sea; Ex. 15:22). "The road to Shur" was an ancient caravan route used to cross the Negev; it went from Hebron to Beersheba and south into Egypt. After Jacob offered sacrifices in Beersheba to the God of his father Isaac (Gen. 46:1,5–7), he must have used the road to Shur to travel with his family into Egypt.

PHOTO CAPTIONS

L-1 Kadesh-barnea was on the southern border of Canaan, 46 miles south of Beersheba. It is spoken of as being located in the wilderness of Zin (Num. 20:1; 27:14; 33:36; Deut. 32:51), which was apparently part of the wilderness of Paran (Num. 20:16). The Israelites remained "many days" in Kadesh-barnea after they left Mt. Sinai. From Kadesh-barnea Moses sent men to spy out the land of Canaan. The spies returned and reported that the land was indeed good, "it does flow with milk and honey! Here is its fruit." They also gave an unfavorable policy evaluation, "We can't attack those people; they are stronger than we are." The people complained. As a result, God decreed that an entire generation would die before Israel would be allowed to enter Canaan (Num. 13; 14; Deut. 1). Kadesh was the place where Korah rebelled (Num. 16–17), where Miriam died (Num. 12:1–15; 20:1; Deut. 24:8–9), and where Moses "struck the rock." As a result of this last incident, Moses was not allowed to enter the promised land. The Lord told Moses and Aaron, "Because you did not trust in me enough to honor me as holy in the sight of the Israelites, you will not bring this community into the land I give them." These were the waters of Meribah (Num. 20:11–12; 27:14; Deut. 32:48–52; Meribah means "quarreling" in Hebrew). The fort of Kadesh-barnea (center left) dates to the 10th century B.C., or the period of the kingdom of Judah.

L-2 Gerar is identified with Tel Haror (center), which is 16 miles northwest of Beersheba. Both Abraham and Isaac lived there and made treaties with Abimelech, king of Gerar (Gen. 20,26). Isaac dug wells "in the Valley of Gerar" (i.e. Nahal Gerar, center), where water flows underground even when the river bed is dry (Gen. 26: 15–22). About 900 B.C., Asa, king of Judah, defeated a Cushite army near Mareshah and pursued them to Gerar; "Such a great number of Cushites fell that they could not recover" (2 Chron. 14:9–14).

L-3 Karka was near Kadesh-barnea on the southern border of Judah (Josh. 15:3). It is identified with one of three springs in the locality of Kadesh-barnea that was probably used by the children of Israel as they wandered in the wilderness.

L-4 Tel Arad is 18 miles northeast of Beersheba. It was an important Canaanite and Israelite city in the Eastern Negev that guarded the roads to Edom, Sinai, and Egypt. Arad is on the list of cities conquered by Joshua (Josh. 12:14), and Shishak, king of Egypt, mentioned two fortresses by the name of Arad (see 2 Chron. 12:1–12). The first was the "Great Arad," identified with Tel Arad; the second was the "Arad of Jerahmeel," identified with Tel Malhata about 8 miles away. It is clear from Shishak's inscription in the temple of Karnak that one of the objectives of his campaign was to gain control of the trade routes in the Negev.

**WESTERN NEGEV
UNIT L1
1 : 200,000**

1 Avedat, H.	5 Beraein	9 Gerar	13 Kadesh Barnea
2 Beer Sheva (modern)	6 Besor, N.	10 Gerar, N.	14 Karka ?
3 Beer Sheva, N.	7 Elusa	11 Goshen ?	15 Makhtesh Ramon
4 Beer Sheva, T.	8 En Avedat	12 Hazar-addar ?	16 Nessana

N

EASTERN NEGEV
UNIT L2

1 : 200,000

1 Arabah, W.
2 Arad (modern)
3 Arad, T.
4 Beer Sheva, N.

5 Beer Sheva, T.
6 Beer Sheva (modern)
7 Dimona
8 En Boqeq

9 Hazeva, Tamar
10 Hormah
11 Makhtesh Gadol
12 Makhtesh Qatan

13 Makhtesh Ramon
14 Mampsis
15 Masada
16 Mezad Tamar

N

L-4   Arad: towards Judean Hill Country   **View: N**

L-5 Beersheba is 50 miles south of Jerusalem. This ancient site is remembered as the ancestral home of Israel's patriarchs: Abraham (Gen. 21:22–34), Isaac (Gen. 26:23–33), and Jacob (Gen. 46:1–7). Abraham lived here and made a covenant of peace with Abimelech, king of Gerar, concerning his well (Gen. 21:22–34; 22:19). Isaac made a similar covenant of peace with Abimelech, also at Beersheba (Gen. 26:26–33). God appeared to both Isaac and Jacob at Beersheba, promising Isaac that he would multiply his seed for Abraham's sake (Gen. 26:23–25), and indicating to Jacob that he should move his family to Egypt where God would make of his posterity a great nation (Gen. 46:1–7).

L-6 The ruins in this picture date to the 10th century B.C., or the time when Samuel's sons were judges in Beersheba (1 Sam. 8:1–3). A street encircled the city an equal distance from the outside wall with rows of buildings on either side. The city's gate (left center) was discovered close to the well (lower center). The expression "from Dan to Beersheba" described the limits of Israelite occupation of Canaan, just as the expression "from Beersheba to Mount Ephraim" (2 Chron. 19:4) or "from Geba to Beersheba" (2 Kgs. 23:8) described the limits of the Southern Kingdom after the division of the United Kingdom. No Middle Bronze (Patriarchal) remains have been found at Tel Beersheba.

BIBLICAL/HISTORICAL REVIEW
Cross references to the Student Map Manual

- **Abraham and Isaac: Sojourn in the Negev**
  Gen. 20, 26; SMM 4-3. There are several sites in the Negev identified with the Patriarchs. The first is Gerar, which is about 16 miles northwest of Beersheba (see **L-5**). Both Abraham and Isaac lived there and made treaties with Abimelech, king of Gerar. Isaac dug wells in the Valley of Gerar (i.e. Nahal Gerar). From there Isaac went to Beersheba where the LORD appeared to him and said, "I am the God of your father Abraham. Do not be afraid, for I am with you; I will bless you and will increase the number of your descendants for the sake of my servant Abraham." Both Abraham (Gen. 21:30–31) and Isaac (Gen. 26:33) dug wells in that area and both called the site Beersheba.

- **Conquest of Canaan: Battle of Arad (13th century B.C.)**
  Num. 13–14, 21; SMM 5-2b, c, d. The spies returned from Canaan to the Israelite camp at Kadesh-barnea (see **L-1**) and they reported on the strength of the Canaanites, saying, "We can't attack those people;

they are stronger than we are." When the people murmured against God, Moses declared that the adults of Israel would not enter the Promised Land. Some rebels decided to invade the land on their own but were soundly defeated by the king of Arad (see **L-4**).

- **Raid on Ziklag: David Defends the Southern Tribes (ca. 1007 B.C.)**
  1 Sam. 29–30; SMM 7-4g. While David and his army were away with the Philistines, the Amalekites invaded the Negev, burning David's city of Ziklag and carrying away its inhabitants, which included David's two wives, Ahinoam and Abigail. David and his men pursued the Amalekites and found them "eating, drinking and reveling because of the great amount of plunder they had taken from the land of the Philistines and from Judah." David fought them from dusk until the evening of the next day and recovered everything the Amalekites had taken. The Amalekites were finally destroyed by the tribe of Simeon who received parts of the Negev as their inheritance (see Josh. 19:1–5; 1 Chron. 4:42–43).

- **Nabatean Kingdom: Settlements (Roman and Byz. Periods)**
  SMM 13–2. When the Edomites took over southern Judea after the fall of Jerusalem in 586 B.C., the Nabateans moved into the Negev. They developed a flourishing economy based on commerce and agriculture. Remains of dams used to store water for the farms are found in the wadis and valleys around the key settlements established to protect their caravan routes. Soubaita (Shivta) was situated on a road linking Ovoda (Avedat) and Nessana. The Nabateans transported the spices, textiles and precious gems from Arabia and India through Petra and Elath across the Negev to their Mediterranean outlets. ∎

L-7 (overleaf) The site of Soubaita (Shivta) is 25 miles southwest of Beersheba. It was founded in the 1st century B.C., but mainly flourished in the Byzantine Period. Between 1,200 and 1,300 rooms were counted on the site over an area of 29 acres. The city's population of about 5,000 survived by cultivating nearly 1,300 acres. Rainwater was brought into the fields by a complicated system of channels that collected water from a drainage area of 77 square miles.

L-5   Beer-sheba, Bersabe   View: N

L-6   Beer-sheba, Bersabe: excavations   View: SW

M-1   Zoara(a) & entry of river Zered (el-Hasa)   **View: SE**

M-2   Mt. Sdom & Dead Sea: salt pans   **View: NW**

M-3   Punon, Phaenon (Feinan)   View: SE

WADI ARABAH   Unit M

The Arabah is a desert region between the Dead Sea and the Gulf of Elath/ Aqabah (Red Sea) and is about 110 miles in length. Directly south of the Dead Sea is the Sodom playa, a mud and salt flat that was partly covered by water when the level of the Dead Sea was higher than it is now (see **M-2**). From the southern end of the playa, the Arabah begins to slope upwards (see **M-1**) over a distance of 48 miles to Jebel el-Khureij. At that point it descends gradually about 46 miles to the site of ancient Elath on the Red Sea (see **M-5**). Here "the valley becomes narrower, 3 to 4 miles wide, and again assumes the typical form of a rift valley; to the west it is bounded by steep scarps, formed by the limestone ranges of the southern Negev Mountains, and in the east it is bounded by an impenetrable wall of granite mountains, which rise to 4500 feet" (Karmon, 292). The average rainfall in the Arabah is less than 1 inch annually. East of the Arabah are the high mountains of Edom (see **Unit O**).

Because the Arabah receives so little rainfall crops were not grown except where necessary to maintain the copper mines (see **M-5**) and rich trade routes. The western side of the northern Arabah opens toward the uplands of the Eastern Negev (see **Unit L**) and once provided the easiest route to the Mediterranean. On the higher, eastern side, the most important trade route ascended to Petra by way of Wadi Musa (see **O-6**). The Arabah "is a land of passage which not only bears lines of traffic between Egypt and Syria and between the Red Sea or Arabia ... and the Levant, but by its very wildness grants its tribes the control, and some of the profit, of that traffic" (Smith, 360–361). The Arabah's main role was not to compete with the north-south trade-routes of Transjordan and Palestine, i.e., the King's Highway and the Coastal Route, but to service east-west communication between these routes and between the mountainous regions east and west of the Arabah that would profit from trade. Edom's territory, for example, stretched across the Arabah into the Negev of southern Palestine while the Israelites were camped at Kadesh-barnea (Num. 20:14,16; see **Unit L**). The kings of Edom and a united Israel (later Judah) competed for control of the routes between Palestine and the Red Sea by capturing each other's lands (see 2 Sam. 8:14; 1 Kgs. 9:26; 22:47; 2 Kgs. 8:20, etc.).

PHOTO CAPTIONS

M-1 Edom, or the "mount of Esau" (Oba. 9; see **Unit O**), is seen here in the distance. George Adam Smith compared the western slopes of Edom to those of Moab: "Whereas looking east on Moab you see an almost unbroken wall of mountain all limestone save for its lower courses of purple sandstone flashing upon the Dead Sea, the western aspect of Mount Esau [Edom] is ... a series of ridges, shelves, and strips of valley, mazes of peaks, cliffs, and chasms that form some of the wildest rock scenery in the world" (Smith, 362–363). The site of biblical Zoar (upper left, in the green area to the right of the wadi) is located 5 miles south of the Dead Sea where "the brook Zered" empties into the Arabah (upper left). The Zered was the border between Moab and Edom. Lot escaped to Zoar when God destroyed Sodom and Gomorrah with fire and brimstone (Gen. 19:18–29).

M-2 This photograph shows the huge salt plug of Mt. Sodom (6.8 miles long and 1.2 to 1.8 miles wide) and the salt pans of Israel's Dead Sea Works. The installations of the Palestine Potash Company, which were set up at the foot of Mt. Sodom in 1937 (right center, left of channel), fell into disuse during the 1948 Israeli War of Independence. In 1957–58 the renewed activity of the Dead Sea Works produced 100,000 tons of potash. By 1970, the potash output reached nearly 1,000,000 tons. By contrast, in ancient times, the Dead Sea was valued only for its salt and bitumen. The area of the Dead Sea south of the Lisan now consists of extensive but shallow evaporation pans.

M-3 Punon (modern Feinan) was at the mouth of an important passage into Edom from the Arabah. It was a well watered mining center with a large smelting operation. The Arabah trade route to southern Arabia and Egypt was used to transport the refined copper to market. The summary of Israel's journey from Egypt to Canaan indicates that the children of Israel "camped at Punon" (Num. 33:42).

M-4 For 40 years the Israelites wandered through "the vast and dreadful desert, that thirsty and waterless land, with its venomous snakes and scorpions" (Deut. 8:15). At sunrise, when the sun first touches the land, the wilderness seems less threatening, as in this photograph. But those who fled here for refuge "wandered in desert wastelands, finding no way

WADI ARABAH (N)
UNIT M1
1 : 200,000

17 Sdom, Mt.   21 Toloha
18 Sela   22 Tsafir
19 Shaubak castle   23 Zin, N.
20 Tafileh   24 Zoar

N

WADI ARABAH (S)
UNIT M2
1 : 200,000

1 Aqabah	5 En Yotvata	9 Paran	13 Ram, W.
2 Ariedela	6 Aqabah, Gulf	10 Petra	14 Ras en-Naqb
3 Biqat Uvda	7 Harun, Jebel	11 Praesidium	15 Timna
4 Eilat	8 Paran, N.	12 Quweira	16 Yutm, W.

M-4   Wilderness of Paran: sunrise   View: SE

to a city where they could settle" (Ps. 107:4–5). Here God tested his people to humble and prove them, and to know what was in their heart (Deut. 8:2).

M-5 In this photograph we look across the southern end of the Arabah to the Gulf of Elath/Aqabah (upper right). Excavations carried out here between 1932–1934 and in 1959 found that ancient mines and mining camps covered an area of 4 square miles. The mines were first worked by the Egyptians during the 19th and 20th Dynasties (14th–12th centuries B.C.). The white puff rising from the valley floor (right center) identifies the area of the modern Timna Copper Works (now disused).

M-6 Elath was an ancient port at the northern end of the Red Sea. According to the account of their wanderings in the desert, the Israelites passed this way (Deut. 2:8). King Solomon later "built ships at Ezion Geber, which is near Elath in Edom, on the shore of the Red Sea" (1 Kgs. 9:26). His servants sailed to Ophir and brought back "four hundred and fifty talents of gold" (2 Chron. 8:18). After Elath was lost to Edom (see 1 Kgs. 22:47–48), King Uzziah restored it to Judah (2 Kgs. 14:22). Elath was lost again during the reign of King Ahaz, this time to the Syrians, and was never recovered (2 Kgs. 16:6). In the Hellenistic period, Elath was under the control of the Ptolemies and was called Berenice after a queen of Egypt; as a Nabatean port it was called Aila, and in Arabic it is called Aqabah.

BIBLICAL/HISTORICAL REVIEW
Cross references to the Student Map Manual

- **Campaign of Northern Kings: Abraham Rescues Lot**
  Gen. 14; SMM 4-3c. The account of the four kings from the north who attacked the five kings in the Dead Sea region (Gen. 14) also informs us that they defeated "the Horites in the hill country of Seir, as far as El Paran near the desert." El Paran may possibly be an earlier name for Elath or Ezion Geber, the port on the Red Sea (see **M-6**). Seir, of course, is Edom (see **M-1**). Another city that may lie in the Arabah is Hazazon Tamar. This is a city of the Amorites situated not far from Sodom. This site is placed near or identified with En Gedi (2 Chron. 20:2), and located by Ezekiel in the southeast corner of the land of Israel (Ezek. 47:19; 48:28). This may also be the same as the Tamar fortified by Solomon (1 Kgs. 9:18; sometimes read as Tadmor). This itinerary of the kings again calls attention to the importance of the trade routes.

- **Moses Leads Israel into Transjordan**
  Num. 21; 33:34–44; SMM 5-2e. A detailed account of Israel's travels in the wilderness indicates that "the Israelites moved on and camped at Oboth" after leaving the place where they "spoke against God, and against Moses" and were plagued with fiery serpents (Num. 21:5). Comparing this passage with Num. 33:42, it is likely that Punon (see **M-3**) was the place where the story of the fiery serpent took place. The Israelites had "traveled from mount Hor along the route to the Red Sea, to go around Edom. But the people grew impatient on the way; they spoke against God and against Moses." As a result of their murmuring, "the Lord sent venomous snakes among them; they bit the people and many Israelites died."

- **Victories in the Valley of Salt: David and Amaziah**
  2 Sam. 8:13–14; 1 Kgs. 11:15–18; 2 Chron. 18:12–13; 2 Kgs. 14:1–22; 2 Chron. 25; SMM 7-7e; 9-1/2g. The Bible seems to indicate that the region south of the Dead Sea is the "Valley of Salt" where David smote Edom: "He put garrisons throughout Edom, and all the Edomites became subject to David." Amaziah, king of Judah, also smote the Edomites in the "Valley of Salt" to gain control of all northern Edom and the trade-routes to Arabia.   ∎

M-7 (overleaf) En Avedat, which is 30 miles south of Beersheba, captures the runoff water from a very large area of the Negev. It is at the head of Nahal Zin, which opens into the Arabah and was a major passageway to the Mediterranean. This incredibly barren wilderness was crossed by a road that went from Gaza to Oboda (Avedat), then passed through the broad basin of Nahal Zin across the Arabah to Punon (see **M-3**). From Punon the road ascended the embayment of Punon (see **O-3**) to Bozrah (see **O-5**). The Arabs call this road the Darb es-Sultan.

M-5   Timna: ancient & modern copper mines   View: S

M-6   Ancient Elath, Aila, Berenice (Aqabah)   View: SE

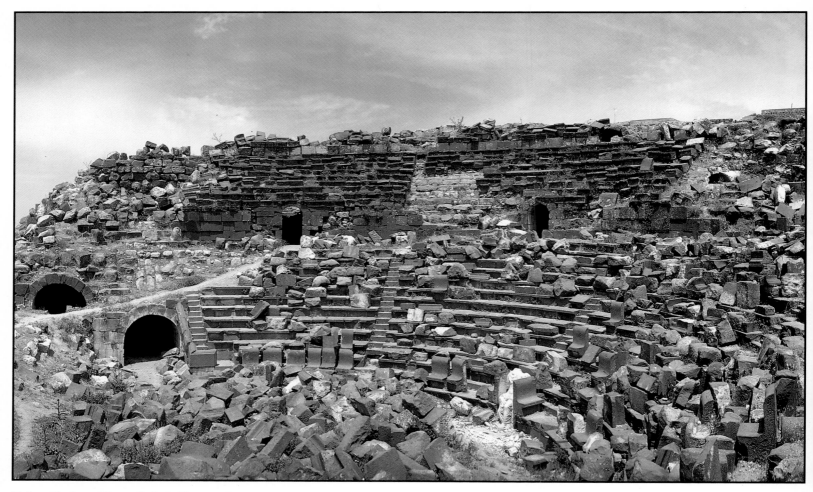

N-1   Gadara (Umm Qeiss): Roman theater   View: NE

N-2   Rabbath-ammon, Philadelphia (Amman): citadel   View: N

GILEAD & AMMON   Unit N

Gilead was a region east of the Jordan Valley from the Yarmuk River in the north to an ill-defined boundary between Heshbon and the Medeba Plateau in the south. The southern boundary is difficult to define because there is no natural border between the regions of Gilead and Moab. Gilead was divided into halves ("half the hill country of Gilead") by the Jabbok River (Deut. 3:12). The northern half of Gilead was ruled by Og, king of Bashan. The southern half was ruled by Sihon, king of the Amorites. Manasseh inherited the northern half of Gilead, and Gad the southern half (Josh. 13:28–31). The western slopes of northern Gilead consist of a rugged mountainous terrain that was covered by forests in antiquity, called the "forest of Ephraim" (2 Sam. 18:6). The forests diminished south of the Jabbok toward the Medeba Plateau. East of its western rim, this high plateau extends 25 to 30 miles before giving way to the Syrian Desert. The Bible distinguishes between the highlands of Gilead and the tablelands north and south of it, referring to "all the towns on the plateau [Hebrew, the Mishor (Medeba plateau)], and all Gilead, and all Bashan" (Deut. 3:10).

The territory of Ammon coincided with the lands along the upper and central Jabbok River and its tributaries. The central Jabbok was the northern boundary (Josh. 12:2), while the other boundaries were not so well defined (see **N-2**). The Ammonites appeared in the Bible for the first time in an active military role when they joined a coalition of Amalekites and Moabites in an effort to help Eglon king of Moab regain some of the territory lost to Israel. (Judg. 3:12–14). Most of the cities of the Decapolis lay in the area of Gilead and Ammon, e.g. Geraza, Abila, Gadara, Pella, and Philadelphia. They still show impressive remains.

PHOTO CAPTIONS

N-1 Gadara was a city of the Decapolis, 5 miles southeast of the Sea of Galilee. The ruins at Gadara include a colonnaded street paved with basalt stones, a basilica, baths, and two theaters, one of which is pictured here. It also controlled the hot baths at Gamat (?). After the death of Herod the Great, Caesar Augustus distributed Herod's kingdom among his sons. Half the kingdom went to Archelaus, "but the Greek cities of Gaza, Gadara and Hippus were detached from his realm and added to Syria" (*War* 2.6.3). The New Testament manuscripts speak of Gerasa, Gadara, and Gergesa in connection with the healing of a man whose evil spirits

"went into the pigs" (Mark 5:1–13). These variants in the text reflect some confusion over the proper locale for the story. Gadara was a famous center of Hellenistic culture. Menippus, the developer of satire, came from there, as did Philodemus, the Epicurean philosopher of the first century B.C., whose library was discovered at Herculaneum, and Theodorus the orator. Gadara was the home of some well known teachers of rhetoric. Near here are the hot springs of Ematha (Hammath Gader), described by Strabo.

N-2 Ammon was a small frontier country, east of Gilead, without natural borders except in the north. The population of Ammon lived from the grazing of cattle and from the merchant caravans that passed along the King's Highway (2 Chron. 27:5). The rise of the kingdom of Ammon and the establishment of its capital at Rabbath-ammon (center) coincided with the founding of Moab, Edom, and Israel during the Late Bronze and Early Iron Ages (ca. 1500–1000 B.C.). Rabbath-ammon (Rabbah of the Ammonites) was founded on a naturally fortified hill at the junction of the King's Highway and Desert Road. It occupied the same site as the modern 'Amman and is the only city in the Bible that is mentioned specifically as belonging to Ammon (Jer. 49:2; Ezek. 21:20). Uriah the Hittite was killed at the walls of Rabbah after David ordered Joab to send Uriah to the "front line where the fighting is fiercest" (2 Sam. 11:15–20). The Ammonites were cursed by Moses because they refused to provide food and water for the Israelites during the wilderness journeys toward the Promised Land (Deut. 23:3–4). In the time of the Judges, Jephthah defeated Ammon and "devastated twenty towns" (Judg. 11). During the Roman period, Rabbath-ammon (renamed Philadelphia) was one of the cities of the Decapolis.

N-3 The Yarmuk River enters the Jordan Valley 2 miles southeast of the Sea of Galilee. It was the natural boundary between Bashan and Gilead, and the largest eastern tributary of the Jordan River. On August 20, A.D. 636, a famous battle was fought beside the Yarmuk, in which the Muslims defeated the Byzantines and won control of Syria. The Byzantines, blinded by a sandy, desert wind, perished in the ravines of the Yarmuk Valley. Before the Yarmuk's waters were diverted for irrigation into a canal along the eastern side of the Jordan Valley, its outflow was nearly equal to that of the Jordan River.

N-4 The whole of the region of Wadi es-Sir was territory disputed by Ammon, Moab, and the tribe of Gad. The biblical city Jazer, which was

GILEAD
UNIT N1
1 : 150,000

1 Abel-meholah ?	5 Arab, W.	9 Dibbin forest	13 Gerasa; Jarash
2 Abila	6 Beth-arbel; Irbid	10 Dium ?	14 Hammat Pella
3 Aenon ?	7 Beth-shan	11 Enganna; Ajlun	15 Hammath Gader
4 Ajlun castle	8 Capitolias	12 Gadara	16 Jabbok, R.; Zarqa

17 Jabesh-gilead
18 Jordan, R.
19 Kufrinja, W.
20 Lo-debar ?

21 Mahanaim ?
22 Maked ?
23 Pella
24 Penuel

25 Salim ?
26 Shallala, W.
27 Succoth ?
28 Yabis, W.

29 Yarmuk, R.
30 Zaphon ?
31 Zarethan ?
32 Zeizin

N

AMMON & MADABA
UNIT N2

1 : 150,000

1 Abel-keramim ?	5 Baaras	9 Bethennabris	13 Gedor
2 Adam	6 Baca	10 Callirhoe	14 Heshbon, Esbus
3 Aenon ?	7 Beth-baal-meon	11 Dabaloth	15 Jabbok, R.; Zarqa
4 Ain Musa	8 Beth-jeshimoth	12 Elealeh	16 Jogbehah

17 Jordan, R.
18 Lemba
19 Livias, Julias
20 Madaba

21 Nebo
22 Nebo, Mt.
23 Philadelphia; Amman
24 Ramoth-mizpeh ?

25 Salt
26 Shueib, W.
27 Siyagha
28 Tyre, Tyrus

29 Yaduda
30 Zarethan ?
31 Zarqa Main, W.
32 Ziza

N

included in the territory given to Gad (Josh. 13:25), was between two tributaries of Wadi es-Sir, 6 miles west of Rabbath-ammon on the edge of the plateau overlooking the Jordan Valley. This photograph depicts the fertility of the Wadi es-Sir region, which was densely settled during the Iron Age.

N-5 After Moses blessed the tribes of Israel (Deut. 33), he "climbed Mount Nebo from the plains of Moab to the top of Pisgah, across from Jericho" (Deut. 34:1). Mt. Nebo (right center) is 12 miles east of the mouth of the Jordan River. It is separated from Pisgah by a slight depression. From Pisgah, Moses had an unobstructed view of the Jordan Valley, the Judean Hill Country, Mt. Ephraim, and Mt. Hermon (which was over 100 miles to the north; see Deut. 34:2–4). Moses was not allowed to enter the Promised Land because of the incident at Meribah in Kadesh (see **L-1**).

N-6 According to Josephus, John the Baptist was a prisoner in Machaerus (center) when Herod Antipas ordered his execution (see Matt. 14:10; Mark 6:14–29). Josephus also described Machaerus' fortifications, saying that "the character of the place might well embolden its occupants with high hopes of security and cause fear and alarm among those attacking it" (*War* 7.6.1). In the First Jewish Revolt, Machaerus was a Jewish stronghold that fell to the Romans in A.D. 72. The outlines of two Roman camps are still visible west of Machaerus (lower and upper left). Describing the view from Machaerus on a clear day, Ridgaway said that "some of the buildings near Bethlehem and Jerusalem can be distinctly seen" (Ridgaway, 406).

BIBLICAL/HISTORICAL REVIEW
Cross references to the Student Map Manual

- **Jacob's Travels in Transjordan (Gilead)**
  Gen. 28; 31–35; SMM 4-4a,b. Jacob was sent by his father, Isaac, to Padan-aram, where he was to take a wife from among the daughters of Laban, his mother's brother. After twenty years, the Lord commanded Jacob to return to Canaan. He left secretly, but his father-in-law caught up to him in the hill country of Gilead. A covenant and non-aggression treaty was made between them. After he crossed the ford of the Jabbok River, he met his brother Esau and was reconciled to him. "Esau ran to meet Jacob and embraced him; he threw his arms around his neck and kissed him. And they wept." Jacob then went to Succoth and stayed there for some time.

- **Saul Rescues Jabesh-gilead from the Ammonites (ca. 1025 B.C.)**
  1 Sam. 11; SMM 7-4c. When Nahash the Ammonite besieged Jabesh-gilead, messengers were sent to Saul to request his help. Saul responded by attacking the Ammonites "during the last watch of the night…and slaughtered them until the heat of the day." He rescued the inhabitants of Jabesh-gilead; they repaid Saul for his help when they retrieved his body from the wall of Beth-shan and gave it proper burial.

- **The Decapolis: A League of Ten Cities**
  SMM 12-3f. The decapolis was a federation of ten Hellenistic cities east of Samaria and Galilee. The Roman historian Pliny the Elder (1st century A.D.) listed the cities as Damascus, Philadelphia (Rabbath-ammon in the Old Testament), Raphana, Scythopolis (Beth-shan in the Old Testament), Gadara, Hippus, Dion, Pella, Gerasa, and Canatha. Scythopolis was the chief city of the Decapolis, and the only one west of the Jordan River. ∎

N-7 (overleaf) Gerasa was a city of the Decapolis, 20 miles east of the Jordan and 26 miles north of 'Amman (Rabbath-ammon) (see **N-2**). Its position on the King's Highway brought prosperity to the city through trade, especially with Petra to the south and Palmyra to the north. The ruins of the Roman forum (lower right) connect with the cardo (columned street) leading north. Behind the ruins of a theater (left), which seated 3,000 people, are the remains of the Temple of Zeus. The ruins of the Temple of Artemis are visible northwest of the forum in the center of the photograph. Gerasa existed as a city by the time of Antiochus IV of Syria (ca. 170 B.C.). In ca. 82 B.C., Gerasa was captured by Alexander Jannaeus, and it remained a Jewish possession until it was taken by the Romans in 63 B.C. and turned into one of the cities of the Decapolis. Even after Roman intervention, the Jews of Gerasa maintained friendly relations with the other inhabitants. As a result, the inhabitants of Gerasa sent the Jewish population away unharmed after the outbreak of the First Jewish Revolt against the Romans. Christians were found in Gerasa by the 2nd century A.D., and by the 4th century the city had become a strong Christian center. The city fell in the Muslim conquest of A.D. 635 and was finally destroyed by an earthquake in ca. A.D. 746.

N-5   Nebo, Pisgah (Siyagha) & Lower Jordan Valley   **View: NW**

N-6   Machaerus & Roman camps   **View: NW**

O-1   Kir-hareseth, Charachmoba (Kerak)   View: NW

O-2   Aroer & River Arnon (Mujib)   View: SE

O-3   **Wadi Bustan / Ghuweir: descent to Feinan**   View: N

MOAB & EDOM   # Unit O

Moab was the land east of the Dead Sea that extended southward to the Zered Valley (Deut. 2:13–14), eastward to the desert, and westward to the Dead Sea. It was about 25 miles wide from east to west, which included the "steep and frightening ascents" that separated the high tableland of Moab from the eastern shore of the Dead Sea (Aharoni, 39). The northern border was much disputed and only sometimes included the Medeba Plateau. At other times the border was placed at the deep canyon of the Arnon River (see **O-2**). Moab becomes increasingly dry to the east, leaving a relatively narrow north-south strip of land that is abundantly watered and able to produce fine crops of wheat and barley. The economy of Moab was based on raising sheep and goats, for "Mesha king of Moab raised sheep, and he had to supply the king of Israel with a hundred thousand lambs and with the wool of a hundred thousand rams" (2 Kings 3:4). The Moabites must also have benefited from the trade that came from southern Arabia along the King's Highway.

Edom was bound in the north by the Zered Valley, which separated Edom from Moab. In the south, the high Edomite plateau dropped off into the wasteland of the Plain of el-Quweira. The north-south length of Edom was about 110 miles (the region between the southern end of the Dead Sea and the northern end of the Red Sea, or gulf of Elath/Aqabah). Edom was bound on the east by the desert and on the west by the steep slopes overlooking the Arabah (see **Unit M**) and had an average width of only 15 miles. In the Bible, as well as in early Egyptian documents, Edom is also called "the hill country of Seir" (Gen. 36:9), "Mt. Seir" (Deut 1:2), "the land of Seir" (Gen. 36:30), and "Seir" (Judg. 5:4).

PHOTO CAPTIONS

O-1 The huge Crusader castle of Kerak (lower center) was built on the ruins of the Moabite capital of Kir-hareseth. The castle was strategically located on the King's Highway about midway between the Arnon and Zered Rivers, overlooking a major descent to the Dead Sea (upper left). After the revolt of Mesha king of Moab, the king of Israel (Jehoram) joined forces with the king of Judah (Jehoshaphat) and the king of Edom (evidently a vassal of Judah) in an attempt to reduce Moab to her former status when Mesha paid tribute to Israel (2 Kings 3:4). The Israelites "rose up and fought them [Moabites] so that they fled .... Only Kir Hareseth was

left with its stones in place " (2 Kings 3:24–25). After Mesha failed with 700 men to break through the lines of the Israelite force, he "took his firstborn son, who was to succeed him as king, and offered him as a sacrifice on the city wall. The fury against Israel was great; they withdrew and returned to their own land" (2 Kings 3:26–27). On a black basalt stone, commonly called the "Moabite Stone," Mesha has left us an inscription to commemorate his successful revolt against Israel and his rebuilding of several towns by using Israelite slave labor. During the Roman and Byzantine periods, Kir-hareseth was called Charachmoba.

O-2 Sihon king of the Amorites, ruled from Aroer on the "rim of the Arnon Gorge" (lower center; Josh. 12:2). Aroer was built by the tribe of Gad (Num. 32:34), but was part of the inheritance of the tribe of Reuben (Josh. 13:15–16). Moab extended its borders to include the territory on both sides of the Arnon when it revolted against Israel in the 9th century B.C. (2 Kgs. 3:5; see **O-1**). Mesha king of Moab fortified Aroer, but shortly afterward the entire area was conquered by Hazael king of Syria, who took all the land of "Gilead (the region of Gad, Reuben and Manasseh), from Aroer by the Arnon Gorge through Gilead to Bashan" (2 Kgs. 10:32–33).

O-3 The descent to Punon (modern Feinan) was an important ascent between the Arabah (see **Unit M**) and Edom. This view is across the Punon embayment, which cuts deep into the Edomite plateau. Obadiah's prophecy contains a vivid description of the strongholds of Edom and of the pride of its people, who were overly secure in their mountain fortress: "'The pride of your heart has deceived you, you who live in the clefts of the rocks and make your home on the heights, you who say to yourself, "Who can bring me down to the ground?" Though you soar like the eagle and make your nest among the stars, from there I will bring you down,' declares the Lord" (Oba. 3).

O-4 In 1934 the American archaeologist Nelson Glueck explored the area around Beidha, a Nabatean site. He found that the buildings were similar in architecture to those of the Nabatean capital of Petra, only 4 miles away. Pictured here is a colonnaded tomb that shows the grandeur of Nabatean architecture. The rock-cut stairs (left center) lead to dwellings above the tomb (see **O-7**). Aretas (2 Cor. 11:32) was probably from this area. Close by is neolithic Beidha, a well-preserved prehistoric ruin.

MOAB
UNIT O1

1 : 150,000

1 Adir
2 Arnon, R.; Mujib
3 Aroer
4 Bab edh-Dhra

5 City of Moab
6 Cape Costigan
7 Dhat Ras
8 Dibon

9 Heidan, W.
10 Horonaim ?
11 Ije-abarim
12 Kerak, W.

13 Kir-hareseth; Kerak
14 Lejjun
15 Lisan Peninsula
16 Machaerus

17 Mazraa
18 Motha
19 Muhai
20 Numeira

21 Rabbath Moab
22 Tannur, Kh.
23 Zered, R.; Hasa
24 Zoar

N

EDOM & Mt. SEIR
UNIT O2
1:150,000

1 Adru	5 Dajaniya, Kh.	9 Ellebana	13 Ir-Nahash
2 Arabah, W.	6 Dana, W.	10 Fidan, W.	14 Laban, W.
3 Beidha	7 Dana	11 Gaia	15 Negla
4 Bozrah	8 Dusaq	12 Ghuweir, W.	16 Petra

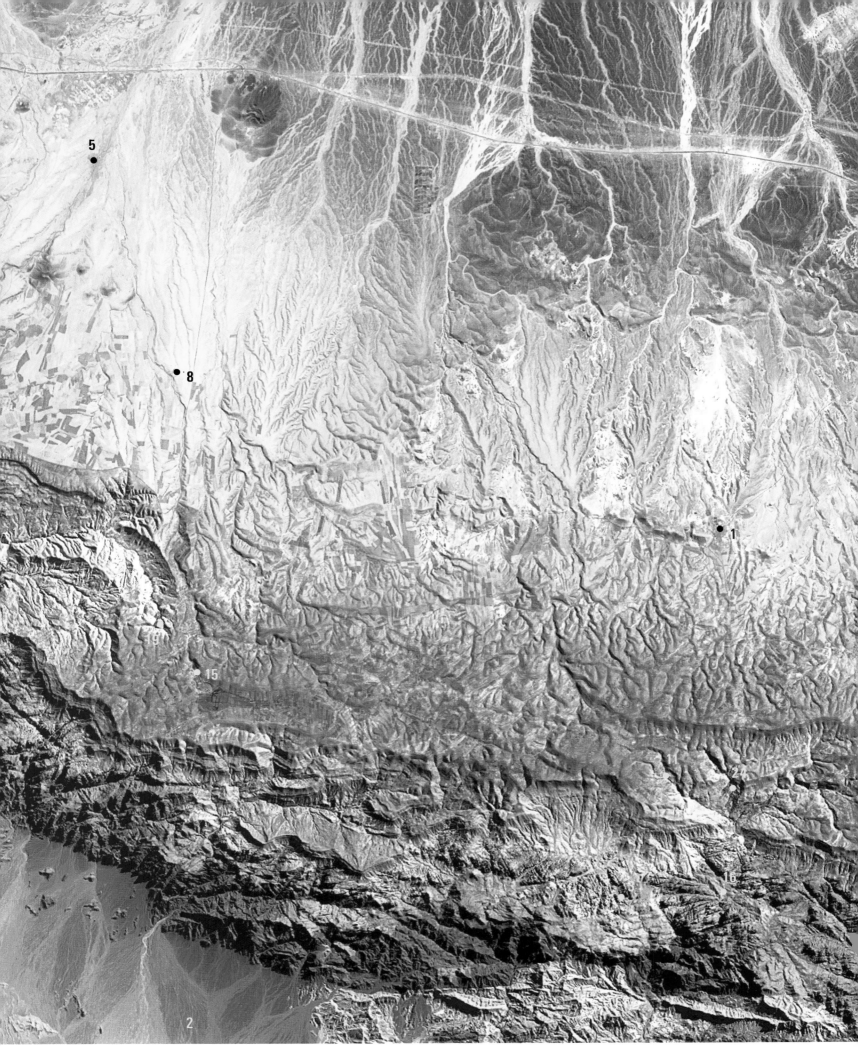

17 Punon
18 Sela
19 Shaubak castle
20 Tafileh

21 Toloha
22 Uneiza, J.
23 Uneiza
24 Wadi Musa

N

O-4   Beidha (near Petra): Nabatean tomb   View: W

O-5 Bozrah, the stronghold of northern Edom, is west of the King's Highway, situated on an isolated spur (center) at the head of Wadi Jamal (left center). The Lord's judgments upon Edom (which was celebrated for its strong fortifications) were couched in a prophecy against Bozrah and Teman, "I will send fire upon Teman that will consume the fortresses of Bozrah" (Amos 1:12).

O-6 East of Petra is an abundant water source called Ein Musa ("Spring of Moses," center). In ancient times, the water from Ein Musa was brought to Petra by means of conduits and earthenware piping. Wadi Musa was important not only because it contained a major source of water but because it was one of the few ascents from the Arabah (see **Unit M**) into Edom. Caravans came to Petra by way of Wadi Musa before continuing on to the plateau and the King's Highway. Local tradition claims that Moses provided water for the children of Israel by striking a rock at Ein Musa, but the Bible places the incident in the vicinity of Kadesh-barnea (see **L-1**; Num. 20:1–13; Deut. 32:48–52).

BIBLICAL/HISTORICAL REVIEW
Cross references to the Student Map Manual

- **Medeba Plateau**
  Josh. 13:9, 16; Deut. 3:10; 4:43. The Arnon River (see **O-2**) divided Moab into halves. The northern half is a plateau rising 2,400 feet above sea level called "plateau of Medeba" (Hebrew, the Mishor). It extended about 25 miles from the edge of Arnon to an ill-defined border with Gilead, somewhere between Medeba and Heshbon. During the period of the Israelite monarchy, this region was known to both Israel and Moab as the "land of Gad" (1 Sam. 13:7). Its economy was based on agriculture, cattle raising (Num. 32:3–4), and trade that came along the King's Highway and other desert routes.

- **Revolt of Mesha King of Moab (9th century B.C.)**
  2 Kgs. 1:1; 3:1–5; SMM 8-6c. Mesha king of Moab erected a stele that was discovered in 1868 by F. A. Klein, a German missionary. Called the Mesha Stone (or Moabite Stone), this stele gives an account of the war between Moab and Israel. The biblical account of the war indicates that "After Ahab's death, Moab rebelled against Israel." This passage probably refers to the later stages of the revolt, which was renewed after Ahab's death. The Mesha Stone reads in part: "As for Omri, king of Israel, he humbled Moab many years ... but I have

triumphed over him and over his house, while Israel hath perished for ever!" (*ANET*, 209–210).

- **Israelite Campaign Against Moab (9th century B.C.)**
  2 Kgs. 3:6–27; SMM 8-6d. In this campaign, Joram king of Israel and Jehoshaphat king of Judah joined forces against Moab. They attacked by way of the Desert of Edom and were aided in their campaign by the king of Edom. What at first looked like a complete victory for Israel turned into defeat when the king of Moab offered his eldest son as a sacrifice on the city wall. The conclusion is very difficult to explain: "The fury against Israel was great; they withdrew and returned to their own land." ∎

O-7 (overleaf) The Bible indicates that Mt. Hor was on the border of Edom. It is the place where Aaron died and was buried (Deut. 32:50). Josephus placed Mt. Hor in the vicinity of Petra, which is now identified with the twin peaks of Jebel Harun (upper center) or the "mountain of Aaron." This is the highest mountain in Edom's range (4,800 feet). The most likely spot for Mt. Hor, however, is at Jebel Madurah about 10 miles northeast of Kadesh-barnea (see **L-1**) "near the border of Edom" (Num. 20:22–23; 21:4; 33:37). Ridgaway commented on the splendor of the region in this photograph and on the tombs of Beidha (see **O-4**) and Petra: "Edom, the much-coveted prize of King David, the entry point of Solomon's gold of Ophir, the gateway through which rolled Oriental commerce for ages, the munition of rocks in which heroism grew, and whence it sallied out to dictate law to semi-barbarous hordes, the city of palaces and temples, whose inhabitants dwelt in luxury while they lived, and at death made their burial with the great, had so perished out of man's knowledge that its very existence had been forgotten until discovered and made known by Burckhardt in 1812. And now of all its monuments those which alone remain, with possibly a few exceptions, to tell the fate of the past, are records of death" (Ridgaway, 154; see **O-4**).

O-5   Bozrah, Bosor (Buseira)   View: SE

O-6   Ein Musa & Wadi Musa   View: E

P1-1   Way of the Pilgrimage (Darb el-Haj)   **View: NW**

P1-2   Ras en-Naqb: descent to Gulf of Aqabah   **View: SE**

P1-3 Nawamis (tombs), near Ein Khudra

View: SE

EASTERN SINAI

Unit P1

The Sinai Peninsula* is situated between the Gulf of Suez on the west and the Gulf of Elath/Aqabah on the east. It was important to Egypt and other nations because of its mineral deposits and lines of communication that connected the continents of Asia and Africa. Thus control of Sinai was an important objective of Egypt, Arabia, Edom, Moab, Israel (later Judah), Philistia, Mesopotamia, and the land of the Hittites (see **P1-1, P1-6,** and **P3-6**). According to one scholar, "the history of Sinai can be traced in terms of the development of its transportation routes—used for carrying provisions to the mine-workers (see **P3-6**) or for carrying goods ... to and from Egypt and the Land of Israel, ... and for conducting the pilgrim-caravans to the monasteries and to Mecca" (Har-el, 110; see **P2-3**). Stanley equated what we remember about Sinai with the exodus of Israel from Egypt, calling the wanderings of Israel Sinai's *only* history.

"The moment the green fields of Egypt recede from our view, still more when we reach the Red Sea, the further and further we advance into the Desert and the mountains, we feel that everything henceforth is continuous, that there is a sustained and protracted interest, increasing more and more, till it reaches its highest point in Palestine, in Jerusalem, on Calvary, and on Olivet. And in the desert of Sinai this interest is enhanced by the fact that there it stands alone. Over all the other great scenes of human history,— Palestine itself, Egypt, Greece, and Italy,— successive tides of great recollections have rolled, each to a certain extent obliterating the traces of the former. But in the Peninsula of Sinai there is nothing to interfere with the effect of that single event. The Exodus is the only stream of history that has passed through this wonderful region,—a history which has for its background the whole magnificence of Egypt, and for its distant horizon the forms, as yet unborn, of Judaism, of Mohometanism [Islam], of Christianity" (Stanley, 3–4).

---

*When "Sinai" is used in the Old Testament, it does not necessarily refer to the Sinai Peninsula, as is the case today. Sinai was only one of five wilderness regions, which included the wildernesses of Shur, Sin, Paran, and Zin. Mt. Sinai was in the Wilderness of Sinai (see P2-7).

PHOTO CAPTIONS

P1-1 The Darb el-Haj or "Way of the Pilgrimage" crosses Sinai north of et-Tih (see **P3-5**). It was used by Muslim pilgrims traveling to the holy place of Mecca in Arabia. Edward Robinson described the route and its significance.

"Such indeed is the importance of this caravan, both in a religious and political respect, that the rulers of Egypt from the earliest period have given it convoy and protection. For this purpose, a line of fortresses... has been established at intervals along the route; with wells of water, and supplies of provisions for the pilgrims of the Haj. At these castles the caravan regularly stops, usually for two days.... The various tribes of Bedawin, through whose territory the route passes, are held responsible for its safety between certain fixed points.... Most of them receive for this service a certain amount of toll from the caravan" (Robinson 1: 253–254).

P1-2 The Israelites must have used the route along the tops of the Ras en-Naqb mountains as they descended from the Wilderness of Sin to the Gulf of Elath (upper right; see **M-6**). Two other routes were much longer and would have taken the Israelites through the Edomite territory of the Arabah; the king of Edom denied them permission to travel that way (Num. 20:14–18; 21:4). This is possibly the "desert road toward the Red sea" used by the Israelites after they departed Egypt (Ex. 13:18).

P1-3 Ein Khudra is identified with biblical Hazeroth, where Aaron and Miriam complained against Moses "because of his Cushite wife, for he had married a Cushite," and because of Moses' role as the sole mediator between God and his people. God said concerning Moses, "With him I speak face to face, clearly and not in riddles" (Num. 12). Ein Khudra is northeast of Mt. Sinai on the way to Elath/Aqabah. Concerning the tombs in this region of Sinai, Stanley said, "The rude burial-grounds, with the many nameless head-stones, far away from human habitation, are such as the host of Israel must have left behind them at the different stages of their progress—at Massah, at Sinai, at Kibroth-hattaavah" (Stanley, 23).

P1-4 Nuweibeh is an oasis on the western side of the Gulf of Elat/Aqabah, about 45 miles south of Elath. Here the coast widens because of deposits

P1-4　Nuweibeh: Turkish fort　　　　　　　　　　　　　　　　　　　**View: NW**

left by run-off water that reaches the gulf from the mountains of Sinai. This Turkish fort is from the turn of the 19th century, when the border in Sinai between the Ottoman Empire and the British protectorate was disputed.

P1-5 This is a model of a Solomonic cargo boat which may have carried gold, silver, almugwood , precious stones, ivory, apes, and peacocks from Ophir (1 Kgs. 9:26–28; 10:11,22; see **P1-6**). The model, which is based upon a tomb painting in Thebes (Egypt), has a single sail elongated horizontally on a central mast with *crow's* nest lookout. There is a single row of 15 oars on each side, with a single large oar on each side of the stern for steering.

P1-6 A port installation from the early Iron Age (ca. 1200–1000 B.C.) was discovered in the bay of Pharaoh's Island (*Jezirat Faraun*) 7½ miles south of the northern end of the Gulf of Elath/Aqabah (see **P1-2**). Some scholars believe that this island may have been the port and shipyard of Ezion-geber, from which Solomon's ships sailed to Ophir (see **P1-5**). It is the only natural anchorage in the Gulf of Elath and was at the end of a strategic route between Egypt and the Gulf. The ruins of a fortress command the height on the northern end of the island (center), on what the Crusaders called the Isle of Graye. The fortress was probably built by Saladin in A.D. 1170. The island was abandoned after A.D. 1300, except as a garrison during the period of Ottoman rule (A.D. 1517–1917). The two hills at the southern end of the island (upper right) contain ruins from the Byzantine Period. Around the island is a casemate wall and nine towers that may date to Phoenician/Solomonic times (10th century B.C.). Some scholars, however, believe that the walls and towers are from the Byzantine period.

ADDITIONAL IMPRESSIONS OF SINAI

Edward Robinson 1: 239–240: "At length, at a quarter past 2 o'clock, we reached the N.W. corner of the Gulf, and entered the Great Haj road, which comes down from the western mountain, and passes along the shore at the northern end of the sea [see **P1-1** and **P1-2**]. Just at this point we met a large caravan of the Haweitat coming from the eastern desert, whence they had been driven out by the drought. They were now wandering towards the South of Palestine, and had with them about seventy camels and many asses, but no flocks. These were the first real Arabs of the desert we had seen; not wearing the turban like the Tawarah, but decorated with the *Kefiyeh*, a handkerchief of yellow or some glaring

colour thrown over the head, and bound fast with a skein of woolen yarn; the corners being left loose and hanging down the sides of the face and neck. They were wild, savage, hungry-looking fellows; and we thought we had much rather be with our mild Tawarah than in their power."

Edward Robinson 1: 228–229: "The first view of the Gulf and its scenery from the spot where we now stood, if not beautiful, (for how can a desert be beautiful?) was yet in a high degree romantic and exciting. The eastern Gulf of the Red Sea is narrower than the western; but it is the same long blue line of water, running up through the midst of a region totally desolate. The mountains too are here higher and more picturesque than those that skirt the Gulf of Suez; the valley between them is less broad; and there is not the same extent of wide desert plains along the shores" (see **P1-2**).

Arthur Stanley, 6–7: "The two great lines of Indian traffic have alternately passed up the eastern and the western gulf; and, though unconnected with the greater events of the Peninsula of Sinai, the commerce of Alexandria and the communications of England with India, which now pass down the Gulf of Suez, are not without interest, as giving a lively image of the ancient importance of the twin Gulf of Akaba. That gulf, now wholly deserted, was, in the times of the Jewish monarchy, the great thoroughfare of the fleets of Solomon and Jehoshaphat, and the only point in the second period of their history which brought the Israelites into connection with the scenes of the earliest wanderings of their nation" (see **P1-5** and **P1-6**).

Arthur Stanley, 83: "The sea on which we descended is the Gulf of Elath [see **P1-2**] and Ezion-Geber, up and down which the fleets of Solomon brought the gold of Ophir: the great channel of commerce till it was diverted by Alexandria to the Gulf of Suez .... Now there is not a single boat upon [the Gulf of Elath] from end to end. Once a-year, and once only, boats come around from Suez to Akaba with provisions for the Mecca pilgrims; at all other times it is desolate as the wilderness. But what a sea! and what a shore! ... On this view [the Israelites] undoubtedly looked. It was a new Red Sea for them, and they little knew the glory which it would acquire when it became the channel of all the wealth of Solomon." ■

P1-7 (overleaf) This is another view of Pharaoh's Island looking northeast toward the sunrise (see **P1-6**).

P1-5 Model: Solomonic cargo boat

P1-6 Pharaoh's Island (Jazirat Faroun)

P2-1   St. Catherine's monastery: art gallery

P2-2   St. Catherine's monastery: library

P2-3 St. Catherine's monastery & Mt. Sinai   View: NW

CENTRAL SINAI   Unit P2

Because of harsh living conditions, the population of Sinai has always been relatively small. Today the Bedouin number about 80,000, with about 10,000 living in the mountainous region of southern Sinai and about 15,000 living in central Sinai south of the et-Tih plateau (see **P3-5**). Cut off from the centers of government in Egypt and Arabia, the Bedouin tribes of central and southern Sinai have seldom been subject to anyone but their own tribal leaders (see **P3-6**). They have been the self-appointed guardians of the desert routes, exacting payment from desert caravans and providing protection in return. Looting and pillaging have also been common, as evidenced by the confrontation between the Amalekites and the Israelites at Rephidim (see **P3-1**). The ancient Egyptians also stationed army units in Sinai to protect the roads that led to the turquoise mines (see **P3-6**).

In contrast to the sandy coastal plain of the north, the south of Sinai consists of huge granite mountains. The most notable mountains are Jebel Katerina (8,652 feet); Jebel Musa (the traditional Mt. Sinai: 7,486 feet; see **P2-7**); and Jebel Serbal (6,791 feet; see **P3-7**). The broad valleys (wadis) that run between the mountains served as important passageways through central and southern Sinai. The wadis are, for the most part, devoid of vegetation, which is the result of the arid conditions of Sinai.

PHOTO CAPTIONS

P2-1 The art gallery of St. Catherine's Monastery contains over 2,000 icons with religious and historical significance (*icon* is Greek for "image"). It is, in fact, the most important collection of early icons in the world. One of the treasures in the art gallery is a scroll signed by the prophet Muhammed. The story is told that a young camel driver was seeking refuge in the monastery when the monks recognized him as the prophet Muhammed. In return for their help, Muhammed signed a scroll promising his patronage and protection.

P2-2 The library of St. Catherine's Monastery is one of the oldest in the world. It was made famous when the German theologian Tischendorf came to the monastery in 1863 and discovered the Codex *Sinaiticus*, a Greek translation of parts of the Old and all of the New Testament which dates to the 4th century A.D. (Tischendorf purportedly found 43 leaves of

the Codex in a wastebasket that would have been used to light the monastery's oven!) After the Codex was sent to the Russian Czar and never returned, it was purchased by the British Museum for £100,000 in 1933. Additional pages of Codex Sinaiticus were discovered in recent years. The library contains some 3,400 manuscripts written in Greek, Arabic, Syriac, and Georgian, as well as ancient church Slavic, Ethiopian, Coptic, Armenian, Latin, and Persian. The library is restricted to only those visitors who obtain written authorization from patriarchates. The Rockefeller foundation paid for the modern library shelving in the library. In 1950, an American expedition microfilmed two million pages in twelve different languages.

P2-3 St. Catherine's Monastery was built at the foot of Mt. Sinai (Jebel Musa) to protect the burning bush where God appeared to Moses. "So Moses thought, 'I will go over and see this strange sight—why the bush does not burn up.' When the Lord saw that he had gone over to look, God called to him from within the bush, 'Moses, Moses!'...'Do not come any closer.... Take off your sandals, for the place where you are standing is holy ground'" (Ex. 3:3-5). The oldest building of St. Catherine's Monastery is a chapel in the center of the compound named after the "Burning Bush," which dates to the time of Constantine the Great (4th century A.D.). There have been as many as six monasteries in southern Sinai and thousands of monks. Today, however, there is only the monastery of St. Catherine with only a few monks. The walls of the monastery were built in the 6th century by the Emperor Justinian to protect the monks in the Sinai region, who were being persecuted by the Saracens (Arabians). The monastery's walls are 33 to 49 feet high, and 279 feet by 312 feet in length. Catherine, after whom the monastery is named, lived in Alexandria in A.D. 307 during a period of Christian persecutions. After Catherine was publicly accused of idolatry by the emperor Maximinus, she was tortured and put to death. According to tradition, her body was transported by angels to a peak (Mt. Catherine) south of Jebel Musa. Three centuries later, monks from Justinian's monastery found her bones and brought them to the monastery church.

P2-4 This is one of the suggested sites of Rephidim, a stopping place of the Israelites on their way to Mt. Sinai and the center of the Amalekites during the time of the Exodus. Three biblical events are connected with Rephidim: (1) Israel murmured against Moses for want of water. "The

P2-4   Watiya pass: excavations   View: W

whole Israelite community set out from the Desert of Sin, traveling from place to place as the Lord commanded. They camped at Rephidim, but there was no water for the people to drink. So they quarreled with Moses and said, 'Give us water to drink.'" Moses struck a rock in Horeb and water came out for the people to drink (Ex. 17:1–7); (2) "The Amalekites came and attacked the Israelites at Rephidim." Joshua fought the Amalekites as Moses stood on the top of a nearby hill. "As long as Moses held up his hands, the Israelites were winning, but whenever he lowered his hands, the Amalekites were winning....Aaron and Hur held his hands up… So Joshua overcame the Amalekite army with the sword" (Ex. 17:8–16); and (3) Jethro's visit to Moses may have taken place in the vicinity of Rephidim. On that occasion, Jethro counseled Moses to teach the law and delegate power to lesser judges (Ex. 18). South of the Watiya pass (see **P2-5** and **P2-6**) is St. Catherine's Monastery and Mt. Sinai (see **P2-3** and **P2-7**).

P2-5 The Watiya pass crosses the central mountains of southern Sinai and is the gateway of Wadi esh-Sheikh, where the wadi sweeps round toward Jebel Serbal (see **P3-7**). According to Ridgaway, the Watiya pass "is the immediate gate-way to the whole region lying north and northeast, which is the country of the Amalekites, known as such then and afterward." Ridgaway continues, "The nearness of this pass to Mount Sinai seems to fulfill the condition that Moses and the elders went in advance of the tribes to the 'rock that is in Horeb.'... But where were the Amalekites while Moses and the elders went on to the rock in Horeb? It appears from the narrative (Ex. 17:8) as though they were not gathered at the point where the battle took place till after the smiting of the rock: 'Then came Amalek, and fought with Israel in Rephidim.' Is it improbable that Amalek now, convinced through their scouts that Israel meant to force their way to Mount Sinai, and obtain possession of the entrance to their whole territory, determined for the first time to oppose their further progress?" (Ridgaway, 60–61; see **P2-4**).

P2-6 This is a detailed view of the Watiya pass and the country of the Amalekites (see **P2-5**). As recorded in the Bible, Amalek was one of the grandsons of Esau (Gen. 36:12; 1 Chron. 1:36). Their territory seems to have ranged from central Sinai to the Negev (see **Unit L**) and from the Arabah (see **Unit M**) into Arabia.

ADDITIONAL IMPRESSIONS OF SINAI

Henry Ridgaway, 70–74. "In the morning ... we left ... for the ascent of Jebel Musa [Mt. Sinai]. The wind was blowing strong from the northwest, and the atmosphere was favorable for climbing. We took the usual path, lying back of the convent, which winds up the gorge between Jebel Musa and El Birell. The boulders, for quite a distance up, have been so placed as to form a rude stairway, which greatly facilitates the ascent....A large spring of ice-cold water is passed, and then all along, for an hour, a beautiful stream gurgles and dashes through the opening rocks....It was near noon when we reached the summit, so that we had been three hours and ten minutes in accomplishing the ascent. A huge flat rock extends nearly over the summit ....Immediately below the chapel [the Greek Chapel of the Transfiguration which crowns the highest peak], the rock on which it stands has a slight cave-like appearance, with a crevice in which, tradition says, Moses was placed when the Lord God passed before him and proclaimed his name (Ex. 34:6–7) ....Mountains of various elevations and shapes, gray, reddish, and dark, with no vestige of green, no sign of life, but looking cold, hard, and stern, as if, when plastic, an omnipotent hand had suddenly squeezed them into unyielding fixedness:—all combine to form, in their grandeur, a fit scene for the delivery of that law, one of whose properties is its unchangeableness" (see **P2-7**).   ∎

P2-7 (overleaf) The Bible indicates that Mt. Sinai was in the Wilderness of Sinai between the Wilderness of Sin and the Wilderness of Paran. The Plain of Rafah, at the foot of the mountain, is the traditional place where Israel camped while "The Lord descended to the top of Mount Sinai and called Moses to the top of the mountain. So Moses went up." On Mt. Sinai, Moses received the Ten Commandments (Ex. 19:17–20; 20:1–17). But "when the people saw that Moses was so long in coming down from the mountain," they asked Aaron to make gods for them to worship. Still on the mount, Moses was warned by the Lord that his people had corrupted themselves. When Moses and Joshua returned to camp, they saw the calf and the dancing, and Moses' "anger burned and he threw the tablets out of his hands, breaking them to pieces at the foot of the mountain. And he took the calf they had made and burned it in the fire; then he ground it to powder, scattered it on the water and made the Israelites drink it" (Ex. 32:1–20).

P2-5   Watiya pass: approach to Mt. Sinai   **View: S**

P2-6   Watiya pass   **View: S**

P3-1   Wadi Feiran: oasis   View: NW

P3-2   Tell Feiran   View: SW

P3-3   Wadi Feiran: oasis   View: E

WESTERN SINAI   Unit P3

The Bible makes it clear that the Israelites did not reach Canaan by the road through the Philistine country that crossed northern Sinai (Ex. 13:17). This route was the southern portion of the international Coastal Route. It was guarded by a chain of forts that protected merchant caravans as well as by the Egyptian army. The Israelites did not travel the Coastal Route "though that was shorter. For God said, 'If they face war, they might change their minds and return to Egypt'" (Ex. 13:17).

After crossing the Red Sea, Moses brought the Israelites into the Desert of Shur (Ex. 15:22; see **Unit L**). The people murmured about having no water and were then brought to Elim, where they found 12 wells of water and 70 palm trees (Ex. 15:23–27). In the Desert of Sin, which was between Elim and Sinai, the Israelites again grumbled against Moses and Aaron because they had brought them "into this desert to starve this entire assembly to death" (Ex. 16:2–3). Here manna was given for the first time (Ex. 16:13–36). After leaving Mt. Sinai (see **P2-7**), the Israelites camped in the Desert of Paran. From Paran, Moses sent twelve spies to explore the land of Canaan (Num. 13:3–26). (The Desert of Zin was associated with the Desert of Paran; see **M-4** and **M-7**; Num. 13:26; 20:1.) Kadesh-barnea was in the Desert of Paran, near the border between Sinai and the Negev (see **Unit L**) and the territory of Edom (see **Unit O**).

PHOTO CAPTIONS

P3-1 Travelers to Sinai talk about the "endless windings of [Wadi] Feiran." Ridgaway referred to it as the "gem of the desert" and said, "there is an ample stream of water flowing through the wady for a mile at least, and its course is fringed with palms, the tamarisk...and other trees" (Ridgaway, 52). This is the traditional route taken by the Israelites. "The mouth of this wadi is just off the east bank of the Gulf of Suez, some 2 miles south of Abu Rudeis, and it winds eastwards into Sinai, climbing between tall granite mountains until it reaches a magnificent oasis, some 2,000 feet above sea level, set amidst lofty peaks. Lush and picturesque, well-watered and thick with palm trees and tamarisks, it is one of the surprises of arid southern Sinai" (Pearlman, 102). From the 4th century A.D., the Feiran oasis has been identified by some as the site of Rephidim, by others as Elim.

P3-2 The Feiran oasis now contains a small farm headed by a monk, many Bedouin farms (left center), and a tell surrounded by a wall that extends over an area of about 10 acres (center). The tell has remains "from the Iron Age (ca. seventh century B.C.) up to the Arab period without any noticeable gap" (Aharoni, 199). At the foot of the mountains surrounding the oasis are caves where many early monks lived. A little to the south of the oasis are the ruins of a large Byzantine city (not pictured). Stanley gave this description of the Wadi Feiran: "We passed into the endless windings of the Wady Feiran [see **P3-1**]. I cannot too often repeat, that these wadys are exactly like rivers, except in having no water; and it is this appearance of torrent-bed and banks, and clefts in the rocks for tributary streams, and at times even rushes and shrubs fringing their course, which gives to the whole wilderness a doubly dry and thirsty aspect" (Stanley, 71).

P3-3 The oasis of Feiran lies on an important trade route that links the Gulf of Suez with the Gulf of Elath/Aqabah (see **P1-2**). The oasis extends over an area of approximately 3 miles and has a very large palm grove. It receives its water from the springs and wells that flow from Jebel Serbal (see **P3-7**). For many centuries, its refreshing shade and water have been a welcome site to weary travelers as they traveled the desert of Sinai. Stanley described the oasis of Feiran: "The palm-groves of Feiran I saw only by the clear starlight; yet it was still possible to see how great must be the beauty of the luxuriant palms and feathery tamarisks—the wild glades below, the vast mountains above" (Stanley, p. 72). The present date groves belong to several Bedouin tribes. When the Romans ruled this area, they had a monopoly on the fruit.

P3-4 Serabit el-Khadim was discovered in 1761 by Karsten Niebuhr, who was looking for the inscriptions of Wadi Mukkatab. He was taken by his guides to this place because of its "greater interest and wonder" (Ridgaway, 115). (In Wadi Mukkatab, 1 mile south of Maghara (see **P3-6**), archaeologists and other explorers have found inscriptions, extending over a distance of about 6 miles, written in Greek, Latin, Arabic, Coptic, and Nabatean. Some were left by workers connected to the turquoise mines, as well as by early Christian pilgrims who came to Sinai beginning in the 4th century.) The next travelers to Serabit el-Khadim came in the early part of the 19th century. "All these travelers, with the exception of two Englishmen...pronounced [Serabit el-Khadim] to be an ancient Egyptian cemetery" (Ridgaway, 115). In fact, Serabit el-Khadim was a famous

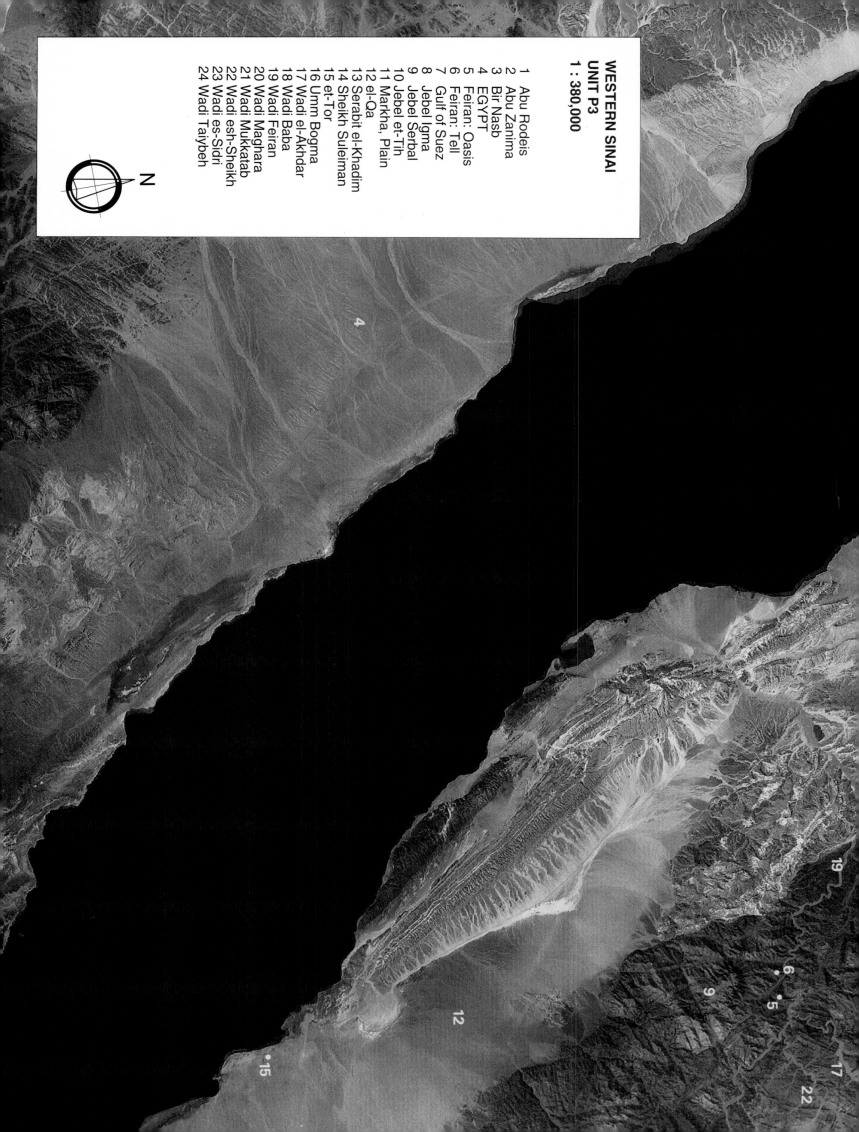

WESTERN SINAI
UNIT P3
1 : 380,000

N

P3-4   Serabit el-Khadim   View: N

mining area and the site of a temple dedicated to the Egyptian goddess Hathor, also known as the "Lady of the Turquoise" (see **P3-6**). Other significant discoveries at Serabit el-Khadim include the "proto-Sinaitic inscriptions" from the 15th century B.C. that are closely related to Hebrew, ancient tools of the mining trade, and molds for making the tools.

P3-5 The vast et-Tih plateau (top of picture) occupies about 60 percent of Sinai's total area. The strip of Nubian sandstone between the et-Tih plateau and the granite mountains of southern Sinai is said to contain the richest mineral sources of the Sinai Peninsula. The region is also said to epitomize "the vast and dreadful desert, that thirsty and waterless land, with its venomous snakes and scorpions" (Deut. 8:15). The Israelites were tested in the wilderness for 40 years before they were allowed to enter the Promised Land. Tih means "wanderings" in Arabic. Archaeologists have reported finding seasonal camps here that were identified by the discovery of cisterns, wells, potsherds, and flint implements.

P3-6 Turquoise is a semi-precious blue-green stone used to make jewelry. It was mined by the Egyptians with flint chisels and stone hammers. Maghara means "cave" in Arabic, but what the Bedouin thought were caves were actually Egyptian mine shafts. Because Egypt had few metals of its own, it desperately needed the mines of Sinai and southern Arabah (see **Unit M**). This relief depicts Pharaoh Sekhemkhet (2648–2642 B.C.) wearing the crown of Upper Egypt and smiting an asiatic prisoner (Pharaoh is to the far left). The other figure is also of Sekhemkhet (center). Here, he is wearing the crown of Lower Egypt with the long feather curling out in front. Reliefs such as this one seem to suggest that, from early times, an Egyptian army was stationed in Sinai to protect the routes and Egyptian mining activity. The turquoise mines of Wadi Maghara and Serabit el-Khadim were the only turquoise mines in the entire eastern Mediterranean. The closest turquoise mines outside Sinai were in Persia (Iran). Stanley noted that "the Egyptian copper-mines and monuments and hieroglyphics, in Surabit el-Khadim and the Wady Mughareh, imply a degree of intercourse between Egypt and the Peninsula in the earliest days of Egypt, of which all other traces have long ceased" (Stanley, 26–27).

ADDITIONAL IMPRESSIONS OF SINAI

Ridgaway, p. 111 (region of Jebel et-Tih in P3-5): "From this spot we had a wide view over the surrounding country. On our left was the Tih, a long, lofty, level, unbroken ridge [top of picture from left to right]...

stretching off eastward as far as the eye could reach, apparently of limestone. On our right, and before us, along the foot of the Tih, lay an uneven sandy plain, several miles in breadth, full of low broken ridges and water-courses. This sandy plain extends, as we afterwards found, through the whole interior of the peninsula, almost to the eastern coast. It lies between the Tih and the proper mountains of the peninsula, which rose on our right in fantastic shapes and wild confusion." ∎

P3-7 (overleaf) Wadi el-Akhdar joins the Wadi esh-Sheikh before reaching Jebel Serbal. Together they pass into Wadi Feiran, which runs north of Serbal down to the Gulf of Suez (see **P3-1**). Robinson described Jebel Serbal as having "the appearance of a long, thin, lofty ridge of granite, with numerous points or peaks ... a grand and noble object" (Robinson, 1: 126). Because of its height and proximity to the sea, Jebel Serbal receives large amounts of rainfall, and in the winter it is capped with snow. Many early Christians considered Jebel Serbal to be the original Mt. Sinai. Ridgaway described it as standing "in dark and solemn grandeur, prominent, not alone for its physical pre-eminence, but also for its historical association" (Ridgaway, 56). In time, however, the identification of Mt. Sinai with Jebel Musa prevailed (see **P2-7**). Wadi esh-Sheikh (foreground) is one of the largest and most famous passageways of the Sinai Peninsula. "It takes its rise in the very heart of Sinai, whence it issues a broad valley at first in an eastern direction, and then sweeping round to the North and West, it passes down towards Serbâl" (Robinson, 1: 125–126).

P3-5   Serabit el-Khadim & Jebel et-Tih

View: N

P3-6   Wadi Maghara: ancient Egyptian relief

Q-1   Tanis (San el-Hagar): excavations   View: E

Q-2   Painted relief (captives): Temple of Rameses II, Abydos

Q-3   Tanis (San el-Hagar): excavations   View: S

Q-4   Nile Delta (Goshen): Baking bricks   View: NE

LOWER EGYPT   Unit Q

Egypt was the second great center of ancient civilization along with Mesopotamia. This is remarkable given that Egypt is 84 percent desert and, like its north-Africa neighbors, one of the driest countries in the world. But, unlike its neighbors, Egypt had the Nile, and for an average of 12 miles on either side of the Nile's banks Egypt was as fertile as any country in the world. It has been estimated that 97 percent of the people in Egypt live on only 4 percent of the land, a fact that prompted the 5th century B.C. Greek historian Herodotus to comment that "Egypt is the gift of the Nile."

Ancient Egypt was geographically divided into two zones. The northern zone, called Lower Egypt, contained the delta, which is 100 miles long by 150 miles wide (see **Q-6**, **Q-7,** and **Q-9**). The southern zone, called Upper Egypt, included the cultivable land as far south as Aswan (about 400 miles south of modern Cairo). The Nile flows from south to north and empties into the Mediterranean Sea. The chief commercial and military road ran along the coast of northern Sinai to Gaza on the southern coast of Canaan. Moses wanted to avoid the Egyptian military posts and, for this reason, led the children of Israel "by the desert road toward the Red Sea" rather than "on the road through the Philistine country" (Ex. 13:17–18; see Ex. 14:12; Num. 14:4). In ancient times, roads were designated by the name of their terminal point (see above, p. 13).

PHOTO CAPTIONS

Q-1 The central authority of Egypt declined during the Middle Kingdom (18th century B.C.), opening the way for foreign rulers called Hyksos to subjugate Egypt. The name "Hyksos" means "foreign rulers," and was a term used by the Egyptians for these new conquerors. The Hyksos' capital was established at Avaris, whence they ruled Egypt for about 100 years (ca. 1650–1542 B.C.). In the opinion of some, it was during the Hyksos period that Pharaoh "set [Joseph] over all the land of Egypt" because he interpreted Pharaoh's dreams and suggested a plan of action to save the country. "Then Pharaoh said to Joseph, 'Since God has made all this known to you, there is no one so discerning and wise as you. You shall be in charge of my palace, and all my people are to submit to your orders. Only with respect to the throne will I be greater than you'" (Gen. 41:39–41; see **Q-3**).

Q-2 The painted relief in this photograph is from the temple of Rameses II (ca. 1290–1224 B.C.) at Abydos, 322 miles south of Cairo. Abydos is north of the Valley of the Kings and the site of ancient Thebes (Luxor). The Tombs of the first Pharaohs (ca. 3100–2686 B.C.) are in Abydos, as well as temples of Seti I and Rameses II. This scene portrays Asiatic captives bound with papyrus stems.

Q-3 In the Eastern Delta near modern Qantir, Rameses II built a new capital city which he named Pi-Rameses. Contemporary records and archaeological evidence suggest that the palace was large and lavishly decorated. The massive mudbrick walls were overlaid with glazed faience tiles showing foreign captives, vassals paying tribute, and prisoners being eaten by lions, all designed to create awe in the observer. This "House of Rameses" is probably the city referred to in the Bible that the Israelites built for Pharaoh: "So they put slave masters over them to oppress them with forced labor, and they built Pithom and *Rameses* as store cities for Pharaoh" (Ex. 1:11; italics added). Little remains of his capital today. The river branch which flowed to the west of the city silted up and changed course northward. Pi-Rameses was cut off, and the rulers of Dynasty XXI carried most of the usable materials to Tanis and used them to construct a new capital. Among the granite blocks of the temple at Tanis, Flinders Petrie discovered the remains of a colossal statue of Rameses II, originally about 33 feet high, which had been cut up for building stone.

Q-4 Mud bricks were used in the construction of village houses and sometimes for royal palaces, whereas stone was used in the construction of tombs and temples (see **Q-8**). After Moses told Pharaoh to let the Israelites leave Egypt, Pharaoh commanded his taskmasters, "You are no longer to supply the people with straw for making bricks; let them go and gather their own straw. But require them to make the same number of bricks as before; don't reduce the quota" (Ex. 5:6–8). The making of bricks was usually done by captive Asiatics as early as the 18th dynasty. A 15th century B.C. tomb painting of Rekh-mi-Re at Thebes (*ANE* 1: fig. 18; see **Q-5**), shows workmen with hoes kneading clay moistened with water. Other laborers are carrying the material to the brickmakers, similar to the action taking place in this picture .

Q-5 The pyramids of Giza have stood for nearly 4,500 years and are symbolic of the Egyptians' belief in afterlife. The Great Pyramid of

NILE DELTA
UNIT Q
1: 650,000

1 Cairo
2 Damietta (Dumiyat)
3 Giza
4 GOSHEN
5 Heliopolis, On
6 Natrun, Wadi
7 Nile (Damietta)
8 Nile (Rosetta)
9 Pelusium
10 Rosetta (Rashid)
11 Sais
12 Sebkhat el-Badawil
13 Succoth
14 Suez
15 Tanis
16 Tumilat, Wadi

N

Q-5   Pyramids of Giza: Sunset

View: W

Cheops (right) is the largest, covering 13.1 acres and rising to a height of 481.4 feet. It was constructed with 2,300,000 quarried stones averaging $2^1/_2$ tons each. The 9 granite slabs that form the roof of the king's burial chamber weigh about 45 tons each. The middle pyramid belonged to Chephren, and the one on the left to Mycerinus. All three pyramids are from the 4th Dynasty (ca. 2613–2495 B.C.).

Q-6 Egypt's Nile River follows a 600 mile course from the First Cataract to Memphis (near modern Cairo). Each year the Nile would rise some 25 feet to flood the Nile Valley with rich black soil, renewing the soils every year and providing Egypt with a strong, agricultural-based economy (see **Q-7**). Egypt's wealth and power, however, came from trade and from conquering foreign lands. For this reason, Canaan was important to Egypt as a crossroads for trade and as a bridgehead against foreign attack. Egypt traded with Phoenicia for wood with which to build its houses and ships. Goshen, in the eastern Delta, was the place where Jacob and his family lived, as did his descendants (Gen. 45:10; Ex. 9:26). Pharaoh said to Joseph, "the land of Egypt is before you; settle your father and your brothers in the best part of the land. Let them live in Goshen" (Gen. 47:6).

Q-7 The people of ancient Egypt called their land *Kemi*, which means "Black Land." The rich, black soil that resulted from the yearly flooding of the Nile produced crops of barley, wheat, vegetables, and melons. In addition, the flax grown along the banks of the Nile made the linen of Egypt a prized commodity. Harvest scenes are a common theme in Egyptian wall paintings, which show laborers breaking soil and plowing. A scene from a 15th century B.C. tomb in Thebes shows a person, possibly a "slave driver," watching the laborers from a booth. When Pharaoh refused to let the Israelites leave Egypt, Moses commanded Aaron to strike the Nile with his rod in the presence of Pharaoh and his officials; and "all the water was changed into blood The fish in the Nile died, and the river smelled so bad that the Egyptians could not drink its water. Blood was everywhere in Egypt" (Ex. 7:19–21).

Q-8 In this picture men and women are making sun-dried bricks, one of the common building materials of the Near East. The method for making the bricks is much the same today as it was in ancient times. After the clay is thoroughly soaked and mixed with straw, it is carried on a flat board or in baskets to the artisans in charge of molding the bricks either by hand or in wooden molds. Notice the woman below the mud tower mixing the straw and the clay, and the man and woman who are carrying the already mixed clay to the craftsman at the table, who is shaping the wet clay into

bricks. Mixing chopped straw into the mud gives strength to the brick and makes it less crumbly. A scene similar to the one in this photograph is depicted on the wall of a 15th century B.C. tomb at Thebes in Upper Egypt (see **Q-4**). A record of brick-making from the 13th century B.C. lists forty men with a quota of 2,000 bricks for each. The actual numbers delivered are also entered. In one example, there was a deficit of 370 bricks. Bricks for houses might measure 9 x $4^1/_2$ x 3 inches, while those for larger buildings might be 16 x 8 x 6 inches.

BIBLICAL REVIEW

- **The Land of Goshen**
  (Gen. 45:7–11; 46:28–34; 47:1–12). Jacob was embalmed according to Egyptian practice, but was taken to Canaan and buried in the tomb of Machpelah (Gen. 50:2, 13). Joseph also was carried from Goshen to Canaan for burial (Gen. 50:1–14). The plagues did not come to Goshen, as they did to the rest of Egypt (Ex. 8:22; 9:26). According to one tradition, the Israelites lived in Goshen 430 years (Ex. 12:40–41; Gal. 3:17). The Israelites went from Goshen to Succoth, where they escaped Pharaoh (Ex. 12:37; Num. 33:3, 5).

- **Avaris / "House of Rameses"**
  A new capital was built by Rameses II near Avaris (modern Qantir). Pi-Rameses is mentioned with Pithom as cities built by the Israelites for the Egyptians (see **Q-3**). The Exodus began from Rameses (Ex. 12:37; Num. 33:3, 5).

- **Zoan / Tanis**
  About the year 1330 B.C., a celebration was held to mark the four hundredth year of the founding of Tanis (Zoan). According to a biblical reference, "Hebron had been built seven years before Zoan in Egypt" (Num. 13:22; Isa. 19:13; 30:1–4).

- **Joseph takes Mary and Jesus to Egypt**
  An angel warned Joseph in a dream: "Get up," he said, "take the child and his mother and escape to Egypt. Stay there until I tell you, for Herod is going to search for the child to kill him" (Matt. 2:13–23). According to Matthew, the child and his family went to live in Nazareth after their return from Egypt. ∎

Q-9 (overleaf) A view across the Nile through the reeds that line the bank of the river.

Q-6 **Nile Delta: washing beside the reeds**

Q-7 **Nile Delta (Goshen)** **View: E**

Q-8 **Nile Delta: Drying mud bricks (with straw)** **View: NW**

SYRIA (N)
APPENDIX 1
1 : 500,000

1 Alalakh; T. Atchana	5 Antioch a/Orontes	9 Baghras	13 Deir Semaan
2 Alexandretta	6 Apamea; Q. Moudiq	10 Balanea; Baniyas	14 Ebla; T. Mardikh
3 Amik Golu	7 Aradus; Rouad	11 Beroea; Aleppo	15 Emesa; Homs
4 Antaradus; Tartus	8 Arsuz	12 Chalcis a/Belum	16 Gabala; Jablah

17 Hamath, Epiphania
18 Iskanderun, Gulf
19 Jisr el-Hadid
20 Jisr esh-Shugur

21 Laodicea a/Mare
22 Maarat en-Noman
23 Massiaf
24 Posidium; Ras el-Basit

25 Qadmus
26 Raphanea
27 Ras Abu Hani
28 Orontes, R.

29 Seleucia Pieria
30 Shaizar
31 Syrian Gates
32 Ugarit, Ras Shamra

N

**ANTAKYA
APPENDIX 2
1 : 200,000**

1 Al Mina	5 Antioch a/Orontes	9 Jisr el-Hadid	13 Seleucia Pieria
2 Alalakh; T. Atchana	6 Arsuz	10 Kizil Dag	14 Silpius, Mt.
3 Alexandretta	7 Baal Zaphon ?	11 Magaraçik	15 Syrian Gates
4 Amik Golu	8 Baghras	12 Orontes, R.	16 Taiyinat, T.

LATAKYA - BANIAS
APPENDIX 3
1 : 200,000

1 Abu Qobeis castle	5 Laodicea a/Mare	9 Minet el-Beidha	13 Ras Ibn Hani
2 Balanea; Baniyas	6 Maniqa castle	10 Orontes, R.	14 Sahyun castle
3 Gabala; Jablah	7 Margab castle	11 Posidium; Ras el-Basit	15 Sukas, T.
4 Jisr esh-Shugur	8 Mehelbeh castle	12 Qarqar	16 Ugarit; Ras Shamra

BANIAS - TRIPOLI
APPENDIX 4
1 : 200,000

1 Abu Qobeis castle	5 Caesarea a/Lib.	9 Hom's Gap	13 Krak des Chevaliers
2 Antaradus; Tartus	6 Chastel Rouge	10 Hosn Soleiman	14 LEBANON, Mts.
3 Aradus; Rouad	7 Gabala, Jablah	11 Kahf castle	15 Marathus; Amrit
4 Balanea; Baniyas	8 Hermel	12 Khawwabi castle	16 Margab castle

17 Masiaf
18 Oreimeh castle
19 Orthosia
20 Qadmus

21 Raphanea ?
22 Sumur; T. Kazel
23 Tripolis
24 Ullaza ?; el-Mina

N

LEBANON
APPENDIX 5
1 : 300,000

1 Abana, R.; Barada	5 ANTI-LEBANON, Mts.	9 Beit ed-Din	13 Byblos; Jbail
2 Abel, Abila	6 Aphekah; Afqa	10 BEQA (Coele-Syria)	14 Caesarea a/Lib.
3 Aleh	7 Baabda	11 Berytus; Beirut	15 Chalcis a/Lib. ?
4 Amioun	8 Batruna	12 Beth-zabdai	16 Damascus

17 Hasbaya
18 Helbon
19 Heliopolis; Baalbek
20 Hermon, Mt.

21 Ijon
22 Jezzine
23 Junieh
24 Karun

25 Kumidi
26 LEBANON, Mts.
27 Lebo-hamath
28 Leontes, R.; Litani

29 Marjayoun
30 Orontes, R.
31 Tripolis
32 Zahle

N

TRIPOLI - BEIRUT
APPENDIX 6
1 : 200,000

1 Adonis, R.	5 Aphekah; Afqa	9 Beziza	13 Deir el-Ghazal
2 Aleh	6 Baabda	10 Byblos; Jbail	14 Deir el-Qala
3 Amioun	7 Batruna	11 Caesarea a/Lib.	15 Dog River
4 Antoura	8 Berytus; Beirut	12 Chalcis a/Lib. ?	16 Hadet

16

13

18

22

12

32

5

20

31

24

4

1

15

17

26

2

14

6

8

19

21

17 Junieh
18 Kafr Zebad
19 Khaldeh
20 LEBANON, Mts.

21 Naimeh
22 Niha
23 Orthosia
24 Qalat Fakhra

25 Qasr Neba
26 Sarba
27 Shamat
28 Tira

29 Tripolis
30 Ullaza ?
31 Yanuh
32 Zahle

N

BEIRUT - TYRE
APPENDIX 7
1 : 200,000

1 Adloun	5 Barouk	9 Beth-zaith; Zeita	13 Dan
2 Aleh	6 Beaufort castle	10 Bint Jbail	14 Deir el-Qala
3 Awali, N.	7 Beit ed-Din	11 Caesarea Philippi	15 Hasbani, W.
4 Baabda	8 Berytus; Beirut	12 Cheshim	16 Hasbaya

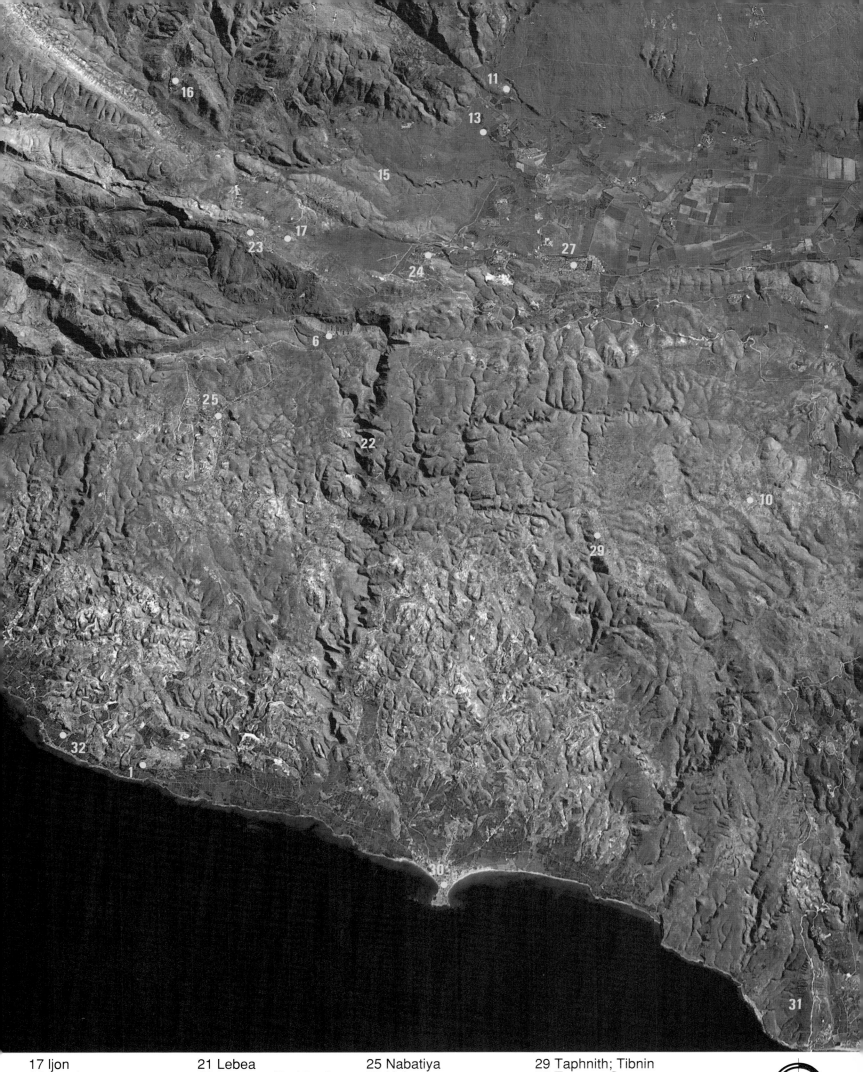

17 Ijon	21 Lebea	25 Nabatiya	29 Taphnith; Tibnin
18 Jezzine	22 Leontes, R.; Litani	26 Naimeh	30 Tyre; es-Sur
19 Karun	23 Marjayoun	27 Qiryat Shemona	31 Tyre, Ladder
20 Khaldeh	24 Metulla	28 Sidon; Saida	32 Zarephath

N

BEQA : South
APPENDIX 8
1 : 200,000

1 Abel-beth-maachah
2 Ain Harsha
3 Beaufort castle
4 Caesarea Philippi

5 Chalcis a/Lib. ?
6 Dakkoueh
7 Dan
8 El-Khiam

9 Hasbani, W.
10 Hasbaya
11 Hebbariya
12 Hermon, Mt.

13 Ijon
14 Ijon, Plain
15 Jezzine
16 Karun

N

DAMASCUS
APPENDIX 9
1 : 200,000

1 Abana, R.; Barada
2 Abel, Abila
5 Beth Zabdai
6 Chalcis a/ Lib. ?

8 Damascus
9 Deir el-Ashayr
10 Dair el-Ghazal
12 Helbon

14 Hermon, Mt.
15 Hosn Niha
17 Kh. Knese
19 Niha

21 Sednaya
23 Yanta
24 Zahle

Glossary

Ain, ayin, ayn. Spring of water.

Jannaeus, Alexander. A member of the Hasmonean family that led the fight for Jewish independence during the intertestamental period. He ruled from 103 to 76 B.C.

Alluvium. Earth, sand, clay, etc. deposited by moving water. An alluvial fan is a sloping deposit of alluvium that builds up and widens out like a fan where a stream enters a plain or reaches the shoreline of a body of water.

Amarna Age/Letters. The Amarna Age was a time of political unrest in Canaan (1400–1350 B.C.). Egyptian authority in Canaan seems to have slackened during this period because of good relations with Egypt's chief rival, Mitanni. Egypt did not become involved in local problems so long as its interests in Canaan were not jeopardized. The Amarna archive was discovered at Tell el-Amarna in Middle Egypt and consists of more than 350 letters written on cuneiform tablets. The vast majority are from the kings of Canaan and Syria to the Egyptian court. Important city-kingdoms of Canaan mentioned in the Amarna letters include those of Gath, Ashkelon, Lachish, Jerusalem, Shechem, Megiddo, and Acco. The Amarna letters provide a picture of Egypt's influence in Canaan during this important period.

Archaeology. The study of antiquity. The term comes from two Greek words, *archaeios* and *logos*, which mean "science of antiquity." Archaeology studies the material remains of past generations, especially artifacts, inscriptions, and monuments that have been uncovered by excavation and research. (See "Tel, Tell.") Types of archaeologists include classical archaeologists, historical archaeologists, underwater archaeologists, and prehistoric archaeologists. The majority of the work in Palestine is done by all except the historical archaeologist, who is mainly concerned with sites that date to recent historical times (Fagan, 8–15).

Bashan. In the Old Testament, Bashan was the region south of Mt. Hermon (see **Unit A1**). In the Hellenistic Period, Bashan was divided into three districts called Gaulanitis (Old Testament Golan; see **A1-4, A1-6,** and **A1-7**), Batanaea, and Trachonitis. Before his death in 4 B.C., Herod the Great willed the districts of Gaulanitis, Batanaea, Trachonitis, and Auranitis (Old Testament Hauran; see Ezek. 47: 16, 18) to his son Philip, as well as the district of Paneas or Caesarea Philippi (see Matt. 16:13, 27; *Ant.* 17.8.1; *War.*1.20.4; *War.*2.7.3).

Bamah. "High place" site of a sanctuary (?)

Bet, beth, beit. House, temple. [Bet and beth, Hebrew; beit, Arabic]

Bronze Age. An archaeological period in Palestine that dates from 3150 B.C. to 1200 B.C. It is divided into three main periods, each with a subdivision of shorter periods. The main periods are: Early Bronze Age, 3150 B.C.–2200 B.C.; Middle Bronze Age, 2200 B.C.–1550 B.C.; and Late Bronze Age, 1550 B.C.–1200 B.C. or the start of the Iron Age. The Bronze Age is characterized by its use of bronze tools and weapons. It is referred to by some Israeli archaeologists as the Canaanite Age.

Byzantine Period/Empire. An historical/archaeological period in Palestine from A.D. 324–640. The Byzantine Empire was the continuation of the Roman Empire after Emperor Constantine I (the Great) transferred the imperial administration from Rome to Byzantium in A.D. 330 (the word *Byzantine* comes from *Byzantium*, a city on the Bosporus strait which connects the Black Sea and the Mediterranean Sea). Constantine renamed Byzantium, Constantinople after himself (Constantinople is now Istanbul, Turkey). The Byzantine Empire is also called the *East Roman Empire*, because it ruled the eastern part of what was once the Roman Empire after it was permanently divided in A.D. 395. Under Emperor Justinian (A.D. 527–565) the Byzantine Empire reached its greatest size and included Asia Minor, the Balkan Peninsula, Egypt, Italy, North Africa, Palestine (see **P2-3**), Syria, and the southern coast of Spain.

Canaan. In the Old Testament, Canaan is generally used as a designation for the territory west of the Jordan River. Abraham, for example, "set out for the land of Canaan" (Gen. 12:5). "On the plains of Moab by the Jordan across from Jericho the Lord said to Moses, 'Speak to the Israelites and say to them: "When you cross the Jordan into Canaan, drive out all the inhabitants of the land before you"'" (Num. 33:50–51). "Canaanite" was also a general designation for the inhabitants of the land called Canaan (see Gen. 12:6 [cf. Gen. 15:18–21]; 50:11; Josh. 7:9). Although its etymology is uncertain, the name Canaan is usually associated with one of Phoenicia's principle products, the purple dye manufactured from sea snails. Other suggestions include the meanings "land of reeds [papyrus?]" or "merchant."

Casemate wall. Two parallel walls divided into narrow sections by perpendicular partitions. "Some of these chambers were filled with stones and earth; others were left empty for use as store-rooms and were connected by doors with the interior of the fortress." The purpose of the casemate wall was to provide the greatest real strength to the wall with the least expenditure of effort (Albright, 121–122).

Cisjordan. The land west of the Jordan River to the Mediterranean Sea. The prefix *cis* has the meaning "on this side," or "on the nearer side." (Compare Transjordan.)

Coastal Route. The name we have chosen to call the international highway that ran from Egypt along the coast of Palestine to the Jezreel Valley (see **Unit D1**). From there, it branched to Phoenicia through the Plain of Acco (see **Unit C2**) and to Syria through Lower Galilee and the Upper Jordan Valley (see **Units B2, A2, and G1**). From Syria the highway continued toward Mesopotamia.

Crusaders. Christians from western Europe who organized eight major military expeditions to the Holy Land between A.D. 1096 and 1270. Their objectives were to (1) recover the Holy Land and (2) protect the Byzantine Empire from the Muslims. Many Crusaders also fought to expand commercial contacts between east and west, and thus used the Crusades for both personal and political gain. Although the Crusaders were able to recapture the Holy Land for a short time, they were unable to establish permanent control. In A.D. 1187 Saladin defeated the Christian army in a battle near the Horns of Hattin (see **B2-2**) which resulted in Muslim control of Jerusalem. Every Crusade after this battle ended in failure.

Darb, derek. Way, road, route, path. [Darb, Arabic; derek, Hebrew]

Decapolis. A federation of 10 Hellenistic cities east of Samaria and Galilee. The Roman historian Pliny the Elder (1st century A.D.) listed the cities as Damascus, Philadelphia (Rabbath-ammon in the Old Testament), Raphana, Scythopolis (Beth-shan in the Old Testament), Gadara, Hippus, Dion, Pella, Gerasa, and Canatha. Scythopolis was the chief city of the Decapolis and the only one west of the Jordan River.

Deir. Monastery. [Arabic]

Diaspora. The term comes from a Greek word which means "dispersion." It refers to the dispersion of the Jewish people throughout the world. Thus, the diaspora is the community of Jews living outside the land of Israel.

265

Dome of Gilead. The highest mountains in Gilead, separated into halves by the River Jabbok.

Ein, en. Spring of water. [Hebrew]

Epigraphic Texts. Inscriptions, especially on buildings, tombs, or statues.

Execration Texts. Two collections of texts from Egypt that contain important information about Canaan in the 20th and 19th centuries B.C. The first collection contains names inscribed on sherds accompanied by a curse, or "execration." The second collection of names was inscribed on small figurines. The lists were compiled to bring disaster to pharaoh's enemies. The first list contains the names of only twenty towns or regions, while the second list contains sixty-four names of mostly well-known towns. According to Aharoni, "the differences between these two collections of execration texts reflect the changes that took place in Palestine during the twentieth to nineteenth centuries B.C., viz. transition from a nomadic to a sedentary way of life and a shift from patriarchal rule by three or four tribal leaders to an urban autocracy, usually under only one ruler" (Aharoni, 146).

Fauna. Animals of a given region or time.

Flora. Plants of a particular region or time.

Har. Mount, mountain. [Hebrew]

Hasmoneans (the "Maccabees" and their successors). A priestly family that headed the rebellion against the Seleucid kingdom to gain religious freedom and establish an independent Jewish state that ruled Palestine from 167 to 63 B.C. They annexed the most important regions of Palestine, including Galilee and Idumea (the Negev region), while absorbing the Semitic people in these regions.

Hellenistic Period. An archaeological period in Palestine that dates from 332 to 63 B.C. It is subdivided into Hellenistic I (332–152 B.C.) and Hellenistic II (152–63 B.C.). The Hellenistic period is the result of the conquest of Alexander the Great (332–331 B.C.), when Palestine came under the influence of Greek culture and thought. References to Grecians are found in Acts 6:1 and Acts 9:29 and probably refer to Greek-speaking Jewish Christians in Jerusalem.

Horevat, horvath. Ruin. [Hebrew]

Hyksos. Asiatics who invaded Egypt at the end of the Egyptian Middle Kingdom (ca. 2040–1633 B.C.), who established their capital at Avaris in the Eastern Delta (see **Q-1**). The military strength of the Hyksos came from their introduction of the horse-drawn battle chariot. The Hyksos are also known for the construction of massive fortifications, which consisted of a large sloping ramp made of earth and a moat at its foot. At the beginning of the 18th Dynasty, the Hyksos were expelled from Egypt by Pharaoh Ahmose (ca. 1550 B.C.), who pursued them into southern Palestine. The best contemporary source for the Hyksos' expulsion from Egypt comes from the captain of a Nile vessel, who wrote, "Then there was fighting on the water in *the canal Pa-Djedku* of Avaris. Thereupon I made a capture ... Then there was fighting in the Egypt which is south of this town [Avaris; the Hyksos possibly forced the Egyptians into a temporary retreat] ... Then Avaris was despoiled. Then I carried off spoil from there: one man, three women, a total of four persons. Then his majesty gave them to me to be slaves. Then Sharuhen was besieged for three years" (*ANET*, 233).

Iron Age. An archaeological period in Palestine that dates from 1200 to 586 B.C. It is subdivided into Iron Age I (1200–1000 B.C.), Iron Age II (1000–800 B.C.), and Iron Age III (800–586 B.C.). It includes the period of Israelite conquest and the establishment of the Israelite monarchy.

Jebel, jebal, gebel. Mount, mountain. [Arabic]

Josephus Flavius (A.D. 37–ca. 100). Jewish commander of Galilee at the outbreak of the First Jewish Revolt against Rome (A.D. 66) and historian, whose writings (*Antiquities* and *The Jewish War*) represent the chief examples of Jewish-Hellenistic literature.

Judas Maccabeus. A member of the Hasmonean family and son of Mattathias, the man who took the first action against the Seleucids in the revolt for Jewish independence (167 B.C.). Judas led the revolt after the death of his father in 166/5 B.C., but was killed 4 years later in a battle north of Jerusalem (161 B.C.). The name "Maccabaeus" was a nickname meaning "the hammer." The revolt is referred to as "The Maccabean Revolt."

Kafar, kefar. Village. [Hebrew]

Khirbeh. Ruin. [Arabic]

King's Highway. Major trade route that runs the length of Transjordan from the Gulf of Aqabah/Elat to Damascus (see p. 13).

Lachish Letters. A collection of 21 ostraca (inscribed potsherds) discovered in the gate house at Lachish by J. L. Starkey in 1935–1938, which were written just before the city was destroyed by Nebuchadnezzar of Babylon in 589 B.C.. The "letters" are military correspondence between a subordinate and his superior at Lachish. One of the sherds mentions that "we are watching for the signals of Lachish, according to all the indications which my lord has given, for we cannot see Azekah." The letter was apparently written after the situation described in Jeremiah 34:7, "while the army of the king of Babylon was fighting against Jerusalem and the other cities of Judah that were still holding out—Lachish and Azekah. These were the only fortified cities left in Judah." Perhaps Azekah had already fallen. (Azekah is located at the entrance of the Elah Valley north of Lachish; see **K-5**.)

Ladder of Tyre. A steep road that connected the Plain of Acco with the territory of Tyre. It was used by the Jewish historian Josephus (1st century A.D.) in his description of the northern boundary of Acco/Ptolemais. It passed *Rosh ha-Niqra*, ("Head of the Cave"), a mountain promontory that enclosed the Plain of Acco in the north. This promontory forms part of the border between Israel and Lebanon today.

Levant. From Greece to Egypt, the countries of the eastern Mediterranean that border the sea. *Levant* is a French word which means rising or raising. It is applied to the East from the "rising" of the sun.

Limes. A fortified line of defense. The Roman limes refers to an "intricate network of watchtowers and forts" that formed the frontier of Arabia. "That zone extended all the way from the great legionary camp that lies at Lejjun in the vicinity of Karak (near the Dead Sea [see **O-1**]) to the detachments in the Wadi Sirhan" (Bowersock, 103–105; the Wadi Sirhan is a long depression that extends about 175 miles to the vicinity of Ammon in Jordan).

Mamelukes. Slaves, mostly Turkish and Circassian, were carefully trained as soldiers; these were mamelukes. They arose in rebellion on May 2, 1250 and murdered their Sultan, Turanshah. This military class ruled Egypt, Syria, and Palestine from A.D. 1250 to 1517. During the 13th century, the Mamelukes expelled the remaining Crusaders from the coastal cities of Palestine.

Mari. One of the largest cities in northern Mesopotamia (see p. 8), located on the western bank of the Euphrates River. Mari was important because of its location on the intersection of two caravan roads: one went across the Syrian Desert, linking Mari with the Mediterranean; the other descended from northern Mesopotamia to Babylon. The site today is known as Tell Hariri.

Mari Archives. An archive of some 20,000 cuneiform tablets found in the palace of Mari, mostly written in Akkadian, and consisting of economic, legal, and diplomatic texts. A number of texts refer to two groups of people that some scholars have equated with the Hebrews. The city of Hazor, located in the Upper Jordan Valley (see **A2-6**), is frequently mentioned as a center for caravans traveling to Babylon.

Massebah A stone monolith or pillar, usually with a sacred or "cultic" function.

Me'arah, me'aroth. Cave, caves. [Hebrew]

Mezad, masada. Stronghold, fortress. [Hebrew]

Nabateans. Apparently Arabic by blood, the Nabateans lived east and southwest of the Dead Sea and played an important role in the intertestamental and New Testament history of Palestine and Transjordan. It is thought that the Nabateans moved into Edom from the northwestern Arabian Desert about the 6th century B.C.

Nahal. The Hebrew equivalent of the Arabic *wadi*. It refers to both a river and a dry river bed. (See "Wadi")

Ostracon (pl. ostraca). A piece of broken pottery (potsherd) with writing on it. The Samaria ostraca, for example, were found in the excavations of the city of Samaria (see p. 92).

Philistines. One of the "Sea Peoples" who, according to Egyptian records, attempted to invade Egypt during the reign of Rameses III (ca. 1188 B.C.). They devastated the land of the Hittites (see p. 9), the coasts of Cilicia and Northern Syria, Carchemish, and Cyprus. After they were defeated by the Egyptians, the Philistines settled the southern Coastal Plain of Canaan, called "Philistia" (see **Unit K**; Isa. 14:29). The word "Palestine" was later derived from the name of the Philistines (see 1 Sam. 4:1), and was used by the Greeks and Romans to denote all of southern Syria. In the Old Testament, there is a constant struggle between the Philistines and Israelites for supremacy in the Holy Land. The power of the Philistines reached its peak after they defeated and killed King Saul and his son Jonathan in the Jezreel Valley (1 Sam. 28, 31; see **Unit D1**), but declined during the reign of King David (see 2 Sam. 5:17–25). The Philistines were conquered by the Assyrians in 734 B.C.

Phoenicians. Semites who occupied the coastal lands from the territory of the Philistines to Jebel el-Akra near the mouth of the Orontes River, a distance of about 250 miles. The Phoenicians developed a maritime empire that lasted for a thousand years. Their cities were founded on islands or near bays that had suitable anchorage. The Phoenicians were never conquered by the Israelites, whose kings often entered into an alliance with them for purposes of trade. This was especially true of David, Solomon, and later, Ahab. The Phoenician religion was disastrous for the Israelites, especially after the marriage of Ahab to Jezebel, a Phoenician princess.

Ptolemies. Ptolemy I was a general in the army of Alexander the Great. After Alexander's death (A.D. 323), Ptolemy gained control of Egypt and the southern part of Palestine. The Ptolemies ruled in Egypt until the Roman Period (see **Seleucid Dynasty**).

Punon embayment. A deep indentation in the Edomite Plateau that divides the plateau into northern and southern sections.

Qal'at, qalat, qasr. Castle, fort. [Arabic]

Ras, rosh. Cape, head, summit. [Ras, Arabic; rosh, Hebrew]

Relief (Bas-relief). A projection of figures or forms from a flat surface that do not stand out far from the background on which they are formed. (see **P3-6**).

Rift Valley. A valley formed when the earth collapses between two parallel faults or cracks in the rock layers below the earth's surface. The Jordan Valley and Wadi Arabah are part of a great rift that extends from Syria to Mozambique in southeast Africa.

Roman Period. An historical/archaeological period in Palestine that dates from 37 B.C. to A.D. 324. It is subdivided into Roman I (37 B.C.–A.D. 70), also known as the Herodian period (after the family of Herod the Great); Roman II (A.D. 70–180); and Roman III (A.D. 180–324).

Seleucid Dynasty. After the death of Alexander the Great (A.D. 323), fighting broke out among his generals. The Seleucid Dynasty was founded by Seleucus I, originally a subordinate of Ptolemy, who established an empire in southeast Asia that extended (at its height) from Turkey to India. The Seleucids finally lost control of Palestine in 142 B.C. (see **Hasmoneans**), while the last of their territory fell to the Romans in 64 B.C.

Stele, stela (pl. stelae). An upright stone slab or pillar engraved with an inscription or other design. Egyptian and Assyrian rulers often set them up to describe victories or other important events.

Tel, tell. "Hill" or "mound" [Tel, Hebrew; tell, Arabic] In archaeological usage, a tell is an artificial mound of accumulated debris left from different periods of human occupation. It is distinctive in shape, with sloping sides and flat top. When excavated, these mounds provide a picture of occupation levels over hundreds or even thousands of years. Outside the Near East, tells are called "occupational mounds."

Transjordan. The high plateau east of the Rift Valley that extends from the Yarmuk River (southeast of the Sea of Galilee) to the Gulf of Elat/Aqaba.

Valley of Lebanon. The valley in Lebanon between the Anti-Lebanon mountain range dominated by Mount Hermon at its southern end, and the Lebanon mountains which run parallel to the Mediterranean coast. In the Classical period it was known as *Coele-Syria* (Latin, "hollow Syria"). Today, it is known as the Beq'a (which means "the valley").

Via Maris. A Latin term meaning "the way of the sea" (see Isa. 9:1). For 100 years it mistakenly has been applied to the international highway that connected Egypt with the countries of the northern Levant and Mesopotamia. Technically, the Via Maris ran from Capernaum (on the Sea of Galilee) to Ptolemais (on the Mediterranean shoreline). See entry under Coastal Highway.

Wadi. A wadi is a dry river bed or, during periods of rainfall, the stream which fills the river bed.

Bibliography

The complete reference for each note in the text of this book may be found in the following bibliography. For example, a note to *The Historical Geography of the Holy Land*, by George Adam Smith, will appear in the text as "(Smith, 45)". Notes to quotations from the works of Josephus appear in the text in the following abbreviated forms: (*Ant.* 3.10.3) or (*War* 3.4.5). The first numeral designates the book in either *The Antiquities of the Jews* or *The Jewish War*. The middle numeral designates the chapter, and the final numeral refers to the paragraph in the book where the quotation is found. *Ant.* is taken from *The Works of Josephus* (Whiston), *War* from *The Jewish War* (Cornfeld). Quotations from the Bible are taken from the New International Version and are cited using standard abbreviations. *Ancient Near Eastern Texts*, edited by James B. Pritchard, will appear as *ANET*, and the condensed version, *The Ancient Near East* as Pritchard plus the volume number.

Aharoni, Yohanan. *The Land of the Bible: A Historical Geography*. Revised Edition. Translated and edited by Anson Rainey. Philadelphia: Westminster Press, 1979.

_____. *The Archaeology of the Land of Israel*. Translated by Anson F. Rainey. Philadelphia: Westminster Press, 1982.

Aharoni, Yohanan, and Avi-Yonah, Michael. *The Macmillan Bible Atlas*. Revised Edition. New York: Macmillan Publishing Co., Inc., 1977.

Albright, William F. *The Archaeology of Palestine*. Harmondsworth, England: Penguin Books Limited, 1940; reprinted., Gloucester, Mass.: Peter Smith, 1971.

Avi-Yonah, Michael. *The Holy Land*. Revised Edition. Grand Rapids: Baker Book House, 1977.

Baly, Denis. *The Geography of the Bible*. Revised Edition. New York: Harper & Row, Publishers, 1974.

Barrows, E. P. *Sacred Geography and Antiquities*. New York: American Tract Society, 1874.

Bowersock, G. W. *Roman Arabia*. Cambridge: Harvard University Press, 1983.

Breasted, James Henry. *Ancient Times: A History of the Early World*. 2nd ed. New York: Ginn and Company, 1944.

Bright, John. *A History of Israel*. 3rd ed. Philadelphia: Westminster Press, 1981.

Cornfeld, Gaalya, gen. ed. *Josephus, The Jewish War*. Grand Rapids: Zondervan, 1982.

Edersheim, Alfred. *The Life and Times of Jesus the Messiah*, 1883; reprint ed, Michigan: Wm. B. Eerdmans Publishing Co., 1971.

Evenari, Michael; Shanan, Leslie; and Tadmor, Naphtali. *The Negev*. Cambridge: Harvard University Press, 1971.

Fagan, Brian M. *Archaeology–A Brief Introduction*. Boston: Little, Brown & Company, 1983.

Farrar, Frederic W. *The Life of Christ*. London: Cassell & Co., Ltd., 1874; reprint ed, Oregon: Fountain Publications, 1980.

Frank, H. T., and Monson, James M., gen. eds. *Student Map Manual: Historical Geography of the Bible Lands*. 2nd ed. Jerusalem: Pictorial Archive (Near Eastern History), Est., 1983.

Fulton, John. *The Beautiful Land Palestine*. New York: T. Whittaker, 1891; reprint ed, New York: Arno Press, 1977.

Hareuveni, Nogah. *Nature in Our Biblical Heritage*. Translated by Helen Frenkley. Kiryat Ono: Neot Kedumim Ltd., 1980.

Hayes, John H., and Miller, J. Maxwell, eds. *Israelite and Judaean History*. London: SCM Press Ltd., 1977.

The Works of Josephus . Translated by William Whiston. Peabody, Mass: Hendrickson Publishers, 1987.

Kallai, Zecharia. *Historical Geography of the Bible*. Jerusalem: The Magnes Press, 1986.

Karmon, Yehuda. *Israel: A Regional Geography*. New York: Wiley-Interscience, 1971.

Kenyon, Kathleen M. *Archaeology in the Holy Land*. 4th ed. New York: W. W. Norton and Co., Inc., 1979.

Monson, James M. *The Land Between*. Jerusalem: By the Author, 1983.

Negev, Avraham, ed. *Archaeological Encyclopedia of the Holy Land*. New York: G.P. Putnam's Sons, 1972.

Newman, J. P. *From Dan to Beersheba*. New York: Harper & Brothers, Publishers, 1876.

Ogden, D. Kelly, and Chadwick, Jeffrey R. *The Holy Land–A Geographical, Historical and Archaeological Guide to the Land of the Bible*. Jerusalem: The Jerusalem Center for Near Eastern Studies, 1990.

Orni, Efraim, and Efrat, Elisha. *Geography of Israel*. 3rd ed. Jerusalem: Israel Universities Press, 1976.

Pearlman, Moshe. *In the Footsteps of Moses*. Tel Aviv: Nateev and Steimatzky, 1973.

Pfeiffer, Charles F., and Vos, Howard F. *The Wycliffe Historical Geography of Bible Lands*. Chicago: Moody Press, 1967.

Pritchard, James B., ed. *Ancient Near Eastern Texts Relating to the Old Testament*. 3rd ed. Princeton, New Jersey: Princeton University Press, 1969.

_____. *The Ancient Near East: An Anthology of Texts and Pictures*. 2 vols. Princeton, New Jersey: Princeton University Press, 1973.

Ridgaway, Henry B. *The Lord's Land*. New York: Nelson & Phillips, 1876.

Robinson, Edward. *Biblical Researches in Palestine*. 3 vols. London: John Murray, 1841.

_____. *Later Biblical Researches in Palestine*. Boston: Crocker and Brewster, 1856; reprint ed., New York: Arno Press, 1977.

Smith, George Adam. *The Historical Geography of the Holy Land*. 25th ed. London: Hodder & Stoughton Ltd., 1931; reprint ed., London: Fontana Library, 1966.

Stanley, Arthur Penrhyn. *Sinai and Palestine*. New York: W. J. Widdleton, 1865.

Thomson, William M. *The Land and the Book*. 3 vols. Hartford, Conn.: S. S. Scranton Company, 1911.

Weitz, Joseph. *Forests and Afforestation in Israel*. Translated by Shlomo Levenson. Jerusalem: Massada Press, 1974.

Wild, Laura H. *Geographic Influences in Old Testament Masterpieces*. New York: Ginn and Company, 1915.

Wiseman, D. J., ed. *Peoples of Old Testament Times*. Oxford: The Clarendon Press, 1973.

Wright, G. Ernest. *Biblical Archaeology*. Philadelphia: The Westminster Press, 1957.

271

Index to Named Sites in Regional Units A1a - O2

T. = Tel/Tell; Kh. = Khirbet; H. = Horevat; W. = Wadi; N. = Nahal; R. = River; J. = Jebel

A

Abel: A1a A1b
Aphek, Upper ?: A1a A1b B1
Ain ?: A1b
Aphek, Lower ?: A1b B2 G1
Ashtaroth ?: A1b
Abel-beth-maacah: A2
Ammud, N.: A2 C1 B1
Anafa (T.): A2
Arbel, Mt.: B1
Afula: B2 C2 D1,2 F1
Azziyeh, W.: C1
Acco/Ptolemais: C2 D2
Achzib: C2 D2
Akko (T.): C2 D2
Aphek: C2 D2
Atlit castle: C2 D2
Aphek, tower: E1,2
Apollonia: E1
Aruna: E1,2
Aphek/Antipatris: E1,2 J2
Adam: F1 G2 N2
Alexandrium: F1,2 G2
Ai: F2 H2 I
Abel Meholah ?: G1 N1
Ajlun castle: G1 N1
Adummim ascent: G2 H1,2
Aenon ?: G2 N1,2
Arnon, R.: H1 O1
Arugot, N.: H1
Anathoth: I J1
Adullam: J2
Adora: J1
Aijalon valley: J2
Ayyalon, N.: J2
Azekah: J2
Ashdod (modern): K
Ashdod (T.): K
Ashkelon (T.): K
Azotus Paralius: K
Avedat, H.: L1
Arabah, W.: L2 O2
Arad (modern): L2
Arad (T.): L2
Adru: M1 O2
Aqabah: M2
Ariedela: M2
Abila: N1
Arab, W.: N1
Abel Keramim ?: N2
Ain Musa: N2
Adir: O1
Aroer: O1

B

Beth-arbel: A1a N1
Beth-shan: A1a B1,2 D1
    F1 G1 N1
Beth-yerah: B1

Belvoir: B1,2 D1 F1 G1
Bethsaida ?: B1
Bersabe: B2 C1 D1
Bet Kerem valley: B2
    C1,2 D1,2
Bet Netofa valley: B2,
    C1,2 D1,2
Beth-haggan: B2 D1 E2
    F1 G1
Baca: C1
Beth Dagon: C1
Beth Shearim: C2 D2
Baddan: F1
Baal Hazor: F2
Beth-horon, Lower: F2 I J2
Beth-horon, Upper: F2 H2 I
    J1,2
Bethany: F2 I J1
Bethel: F2 H2 I
Bir Zaith: F2
Bet Alfa: G1
Beth-hoglah: G2
Bethabara: G2
Bethennabris: G2 N2
Bethlehem: H1,2 J1
Beth-hacc(h)erem ?: I J1
Beth-zechariah: I J1
Beththter: I J1
Beth Shemesh: J1,2
Beth-zur: J1,2
Betogabris: J1,2 K
Bet Guvrin: J2 K
Beer Sheva (modern): L1,2
Beer Sheva, N.: L1,2
Beer Sheva (T.): L1,2
Beraein: L1
Besor, N.: L1
Bozrah: M1 O2
Biqat Uvda: M2
Baaras: N2
Baca: N2
Beth-baal-meon: N2
Beth-jeshimoth: N2
Bab ehd-Dhra: O1
Beidha: O2

C

Caesarea Philippi: A1a A1b A2
Capernaum: A1b A2 B1
Chaspho: A1b
Capitolias: A1A N1
Chastelet castle: A2
Chorazin: A2 B1
Chinnereth: B1,2 C1 D1
Cana, Kh.: B2 C2 D1,2
Caesarea: C2 D2 E1,2
Carmel caves: C2 D2
Carmel, Mt.: C2 D2 E1
Crocodilon Polis: C2 D2 E1,2
Chozba: G2 H2

Cypros: G2
Callirhoe: H1 N2
Cave of the Pool: H2
Cave of Letters: H2
Cave of Horrors: H2
Carmel: I
City of Moab: O1
Cape Costigan: O1

D

Damascus: A1a
Dan: A1a A1b A2
Dium ?: A1b N1
Dan, N.: A2
Daphne: A2
Daberath: B2 D1
Dothan: B2 D1 E2 F1
Dothan, plain: B2 D1 E2 F1
Dishon, N.: C1
Dubbeh, W.: C1
Dor: C2 D2 E1,2
Dead Sea: F2 G2
David, N.: H1
Dibon(-gad): H1 O1
Debir: J1
Dimona: L2
Dana, W.: M1 O2
Dibbin, forest: N1
Dabaloth: N2
Dhat Ras: O1
Dajaniya, Kh.: O2
Dana: O2
Dusaq: O2

E

Edrei: A1a
Eietha ?: A1a A1b
Enab ?: A1a
En Harod: B2 F1,2 G1
En-dor: B2 G1
Ebal, Mt.: E2 F1
En Boqeq: H1 L2
En-gedi: H1,2
Emmaus; Mozah: I J1,2
Emmaus; Qubeibe: I
Ekron: J1,2 K
Emmaus; Latrun: J1,2
Eshtemoa: J1
Elah, valley: J2
Eshtaol: J2
Eglon ?: K
Elusa: L1
En Avedat: L1
Eilat: M2
En Yotvata: M2
Enganna: N1
Elealeh: N2
Ellebana: O2

F

Faria, W.: F1,2 G1,2
Fidan, W.: M1 O2

G

Gadara: A1a B1 G1 N1
Gamala: A1a A1b A2 B1
Golan: A1a A1b
Gergesa: A1b B1
Gennesaret, plain: B1
Gilboa, Mt.: B1,2 D1 F1 G1
Gischala: C1
Garizein: E2
Gerizim, Mt.: E2 F1,2
Geba: F2 H2 I
Gibeah of Saul: F2 H1 I J1
Gibeon: F2 I
Gophna: F2
Gath: J1,2 K
Gezer: J1,2
Guvrin, N.: J1,2
Gaza: K
Gerar: K L1
Gerar, N.: K L1
Goshen ?: L1
Gaia: M1 O2
Gerasa: N1
Gedor: N2
Ghuweir, W.: O2

H

Hazor: A1a A1b A2 B1 C1
Hermon, Mt.: A1a A1b A2
Hippus: A1a A1b A2 B1 G1
Hammath Gader: A1b B1 G1 N1
Hermon, N.: A2
Horshat Tal: A2
Huleh Nature Reserve: A2
Hammath Tiberias: B1
Hattin, Horns: B1,2 C1 D1
Heptapegon; Tabgha: B1
Hannathon: B2 C1,2 D1,2
Haifa: C2 D2
Helkath ?: C2 D2
Hadera: E1,2
Hadera, N.: E1
Harod, N.: F1 G1
Heshbon: H1 N2
Herodium: H1,2
Hyrcania: H1,2
Hebron: H2, J1,2
Hazar-addar ?: L1
Hormah: L2
Harun, Jebel: M2
Hammat Pella: N1
Heidan, W.: O1
Horonaim ?: O1

I

Ijon: A1a A1b
Ijon, plain: A1b
Iyyon, N.: A2